HIGHPOCKET'S WAR STORIES
AND OTHER TALL TALES

HIGHPOCKET'S WAR STORIES

AND OTHER TALL TALES

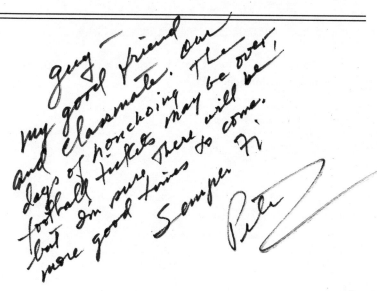

Guy —
my good friend
and classmate. Our
days of homecoming. The
football tickets may be over,
but I'm sure there will be
more good times to come.
Semper Fi
Pete

Peter L. Hilgartner & Henry

Sam Ginder

Guy Henry
I think you will
like this story.
GBu
Sam
4 Aug 2004

Library of Congress Number: 2004092153
ISBN :   Hardcover   1-4134-5267-1
                Softcover   1-4134-5266-3

To order additional copies of this book, contact:
Xlibris Corporation
1-888-795-4274
www.Xlibris.com
Orders@Xlibris.com
24622

CONTENTS

DEDICATION

This book is dedicated to the officers and men I served
during my career in the United States Marine Corps,
and to my family.

Most of all, this book is dedicated to the officers and
men of the Fifth Marine Regiment, Vietnam, with whom
I went to war; especially to the First Battalion.
All were heroes every bit as much as Achilles, Odysseus,
Alexander, Hector, and the other legendary greats of
myth and history. To a large extent, my Marine comrades
shaped my life. I will remain grateful to them all
until the last breath that I draw.

To the families of those who fell, you and your loved ones
are never far from my thoughts. I wish we could have
brought them *all* home!

ACKNOWLEDGEMENTS

This book could not have happened without the encouragement of my U. S. Naval Academy classmates following a speech about combat leadership that I gave to midshipmen and their guests in November 2002. My family and close friends, such as Brenda Glenn, had been pressing me to write this book for a long time. Comments and urgings from family, friends, and classmates lit the spark that fired me to begin collecting material and writing in January 2003.

The two standout Trojans in this effort were my wife, Sara, who put my longhand notes into the computer, and my Naval Academy classmate, Sam Ginder, an author in his own right. Sam used his exceptional talents to smooth out my rough words and make the piece flow. I am deeply grateful to Sara and Sam for their contributions.

I am grateful for the help my daughters, Linda and Dale, and Dale's husband Jim Cirillo, gave me in editing the manuscript drafts. I am also deeply indebted for the many constructive comments I received regarding content from my distinguished group of reviewers. Their recollections of long past events, particularly about the Korean and Vietnam battles, both add to the story and to our Marine Corps history. Memories of those long ago momentous events are no longer as crisp as they once were in our individual recall, but together we have reconstructed those events from our memories, supplemented by historical documents where they exist, to give what we collectively believe to be an accurate account from our perspective.

My Marine Corps reviewers, all retired from active duty, include: Colonel Gerry Turley (also former Deputy Assistant

Secretary of Defense), Brigadier General Gordon Gayle, Major General Kenneth Houghton, Colonel Haig Donabedian, Colonel Jack Grace, Major Gene Balderston, and Major Bill Duncan. Haig, Jack, Gene, and Bill are also my Naval Academy classmates.

The following officers and NCOs of the First Battalion, Fifth Marines were invaluable in helping me reconstruct our actions in the Que Son Valley, and the major battles of Union I, Union II, and Swift: Lieutenant General Arthur Blades, Brigadier General Gerald McKay, Lieutenant Colonel David McInturff, Lieutenant Colonel Dick Alger, Captain James Caswell, Captain Rick Zell, Corporal Bill James, Corporal Tom Mangan, Sergeant Hillous York, PFC Robert J. Pine, Corporal Phil Johnson, and Corporal Brad Silliman. All made substantial contributions to this book, for which I am greatly in their debt. Lieutenant Colonel John D. Murray of the Third Battalion Fifth Marines helped me with his recollections of Operation Swift. John's Mike Company fought under my operational control during that hard-fought battle, and played a significant role in our victory.

I am also grateful to my friends Tom Casmay and Bill Ten Eyck, my nephew Henry Hilgartner, brother Bill Close and his wife Stephanie, and my stepson Greg Fernlund. They all pitched in and helped me with good thoughts, humor, and profound patience.

Gratitude for the help received on this book would not be complete without expressing my deep appreciation for the comments and assistance provided by Admiral Kinnaird R. McKee USN (retired), Vice Admiral William P. Lawrence USN (retired), Lieutenant General Bernard "Mick" Trainor USMC (retired), Brigadier General Edwin H. Simmons, USMC (retired), Historian Emeritus of the United States Marine Corps, Colonel John W. Ripley USMC (retired) Director USMC History and Museums Division, and Ms. Ann Close of Alfred A. Knopf, Inc.

To all of you who helped me with your advice and generous gift of time in reviewing manuscripts, I am deeply indebted. Thank you!

Pete Hilgartner
Great Falls, Virginia
January 20004

Some I Went to War With

In Korea

Pete auditions with ukelele

CWO Larry Betts and Lt Pete
going home

Scout Sgt. Henderson

In Vietnam

"Buck" Darling

Mack McInturff

MSgt Fulmer, Highpockets,
Capt. John Carty

Dick Alger and the
Dragon promote
Lt. Art Blades

Alpha Company Getting Wet

Awards for the Troops

Helo Landing Pad Hill 54

Taking a Break on Patrol

Jim Caswell Hero of Union 1

Ken Houghton, Smart Warrior

Socializing with some Que Son locals

1.0 INTRODUCTION

The paradox of war is that from its brutality, ugliness, and human tragedy it spawns the beauty of heroism.

It was hot, blistering hot, too hot for flak jackets. The heat and humidity sapped the strength and energy from their very souls. Their heads hung on their chests and their eyes had the unfocused glaze of men in a stupor. The battalion moved quietly along the narrow Vietnamese road on its mission to seek out and destroy the enemy. Hilgartner was near the head of the column. You could easily spot him because of his height and the long walking stick he carried.

Wide fields of rice paddies bordered either side of the road, with a copse of thick trees and bushes about 50 feet in diameter rising like an island in the flat sea of paddies two hundred yards on the right. The four Marine scouts guarding the column's right flank moved quickly towards the small island to make sure no enemy troops were hiding there in ambush.

Hilgartner looked at his scouts as they moved toward the copse, and immediately sensed something terribly wrong. The flankers were walking into a death trap! Instinctively he knew there would be no enemy in the copse; instead, the area would be heavily mined and booby trapped.

"Halt," he yelled at the scouts. "Don't go in there!" The Marines didn't hear him.

Then it happened. The island erupted in explosions. Two Marines died; two others were badly wounded. Hilgartner halted the column to call in med-evac choppers for the dead and wounded. He felt nauseous. For a moment he thought he was going to throw up. Hilgartner was deeply affected by what had happened to his Marines, and his failure to stop them before disaster struck.

In the midst of the carnage, Hilgartner saw one of his Marines, PFC Joe Fenech, with his right trouser leg split to his waist. Something, perhaps the force of the blast, had split the trooper's trousers and left his right leg bare, but not wounded. With every step he took, the trooper had to kick the flapping trouser leg out of his way. His trousers flapped back and forth like a circus clown's as he walked. If it hadn't have been for the surrounding tragedy, the sight would have been funny.

"Sergeant Major," Hilgartner called, "have the choppers bring that man a new pair of trousers! When you have him back in uniform, saddle the troops up. We have a score to settle."

When the column moved out it was with new life. No one felt the heat. No one was tired. The battalion had new life and a new sense of purpose. They were going to get 'em!

And "get 'em" they did. When Pete Hilgartner began telling me his combat experiences, I saw a story about the heroism of our Marines in Korea and Vietnam. I saw a story of self-sacrifice and Marines caring for each other as brothers care for each other. However, as Pete's book evolved, it became about more than heroism and caring. It is also about combat leadership.

Pete has an instinct, a gift really, for leading people in combat. It is more than tidy lessons one might find in textbooks or case studies. Pete's leadership is truly instinctual in his *feel* for the right thing to do for his troops, and how to survive in the mayhem of battle. We are all born with individual skills that lead us to prosper in areas of endeavor that suite us best. Some find their destiny in politics, others in education, business, academia, or writing and publishing. Some, like Patton, find their chosen calling in the chaos and heartbreak of war. And so did my friend, Pete Hilgartner.

I have known Pete since we were midshipmen at the United States Naval Academy, more years ago than either of us care to count. We went into different branches of the military to serve our nation, Pete the Marines, and I into submarines. With such divergent paths our lives didn't often cross, but I always heard about Pete's combat exploits. He was not a risk-taker, or a seeker of medals . . . he just happened to be where "shit was happening." Over the years, as I really got to know Pete, to see the midshipman grow to be a combat leader as good as they come, I began to admire Pete Hilgartner the Marine. So, I agreed to work with Pete on his book, not just because of friendship, but because there is a story to be told and lessons to be passed on.

Hilgartner was blessed, or cursed, with being taller than most of us. At six feet six inches tall he stands out in a crowd, and being noticed by Marine troopers is bound to bring a moniker. Pete's was "Highpockets" with his troops.

At a First Battalion, Fifth Marines post Vietnam reunion, one of his troopers told us, "The son-of-a-bitch was so tall that for every step he took, the rest of us had to run three. I used to curse him on those hot patrols through the Vietnam bush when I was so hurting tired I could cry. I was scared, soaked with sweat, and my feet hurt so bad that if I'd have lost one to a landmine it might have brought relief. But as much as I cursed him, I loved that hard-assed S.O.B because I knew he would do everything in his power to get us back alive. He did have a long stride, but we could see him in the lead. That gave us comfort. He was always with us, moving up and down the line, encouraging those who were tired and starting to lag behind."

His troopers called him "Highpockets," but his officers called him "The Dragon." Pete was merciless with officers who would not give and give and give until they had nothing else to give. He expected full dedication from his officers to their troopers, to the battalion, and to their profession. Those who gave less than full measure didn't last long in Hilgartner's unit.

For Pete Hilgartner, Korea was his combat baccalaureate. Vietnam was his post-graduate education. The lessons he learned in Korea made him a better warrior. They also helped him to survive in Vietnam, and to be a better leader. Pete says that the most important lesson he learned from Korea and Vietnam, and the one that he taught all his officers, is that every man in the unit is essential. The unit is like a pyramid. The stones at the bottom carry a key part of the load. If one of those stones is lost, a stone from the level above must take its place to fill the void as well as the place it now occupies. When that happens, the pyramid becomes a weaker structure. In combat, unit strength is necessary for individual survival and unit effectiveness. We all must look out for each other as one brother looks out for another.

That is a simple but profound message for all combat leaders. If any of Pete's officers forgot that admonition, The Dragon was quick to strike.

In researching this book, we talked and corresponded with many of Pete's old comrades in arms. We found that official Marine Corps history about the Union Operations and Swift was sometimes thin, incomplete, and inaccurate. We want to fix this. The world should know what really happened in Union I, Union II, and Swift. This book gives an account of these important events from all levels of perspective: from division and battalion command, company and platoon officers, noncommissioned officers, and troopers. From multiple perspectives, you will get a fuller, richer vision of what happened in the fire and smoke of battle. You will hear it as the troopers and their officers experienced it, not through the dry, clinical account that you might find in an after action report, or a history book. The specifics of individual firefights, be they platoon or battalion size, grow dim and fuzzy around the edges as the years pass. The picture is no longer clear, but the contours of the mayhem remain. We remember those who fell. We remember individual bravery. And it makes us humble.

Just as the paradox of war breeds the beauty of individual heroism that can't be forged in any other crucible, so does the mayhem of combat have its bizarre humor that occasionally shines through the ugliest of moments. This story tells of those insane flashes of absurdity, perhaps gallows humor, that break through even the most terrifying of times.

The U.S. Army in Korea gave the term "grunt" to our Marines. It was a pejorative description of Marine troopers struggling like pack animals through mud, rain, snow, and sleet carrying heavy loads of weapons and ammunition into combat. The Army didn't mean to be complimentary, but our Marines took the name, "grunt," and made it a badge of honor. Grunts are warriors. They are where the action is heaviest. Grunts aren't sitting on their butts miles behind the mainline of resistance pounding on typewriters, answering phones, and preparing briefings for the brass. Grunts are up where the fighting is heaviest, where it's eye-gouging, crotch-kicking, hand-to-hand stuff with guns, knives, bayonets, entrenching tools . . . whatever a grunt needs to kill his enemy. Pete's Marines, officers and troopers alike, are grunts. Hilgartner is a grunt, every man in the First Battalion, Fifth Marines is a grunt, and they're all damned proud of it.

Corporal Bill James, a former First Battalion, Alpha Company trooper during the Union operations tells of an old gunnery sergeant who once squared him away with the grizzled wisdom, "There are two kinds of people in the Marine Corps. There are grunts and the rest are support troops. If you ain't a grunt, you ain't shit." That about sums it up!

This is the grunt's story.

Lord God of Hosts be with us yet,
Lest we forget, lest we forget!

From the Recessional
by
Rudyard Kipling

Sam Ginder
Kensington, Maryland
2003

2.0 THE EARLY YEARS

As the twig is bent so grows the oak

I, Peter Louis Hilgartner, was born in 1927 at the Seton Infirmary Hospital in Austin, Texas. I cite this, not because I claim my entry into this world made 1927 a vintage year, but it *is* a long time ago. If I were a car, or a piece of furniture, 1927 would qualify me as an antique, or at least on the verge of making the transition from old junk to a valuable collectable. So, humor an old man and let me reminisce with you about some of the things that stand out for me in the memories of my childhood. They may give you some insight into why the contours of my life were shaped the way they are.

As a young child, 4 or 5 years old, one of my first memories was being out back in my grandmother's home in the Roland Park section of Baltimore, Maryland. I had created a small oven made out of three bricks placed in a U with one across the top at the back. I gathered some honeysuckle blooms and laid them in the oven. The scent was wonderful!

I was so excited I ran as fast as I could for the house to bring my mother to see what I had created. In running up the steps, two at a time, I tripped and fell sliding into a ragged gutter downspout. I cut a deep gash near my temple that required numerous stitches by a doctor who came to the house. After the painful procedure, I was at last bandaged and standing. Despite the injury and stitches, I still wanted my mother to see this wonderful oven. Understanding my excitement, she went with me to view it and smell the honeysuckle.

Why did I tell you this story? Because after all these years I remember that in my own young way I had a mission, and pressed on with it despite a serious setback. I didn't lose my focus on what, to my young mind, was a very serious mission. I was not destined to be an academic superstar, but I was blessed with something perhaps even more valuable. I have always been able to see my goals clearly and pursue them with tenacious persistence. If I can pass on but one thing to the next generation from the lessons I learned the hard way, it would be this: Find your goals, see them clearly, and pursue them with every bit of determination you have. Never give up. Never give in.

I don't recall moving from Baltimore to Fort Worth, Texas, but I well remember Fort Worth. My mother, brother Fielding, whom we called Tex, and I lived with my grandmother, Alma, and my great grandmother, Ida L. Turner, in a little house on Dorothy Lane. We called Alma, "Mimi" and Ida, "Dama". Mimi was very kind, very artistic, and always had a cigarette in her mouth. Dama also was a kind and loving lady with lots of great stories to tell.

Dama was divorced with two daughters, my grandmother Alma and her sister Faye. Alma the oldest, married John Phelps, a lawyer and writer who also played the flute in the Baltimore Symphony Orchestra. Faye married a banker named Chase, who later became the Chase of Chase Manhattan Bank. Faye became a very wealthy lady.

Dama came to Texas after the Civil War in a covered wagon from Mississippi. In those days, Fort Worth still had a stockade wall around it to keep out Indians on the warpath, marauding Mexican banditos, and other assorted bad guys. Dama was a very talented artist and a well-organized businesswoman. She was the second postmistress of Fort Worth. Dama was in many ways a remarkable lady.

Dama told us that when she was a small child in Natchez, Mississippi, her parents were plantation owners with slaves. One day during the Civil War, she and her little slave girl, a playmate, were sitting on the two front gateposts while Union soldiers were riding along the road. To taunt the soldiers, the two little girls sang an old Confederate song:

Jeff Davis rides a gray horse
Lincoln rides a mule
Jeff Davis is our president
And Lincoln is a fool!

A Union officer on horseback galloped towards them, pulled out his saber and took a swipe at the two little girls, who fell off the gateposts and ran screaming to the house.

Life in Fort Worth was very Southern and pleasant for Tex and me. We built tree houses, forts, and even a clubhouse out of a big box. Dama would take us on the streetcar to the stockyards on Saturdays. We enjoyed seeing the cattle and the cowboys, who all knew her, and tipped their hats when greeting "Miss Ida." One day, she purchased cowboy hats for Tex and me, and a pair of chaps for Tex. I was tall and skinny for my age, and she couldn't find chaps that could fit me. Tex, however, made a big hit with the cowboys who always fussed over that cute little cowpoke.

One day our idyllic life ended abruptly. My father, whom I did not even remember, came to claim Tex and me, and take us to Austin, Texas. The court had ruled that it was now my father's turn to have us under his care for awhile. We were terrified of this stranger. To get away from him, we climbed up a tree to find sanctuary on top of the garage. My father climbed up, captured us, and carried us kicking and screaming to his car. We weren't even given a chance to say goodbye to our mother, or to Mimi and Dama.

The next six years were not very happy ones for me. My father was a firm disciplinarian. When we got in trouble, he whipped us with a horse quirt or his razor strap. I fought him continuously. I tried running away, but he caught me and brought me home. On top of my family problems, I had severe sinus problems and was frequently sick.

My father, a young Austin doctor, was struggling to establish his practice. He worked hard in his office and the hospital six days a week plus a half day on Saturday. On top of this heavy workload, he also made house calls. As he became more successful, we moved from one house to another, each nicer than the last. We had a pinto pony named Jimmy who always went with us. Jimmy nearly drove me crazy because my job was to take care of him. He was the "hard-headedest," meanest, no-account pony in the entire world, I thought then. I still think so . . . the most hardheaded anyway.

One day I was riding the pinto bareback. Jimmy had no saddle and I wasn't wearing a shirt. We were happily galloping through the woods back of our Enfield Road house. I think Jimmy decided that he had galloped enough; so, without any warning he abruptly stopped. This was not an easy slow stop; this was a sudden, full halt! Jimmy stopped, but I didn't. I went sailing over Jimmy's head, loop-the-loop, and landed on my backside in a prickly pear cactus patch.

I was a mess and this was serious trouble. I had cactus thorns in me from the back of my head to my ankles. Jimmy and I walked home, with me sore and angry. I was mad at Jimmy, mad at myself, and dreading the consequences from my father when I got home.

I had to strip down and stand buck-naked in front of my stepmother so she could pull the cactus thorns out of my hide with tweezers. This took all afternoon. Just like the bible says, "The cords of hell entangled me, and death set its snares for me. I called upon the Lord in my distress and cried out for his help." That's a fact!

After my father moved the family to Terrytown, a new area on the outskirts of Austin, I could ride more often. With more open space in the Austin suburbs, I could ride with my best friend, Wilbur Treadwell.

Wilbur had a horse. I still had Jimmy. Wilbur's horse was twice as big as Jimmy, and it embarrassed me to ride with Wilbur. His horse was a fine looking animal. Mine was "Jimmy."

One day Wilbur and I took a longer ride than usual, almost to what is now called Lake Austin. Wilbur and I were riding up a black top road with me leading on Jimmy and Wilbur following on his fine animal. Wilbur stopped and called to me. "Pete, we've gone far enough. It's almost lunchtime. I have to get home."

I stopped and turned Jimmy around facing Wilbur. I think

Jimmy sensed what Wilbur said, because suddenly he took off at a full gallop. Jimmy was going home, with or without me. We were flying towards Wilbur and his horse when we crashed into them. Jimmy and I both went down onto the black top road. Jimmy fell full-force on my right leg. I knew immediately my right foot and ankle were severely injured.

After Jimmy got up I was able to roll into the ditch on the side of the road. My ankle had a big hole in it from a stirrup stud and my foot looked to be at the very least broken. Wilbur galloped off to get help. I lay there moaning. Jimmy stood nearby with reins on the ground. If he told me he was sorry, I didn't hear him. After a while my father came in his car and picked me up. Wilbur took Jimmy back to our house.

My foot eventually healed, but it never developed the way it should have. My right foot is a size and a half smaller than my left foot. Now in my old age, every time I take a step, I am reminded of Jimmy, that miserable creature. Jimmy was one more bump in the rough road of my life.

I had two half-brothers, Andy and Lee, in addition to my brother Tex. They were my father's sons by his second wife. Andy was the older of the two, and Lee was great fun, even as a baby. Lee and I just seemed to gravitate toward each other.

One day while my stepmother, Connie, was shopping, Tex and I had a great idea. We were going to teach Lee some new words and phrases. No one else was around; so, Tex and I repeated the phrase we were trying to teach Lee for what seemed like hours. Finally, we were satisfied that Lee had it down pat.

When Connie returned home, after unloading the groceries she went straight to Lee's crib to see how he was doing. Tex and I were peeking around the door. The big event was about to happen.

In came Connie saying, "And how is my little darling?"

Lee, in diapers, with his happy smile toddled across the crib and with out-stretched arms, cried out, **"You big baboon, you!"**

Connie burst into tears. Tex and I fled for the nearest woods to hide out until the trouble blew over.

When I was twelve years old, after another aborted runaway

attempt, my father removed me from school and put me on a sheep ranch near El Paso, Texas. This turned out to be a Godsend because a wonderful couple, Herman and Becky Sparks, owned the ranch. Everybody called Herman *Buckshot*. To help pay for my room and board, Buckshot taught me how to trap foxes, ringtail cats, and other small animals. Each day I walked the trap line of about 10 to 20 traps to see what I had caught. Half of the approximate $60 per month earned from the hides went to the Sparks. I kept the rest, which I spent when we went to town each month. My father didn't know it, but this was one of the happiest times of my youth. Buckshot was my hero, and I adored Mrs. Sparks.

One day Buckshot sent me to check on the sheep. They were grazing on the top of a small mountain. Since it was a shorter route to the sheep, I decided to climb the mountain's near vertical wall, which was about 200 feet high. The smart thing to do would have been to take the long way around to the back where the grade up to the plateau was much less steep.

Without a rope or climbing gear, I slowly and carefully climbed up. There wasn't much to hang onto, and footholds weren't easy to find. I was about halfway up when I slipped. As I started sliding down I knew I was in big trouble. I was frantically grabbing at anything and everything, all to no avail. My descent became faster and faster until at last I managed to grab a tree root protruding from the rocky wall. It stopped my fall with a big jerk.

I hung there briefly until I could get a foothold and stop shaking. Then I slowly descended to the bottom. Although, substantially scratched and bruised, I was alive and still standing. God put that root there for me, and I was fortunate to have grabbed His gift. After painfully walking the long way around and climbing the hill the easy way—the way the sheep had ascended—I checked on them as Buckshot instructed. I returned to the ranch house and reported that one sheep had a big, wormy wound in its side.

Mrs. Sparks put iodine and bandages on the worst of my cuts. Later that day, Buckshot and I rode our horses to the hilltop to catch and treat the injured sheep. I learned a valuable lesson that day: Don't take unnecessary risks just because they look to be the easy way. The easy way is often the wrong way.

My father decided that my education needed attention; so, he took me away from the Sparks ranch and sent me to a military boarding school, The San Antonio Academy, in San Antonio, Texas. My days on the ranch were some of the happiest of my life, but my education had indeed suffered. My year with Buckshot and Mrs. Sparks was in many ways a learning experience, but it was without formal schooling. I needed to catch up scholastically with my peers. During that first year at the Academy I needed a great deal of extra tutoring to help me catch up, and the school staff patiently gave it to me. I didn't realize it at the time, but this careful tutoring paid big dividends in preparing me for my life to come.

The next school year Tex joined me, and we spent two more years at The San Antonio Military Academy. My father may have sent me away to military school as punishment, but it wasn't a hardship or hateful to me. I thrived there. I always wanted to be a soldier, and the tougher school was, the better I liked it. In my senior year, I was appointed a cadet first lieutenant and company executive officer. This was unusual because I had been at the school for only a year and a half. Most of the cadet officers had been enrolled at the school for three or more years. This was a definite boost to my self-confidence, and convinced me that the military was where I wanted to be.

After I graduated from The San Antonio Military Academy, which was a grade school through the 7th grade, I transferred to the Texas Military Institute, a military high school for grades 8 through 12. Prior to sending me to TMI, my father and stepmother decided that Tex and I should be confirmed in St. David's Episcopal Church in Austin. My father thought that confirmation was important for us even though we only attended church as a family at Christmas. Neither Tex nor I understood why our confirmation was important. The family wasn't big into the church scene; so, we didn't take it seriously.

Each Sunday, Connie, my stepmother, or my father would

drop us off at the church for Sunday school and pick us up after classes. Tex and I found the Sunday school classes boring; so, we found a wonderful way to avoid them. When we left the car on arrival, Tex and I followed Andy and Lee into the Sunday school building. Their classrooms were near the entrance so they would dutifully go into their assigned rooms. Tex and I then marched down the hall, out the back door, and proceeded to the town pool hall. With our Sunday school contribution money, we had enough to shoot pool for the time we were supposed to be in Sunday school. We timed it so that we would return just after the bell rang ending classes. As the kids exited their classrooms, we'd hook onto the end of the column and join Andy and Lee in time for all of us to climb in the car together.

When time came to announce those who were going to be confirmed, Tex and my names were not on the list. Connie was extremely upset. She called the rector of the church to tell him he had made a mistake; our names were not in the confirmation list. "Pete and Fielding were there every Sunday, as were Andy and Lee!"

Believing that nothing was to be gained in a confrontation with Connie, the rector relented and shortly thereafter our names appeared on the list. As we marched down the aisle one Sunday to be confirmed by the Bishop, Tex and I positioned ourselves near the rear of the group. Our stepmother was in the audience, and we could not afford to make a mistake. We watched the kids ahead of us and did what they did; so, all went well.

Years later I told this story to Father Lee Stevens, a monastic of The Holy Cross Order. He had me open the prayer book and we reviewed the ceremony together. I guess that made up for my earlier misconduct of skipping confirmation school to shoot pool, the devil's own game. Well, perhaps I didn't find complete salvation, but I at least started up the steep and bumpy road to redemption . . . haven't made it very far, but I don't go to pool halls anymore.

I spent the academic year of 1940 and 1941 at T.M.I. This was my third and final year at military boarding school. The

Bondurant family owned and operated both The San Antonio Military Academy and Texas Military Institute. They were fine people, and I greatly admired them.

At the end of the T.M.I. academic year, I went to my father's house in Austin for the summer. Shortly after arriving home, my father and I had a major quarrel in the back yard. He threatened to hit me with his quirt, and I told him that would be the last thing he ever did. The next day he put me on a train, and sent me to live with my mother in New York City. I didn't see my father again for nearly ten years, nor did I correspond with him. Had it not been for the influence and counseling I received from Father Lee Stevens, I might never have reconciled with my father. I learned a valuable life-lesson from my father, one he hadn't intended to teach me. Physical or mental abuse is no way to raise your children. Nor is it a way to treat your troops if you want them to follow you.

After six months, my mother and I moved from New York to Newport, Rhode Island when World War II was in full bloom. My stepfather, Commander Forrest (Boney) Close USN was the commanding officer of the destroyer, U.S.S. Hambleton with homeport in Newport. I admired Boney greatly because he was a strong leader, his sailors loved him, and he dearly loved my mother, Tex, and me. Boney was everything I hoped my

Kitty and Boney Close

father would be. Boney was even-tempered, had a good sense of humor, and when it came to discipline, he always treated Tex and me with firm kindness and love. He encouraged me to keep trying when life took its inevitable downturns, and above all he helped my mother, Tex, his son Billy Close, and me to become a true family. Boney became one of my heroes, and a guiding force in my going to the Naval Academy.

Much to my joy, Tex joined us that summer. I not only loved

Tex dearly, but also respected him greatly. He too, had the ability to deal with life's challenges and to land on his feet.

I was enrolled as a day student at St. George's Preparatory School, but Tex went to the local public school where he befriended a number of the local kids. Tex became the leader of a group of youngsters with diverse ethnic and economic backgrounds.

As the weather improved, Tex's group started playing softball after school on a baseball diamond owned by a nearby private school. After the private school softball team completed their day's practice, Tex's group would go up and play on the grounds. I usually accompanied them to watch.

One day a school official, the coach I believe, came out and told Tex to get his group off the field. This annoyed Tex and his band greatly, and more words were exchanged. There were also a few of the school's players around and they joined in, heckling Tex about his dirty, scruffy ruffians. This really got under Tex's skin.

Finally, he spoke back and said to the coach, "Sir, if you all think you are so good, how about playing us?" Tex threw down the gauntlet, and they accepted the challenge. The big day was scheduled for the following week.

During the days before the game, Tex expressed his concerns to me. First, he only had enough teammates to play and no substitutes. He also had only one bat and one ball. We discussed this, and he accepted my offer to be *the* substitute. I told him not to worry about the ball problem. The school had plenty of them, but we'd have to pray his only bat would not be broken. His team had to do the job with only one bat.

The big day came. As Tex and his group approached the field, the schoolboys were already there, resplendent in their team uniforms. They greeted Tex and his group with extensive heckling including many disparaging remarks about his team's lack of proper attire.

The game began with Tex pitching. Soon it was obvious which was the better team. Tex's "scruffians" carried the day. The game ended, and to his credit, the coach walked over to Tex and said in a loud voice, "Son, where can we get uniforms like yours? I think we need to do a lot of improving. Thanks, and you all played a good game."

I have never seen a group of happier kids than Tex and his friends that day.

When school started in the fall of 1943, Boney enrolled Tex and me at St. George Preparatory School as boarders. St Georges was a very fine private school with an excellent reputation for preparing its students for Ivy League universities, West Point, and Annapolis. My education still suffered because of all the disruptions caused by changing schools and not going to class while I was living on the ranch with Herman and Becky Sparks. Moving from Texas to New York City for a semester, and then to Newport was a further disaster for me. The headmaster at St. George's had to create a special curriculum to bring me to the academic level where I should have been. I was a junior, but I took courses at the sophomore level to fill in the gaps in my studies. As I recall, I took sophomore biology, a senior English course, and the remaining courses at the junior level. As a senior, I took no English, but had to take other sophomore and junior level courses as well as senior courses to complete the subject matter the school expected me to master. Even with the special instruction, I still struggled with math and science. When you get behind in these subjects, it's hard to catch up, and school is filled with an ample share of frustration as well as hard work.

As a result of my unique mixture of classes at different levels, I got to know most of the students in the school, but I never became close to any of them. They perhaps didn't know what to make of me, and I didn't feel any class kinship with them, as most freshman, sophomores, juniors, and seniors felt for their classmates. I also played on the football, basketball, and soccer teams, and was captain of the rifle team my senior year; so, St. George's gave me a good balance of academics and athletics.

Tex, in the meantime, was moving smoothly along, becoming a favorite with his classmates and the girls. He was a very handsome and gifted young man. As Tex's older brother, I looked after him as well as I could. I wouldn't let anyone pick a fight with Tex without fighting me first. I was the only one I allowed to fight with him.

Maybe all older brothers aren't protective of their younger brothers, but I sure was.

At Saint George's, all students took turns waiting on tables. One evening, all the table servers were waiting in line to put the food on their trays to carry to their assigned tables. Tex was at the front of the line, and I had taken a place at the end of the line. A junior, (George was his name, I think) came walking in late and went straight to the head of the line and shoved Tex aside. I saw this and reacted immediately.

"You can't do that," I said. "George, I am at the end of the line. You can fall in behind me."

He didn't like that. We had a few more words, and he challenged me to meet him on the football field the next afternoon, after school. I accepted. We were both on the football team; so, the football field seemed to be a good place to duke it out. He was heavier than I was, but I was taller and had a longer reach.

As I walked onto the field the next afternoon in my white football jersey, I noticed that all the windows of the school building overlooking the field were packed with student spectators. They expected to see a big fight, and they did. I also expected this to be a big fight and was determined to win. I blackened his eye, knocked out one of his teeth, and left the field of battle without a scratch.

Later, I learned his parents wanted me expelled, but after hearing the full account of what caused the fight, the headmaster backed me up with no reservations. Afterwards, I noticed that the football coach began giving me more playing time, enough for me to earn a letter.

During the summer of 1944, I "noticed" girls for the first time, especially those whose parents belonged to the Bailey's Beach Swim and Tennis Club. Those folks were the elite of Newport society. My stepfather, Boney, had a guest membership at the club, which I believe was a wartime courtesy extended to military officers stationed in Newport. It was not for altogether altruistic reasons that the club opened its membership, and was also an economic necessity for the club since most men were in the military, and at war, even the Newport blue bloods.

I had a gardening job for a wealthy widow named Mrs. Burden. She was elderly and not much fun to be around. She assigned me to keeping the hedges around her large estate trimmed. This was no small job, but it did have its advantages. Her mansion was located on the corner of two streets, one being the street leading to the Bailey's Beach Club. Sometimes, she would let me hire my brother, Tex, and stepbrother, Bill Close, when she wanted more gardening chores done.

I soon found out that when we had to trim the hedge, if I got the side street section cut quickly I could then cut much more slowly on the hedge that bordered Main Street. The Main Street side was choice because every mid-morning and mid-afternoon many of the young ladies who belonged to the Bailey's Beach Club would pass by on their bicycles. Soon I made friends with several of them by being out front at the right moment. This is when I first learned the value of good reconnaissance.

My friendships with the young ladies of Bailey's Beach Club led me to meeting a young fellow my age named Hugh Auchincloss. Hugh had enlisted in the Marine Corps while under age. The Marine Corps found out about the fraudulent enlistment when Hugh was still a recruit, quickly discharged him, and sent him home. Hugh and I hit it off right away. We were great friends, and spent many hours swimming and riding bicycles together. Hugh had two beautiful stepsisters, Jackie Bouvier and her younger sister Lee. I had a secret crush on Jackie.

My Friend Jackie Bouvier

The Beach Club members planned a big dance during the summer, and my mother said, "Why don't you invite that lovely Jackie Bouvier?" The group of good friends that I hung out with included Jackie, her sister Lee, stepbrother Hugh, my brothers Tex and Billy, and a few others. So my mother's suggestion wasn't totally ludicrous. Well, that parental support was all I needed. I invited Jackie, she accepted, and I was elated.

I bought a gardenia for Jackie with some of my gardening money, and had it delivered by taxi to the Auchincloss mansion. My mother said that was way too extravagant. It was, but I thought it showed a touch of class.

Since I was too young to have a driver's license, I had two choices. I could have my mother drive us to and from the dance—God forbid!—or I could hire a taxi. Even though the taxi would take almost the rest of my earnings, I elected to have a taxi take Jackie and me to the dance and bring us home. It was definitely better than having my mother drive us. To a fifteen year old, having his mother chauffer him and his date was humiliating!

The big night came for my date with Jackie. I know I had a good time and I believe she did too. When the evening ended and I took her home, our goodbye was cordial and polite, but I was not about to kiss her goodnight in front of the taxi driver. Besides, she might rebuff me, and with the taxi driver as witness, my humiliation would be complete.

As you know, Jackie Bouvier married Senator Jack Kennedy who became President of the United States. And Pete Hilgartner went on to do what he most wanted to do in life, to be a soldier. He also carried with him a memory of a very happy time that still brings a smile to his face.

All in all, my years at St. George's were mostly study and hard work. I had a lot of catching up to do. It was not bad though. My goal then was to go to West Point and be a career Army officer. In those days, West Point, the Naval Academy, and the Ivy League schools had very rigorous entrance exams that took three days, one subject in the morning and another in the afternoon. By the time you were finished, you knew you had been through an ordeal. Today, entrance to the military academies and Ivy League schools is determined by SAT scores, which we didn't have back then.

While at St. George's, I took the entrance exams for West Point and flunked the math part; so, after I was graduated from Saint George's, I enrolled in the Severn School in Annapolis, Maryland to work on my math. In those days, Severn had a preparatory school for students taking the entrance exams for West Point, Annapolis, and the Ivy League colleges. Severn was one of many such "prep schools" that gave a cram review of everything offered in the most academically advanced high schools. They also gave frequent tests to prepare students for taking the high pressure entrance exams without clutching. The Severn School cram course was eight hours a day for six and a half days each week. Those students who didn't do well during the week had to go to special classes on Saturday and Sunday to cover material they hadn't mastered. This was no easy trip, and offered a glimpse into what I could expect at either West Point or Annapolis. It also served as the first filter to eliminate those who weren't really committed to the service academies, and weren't prepared to work hard.

I took a long and hard look at what lay ahead. I knew I had problems academically because of my many school disruptions, but I damned sure wasn't going to quit because the road was hard. I wanted to be a soldier, and I wanted the best road to my objective. But before I could go to either West Point or Annapolis, fate had another detour for me.

3.0 MY MILITARY SERVICE BEGINS

In September 1945 our country was still at war. After seeing the movie, *Guadalcanal Diary*, I decided to enlist in the Marine Corps. All my friends had gone to war, and I too had to be in it. However, in mid-September, the war ended and so did my chance to fight. I enlisted anyway. The Marine Corps accepted my enlistment, and Private Hilgartner reported to boot camp at Parris Island, S. C. on October 8, 1945.

Boot camp was tough, as it is supposed to be, but things happened that make for memories and interesting stories. I did well at boot camp. I was a squad leader in my platoon, and held this job the entire time.

Because I was tall and skinny, my G. I. utilities were not long enough. The poor fit of my trousers caused me great grief because I didn't project a proper military image. I looked like Ichabod Crane. When we wore leggings though, it wasn't so bad. They covered the gap between trouser bottoms and field shoes. Still, I was the butt of many jokes.

I had a scary experience while my platoon was on mess duty. My job in the galley was "gofer" and floor swabber. One day the chief cook sent me to the storeroom for potatoes. As I was searching the storeroom for the potatoes, a tough looking Marine truck driver came in to deliver supplies. About the same time, a "BAM" (for Broad Assed Marine as we called female Marines in those politically incorrect days), came in. It was immediately clear that they did not know I was there. Rather than cause an unpleasant scene, I decided that I'd better not let them know I was there. That truck driver would have killed me. From my position behind some shelves, I witnessed a very passionate encounter, of the "bam, bam, thank you ma'am" variety. When I returned with the potatoes, the sergeant cook asked why it took so long. I forget what I told him, but it wasn't about what I'd just seen. In fact I told no one about this for years. I was afraid that truck driver would find me out and do me bodily harm.

I have two other boot camp memories, one fun the other sad. I always enjoyed shooting at the rifle range. It was not supposed to be entertainment, and the gunnery sergeants didn't ease up on those who failed to shoot with proper technique. In spite of the discipline, for me the rifle range was great fun. On the dark side, that Christmas was one of the worst days of my young life. Our platoon was supposed to graduate before Christmas, and I had never before been away from home over The Holidays. Well, we did something to make our gunny sergeant unhappy, and he held us over Christmas Day as punishment. There was only one telephone booth for us to call home, and it seemed endless waiting in a line for my turn. There weren't many dry eyes in that long line of "tough Marine warriors" that day, including mine.

My first orders as a Marine were to duty in Peking, China, but I was pulled from the Ninety Second replacement draft and ordered to report for duty at the Naval Academy Preparatory School (NAPS) at Camp Perry, near Williamsburg, Virginia. My mother had secured a Congressional Third alternate appointment to West Point for me, and my change of orders was in response to my receiving that appointment to the Military Academy.

NAPS prepares candidates to take both service academy's entrance exams. After reporting to NAPS at Camp Perry, I took the West Point exams and passed, as did the principal appointee; so, once again I was foiled. But the disappointment was eased by my new interest in the Naval Academy generated by my stepfather, Boney Close, and the fact that I was now a Marine ensured my reentry into the Marine Corps after graduation.

Since I had passed the entrance exams, West Point offered me an athletic appointment to play basketball, but I could not enter the Military Academy until the following year. Also, since I had passed the West Point exam, the Navy and the Marine Corps gave me a Fleet appointment to the Naval Academy; consequently, I received orders back to NAPS.

In the summer of 1946, the Navy relocated NAPS to Bainbridge, Maryland; so, I reported to Bainbridge. Because I had been to the Camp Perry NAPS, I was called a NAPS *sophomore* along with several other Marines and sailors who also had been to NAPS Camp Perry. I was an old hand at the Navy School routine by this time, and I made some life-long friends at Bainbridge. Men like "Gunny" Balderston, Jack Grace, Haig Donabedian, Bill Duncan, Milton Shaw, Pete Hill, Bill Gorski, Bill Holmberg, and Warren "Kit" Kitterman were with me at the Naval Academy, in the Marines, and later on in civilian life. These are some of the finest men I have ever known.

Among the Marines assigned to NAPS Bainbridge were two young men of future fame and fortune. One was Gus Pabst, scion of the Pabst Brewery. Gus didn't go to the Naval Academy, but went on to enter his family business. We should all thank Gus for providing party fuel for his brothers in arms. The other future superstar was Hugh Krampe. Hugh had been a drill instructor at Parris Island, and had a reputation as an "old salt." Hugh didn't make it to the Naval Academy either, but he went on to distinguish himself in another way. He became actor Hugh O'Brien, whom you know as Wyatt Earp of the long running television series by that name in the late 1950s and early 1960s.

At NAPS, I was now taking the cram course for the third time; so, the studies were not as difficult. With life a bit easier I had time to take advantage of all the liberty and entertainment available to young Marines. Balderston and Donabedian, being the two senior Marine noncommissioned officers, made every effort to rein me in, but it was mostly to no avail. (For those not familiar with Marine Corps officer ranks and enlisted ratings, see Appendix A.)

One time I had to wash the windows in their room in the barracks as unofficial punishment. I don't recall that the punishment did much to catch my attention or square me away. Another instance

I remember, Gunny was planning to put me on a work detail. I found out about Gunny's plans, and slipped away. He chased me all over the base. He spotted me just as I got on a bus to go to the Post Exchange (PX), and I saw Gunny jump on the next bus in hot pursuit. I don't recall how long the chase lasted, but I escaped being put on that particular work detail. I just rode the bus full circuit until it returned to my starting point. Then I hopped off and slipped back into the barracks. I won that engagement, but Gunny had a long memory. He nailed me for countless work details and unpleasant extra duty for the rest of the time we were at Bainbridge. I won the battle, but Gunny won the campaign.

Once again the Naval Academy entrance exams were upon us; this time I passed! I also had the West Point appointment to play basketball; so, I now was accepted by both service academies. The day I was to take the Army physical, I came down with a bad case of the flu. I was too sick even to go to sickbay. Bill Gorski, Bill Holmberg, and our Navy Corpsman, Doc Groner, attended to me. They brought me medicine, water, and food to pull me through. Holmberg got the Navy chaplain involved. The chaplain sent a telegram to West Point explaining my illness, and requesting another date for me to take the physical.

But my destiny was not to follow the road to the Military Academy. The date I was to report to West Point for the physical was the same date I was to be sworn into the Naval Academy. The choice was easy: Once a Marine, always a Marine, and I knew Annapolis would make my mother and Boney very happy.

In June of 1947, those Marines at NAPS who passed the entrance exams received orders to the Annapolis Marine detachment to await discharge from the Marine Corps and induction into the Naval Academy. We weren't in the Marine detachment long, and weren't given any duties the few days we were there.

The day before I was to enter the Academy, I walked around the Academy yard looking at the buildings, monuments, athletic fields, and parade grounds to absorb the history, sights, sounds, and feel of the place that would be my home for the next four years. It was an overwhelming experience! I was alone when I stopped in front of the majestic statue of Tecumseh, the Delaware Indian Chief who brings midshipmen good luck in their examinations and athletic contests with West Point. Every year, the Brigade of Midshipmen decorates Tecumseh in elaborate war paint before the Army-Navy Game to bring them good luck in their football encounter with the cadets. Midshipmen also throw pennies at Tecumseh and render him left handed salutes as they march by on their way to academic examinations in hopes the *God of 2.5*, a passing grade, will smile upon them and bring them good fortune.

Tecumseh overlooks the huge courtyard in front of Bancroft Hall where the Brigade forms up for meals. I looked down, and there on the ground at the base of the statue was a wallet. I opened the wallet and saw that it belonged to Captain Blue, United States Navy who was the senior doctor at the Academy. I located his office and immediately went there to return the wallet. I walked into Captain Blue's office and was greeted by his secretary, who asked me what I wanted.

"I found this wallet," I said, "and I believe it belongs to the Captain."

She replied, "Thank you, I'll take it to him."

I told her that I wanted to give it to him myself. When I was ushered into his office and gave the Captain his wallet, he was most grateful. He said he would like to give me a monetary reward, but I told him I couldn't accept that.

He asked me what my business at the Academy was, and I told him I was entering tomorrow if I passed the physical exam to be given in the morning.

Captain Blue then asked me, "Well, son, how's your health?"

"Sir," I said, "my health is fine except I'm a little too tall and a little underweight. I'm six feet five inches tall and weigh 165 pounds. The Academy height limit is six feet four and 170 pounds for that height."

He replied, "You look like you're in good health to me. Thanks for returning my wallet."

The next morning I was dressed in my midshipman's "white works" uniform with my name stenciled across the chest of my jumper. At the required time, I reported to the Academy Sick Bay for my physical exam. When my turn came to be weighed and my height measured, the corpsman looked at me as I was about to step on the scale and said, "Move on midshipman. You've *been* weighed and measured!"

And for the next four years, including my commissioning physical, I was never weighed or measured. This was Captain Blue's thanks for returning his wallet. I was then, and am now, most grateful to him for overlooking my height problem.

On 18 June 1947, my life as Midshipman Peter L. Hilgartner, United States Navy began. After we were sworn in, I was assigned to a plebe cutter crew. All the plebes were assigned to cutter crews, which were the organizations by which we held muster, marched to the mess hall, were assigned to training exercises, classroom instruction, and all the many activities of the very hectic plebe summer. My NAPS gunnery sergeant, Gene Balderston, was in my cutter crew, and was also my Bancroft Hall roommate. At NAPS we called Gene 'Gunny' (as was every gunnery sergeant in the Marine Corps), and the nickname stuck with him throughout his Academy years and the rest of his Marine Corps career. Gunny, by the way, was one of the oldest midshipmen in the Class of 1951.

Our first night in Bancroft Hall, as we were getting ready for bed, Gene climbed into his lower bunk first. Gunny had commandeered the lower bunk because it was more desirable than the top bunk. It was easier to get into. Even though we were lowly plebes, Gunny still felt senior to me.

Then he said to me, "Pete, turn off the lights before you get into your bunk."

It seemed I had been taking orders from Gunny forever. Now he had given me the opportunity of a lifetime. I couldn't resist. So, I said, "Gunny, I've been waiting a long time to say this. Fuck you! Turn the lights off yourself!" Then I climbed into the top bunk leaving the lights on.

Gunny got up laughing and said, "Pete, you are a real S.O.B!"

Then we both laughed. Gene and I saw each other often during our Academy days and Marine Corps careers. He is a wonderful person and great friend.

Plebe Summer was a tough grind, as it's supposed to be. The eight-week ordeal filters out those who don't have a real commitment to the Navy, the Marine Corps, and the Academy. It is a training regimen of long days, constant running, classroom instruction, and being barked at by officers and senior enlisted men who are there to oversee the process of converting civilians into midshipmen. Plebe Summer quickly shapes up those who are in marginal or poor physical condition. Even those who thought they were in great physical condition before entering the Academy became "leaner and meaner" during Plebe Summer. You either "shaped up," or "shipped out." The heat and humidity of an Annapolis summer are stifling. Most of us lost about ten pounds, and I didn't have ten extra pounds to lose. We also lost an average of 2 to 3 people each week who decided this was not the life for them. By the end of the eight weeks of Plebe Summer the survivors were ready to join the Brigade of Midshipmen.

After Plebe Summer, the academic year began. I quickly found that The Naval Academy is a rough road for those who are not well prepared academically, physically, and psychologically. The Naval Academy academic workload is intense and fast paced. Academics are heavily oriented to mathematics and science. If those aren't your strong suite, woe be unto you. Those who don't pick academic subjects up quickly are soon left behind, and they have to run hard to catch up.

Those who aren't prepared psychologically find the rigors of Academy life more than they can handle. Between academic failure and psychological failure in the form of resignations, we lost 21 percent of my Naval Academy class, which is about average. The next four years were to test my mettle, my resolve, and my desire to attain my goal of being a Marine officer. I was being tested like never before, and I resolved that I would not be defeated or quit because the trip was too hard.

Christmas 1947 was approaching fast. My NAPS friend, Bill Holmberg, and I had no home to go to for the occasion. My mother and Boney were in China, and Bill's parents were on the West Coast. Back in those days, a trip from the East Coast to California was a major undertaking that took almost as much time as we had for Christmas leave. Flying was not an option and the train took five days each way. That would have given Bill two days at home before getting on the train to come back to Annapolis.

Both of us were products of the Naval Academy Preparatory School in Bainbridge, Maryland, Marine Detachment. Since we had not taken our allotted thirty days leave, we still had our unused leave pay of about sixty dollars each. This was a small fortune for two plebes of the class of 1951.

So what to do for Christmas that would be fun? It didn't take long for a bold plan of action to develop. We would take the train to Boston, stay in a fancy hotel and find some girls willing to go out with two of the world's finest and most handsome young men . . . "the spoiled and pampered pets of Uncle Sam," as midshipmen were called back then.

When the great day for Christmas leave arrived, Bill and I were ready, and off to Boston we went. Somehow, I recall our fortune had grown to about a hundred dollars each, which went a long way in 1947.

Boston was beautiful. Snow was on the ground, and the view from our hotel room was spectacular. Breakfast in bed was even better. We weren't plebes anymore; we were kings! Shortly after breakfast, I called an old friend's sister, and asked her for a date. She accepted and said she could also find a date for Bill. The next three days flew by. Patty, my date, had a car, and we went all over the Boston area sightseeing and having a great time. Then came the day to depart, and the hard facts hit us. We only had funds for two tickets to New York City, and about four dollars left to spend there.

No problem! When we got to New York City we would stay at

the Soldiers and Sailors Club for fifty cents a night. Someway fate, or dumb luck, would provide for our other needs.

Arrival in New York went according to plan. Since we were wearing our Naval Academy uniforms, the club hostess gave us a friendly greeting and asked about our plans while in the city. Our answer was stone silence.

Then she said, "Would you boys like a couple of tickets to the radio show, *Break the Bank*? Before the days of television, this was a popular radio show emceed by Bert Parks, future host of the *Miss America* TV show. It was comparable to getting two tickets to a major TV game show today, such as *Jeopardy*. We jumped at the offer, and accepted the two tickets. We did high-fives all the way to our bunks in the club.

The next day Bill found a date for himself; so, I went solo with the two tickets to the Radio City Music Hall. There was a long line when I arrived. In response to an old lady's plea, I gave Bill's ticket to her and went inside. Looking over the audience I spotted a West Point cadet in uniform. He was sitting with an empty seat beside him. I headed for that seat like a man with a mission.

When he spotted me in my Naval Academy uniform, he jumped up and said, "Are you thinking what I'm thinking?"

I answered, "You bet, partner."

We then shook hands and introduced ourselves. His name was Dene Balmer, USMA, Class of 1950.

The announcer came out and asked if any in the audience wanted to be contestants, they should raise their hands. Dene and I stood up, raised ours, and we were immediately selected. Just getting onstage meant we each got $25. This was enough for two train tickets back to Annapolis.

Our next challenge was to survive the cut to determine those who would be contestants on the program. We were again selected. They just couldn't resist the appeal of a West Point cadet and Naval Academy midshipman team. After making the first cut, we progressed to the quiz part of the program. I answered the first question correctly. Then Dene took charge. We were up to $400 before we missed a question. We were not disappointed. Two very happy young men walked off the stage, each with $200 in his pocket, and Joint Operations had its first big success.

I immediately headed for the train station, purchased two tickets to Annapolis, and then called Bill. He informed me he and his date had not been able to find a date for me. They had done the best they could, but I was solo. I told them not to worry, and for them to meet me in the ballroom of the Waldorf-Astoria. We were going to celebrate!

I arrived at the Waldorf well ahead of Bill and his date. In fact, I had time to eat something and listen to Russ Morgan's Band. He had a lovely young singer named Pat Laird. After a few songs, the band stopped for a break and the drummer came over and asked me if I'd like to meet the singer.

"I sure would!" I exclaimed.

So, Pat Laird came over and sat down to talk with me. About that time Bill and his date arrived. We asked Pat if she would like to go out with us after her show. She accepted, to my great pleasure.

That evening and the next two nights, the four of us had a wonderful time. Our last night was New Year's Eve at the Diamond Horseshoe, where we were guests of Billy Rose, the owner. At midnight when the balloons came floating down, each girl popped a balloon and won a gift. Despite our special treatment at the Diamond Horseshoe, when we parted company with the girls, our pockets were empty, but our hearts were full. An officer and a gentleman does not concern himself with pecuniary minutia when he is attending to the delights of fair maidens.

The following morning two exhausted, happy, and broke midshipmen boarded the train to Annapolis. We had the Christmas vacation and adventure of a lifetime! Our small wealth was gone, but we were psychologically refreshed and ready to meet the remaining challenges of plebe year.

Our youngster (sophomore) year began with a cruise on the USS Missouri (BB-63). At the end of WWII, the Japanese surrendered in ceremonies on the Missouri's flag quarterdeck, which were attended by all the Allied senior military officers and the Japanese senior military and diplomatic corps. The site is marked with a commemorative plaque, and the Mighty Mo became a national shrine. She is a truly beautiful ship that has an indelible place in the hearts of every member of The Class of 1951.

As youngsters on our first training cruise, we did the work of ordinary seamen. We scrubbed and holystoned the Missouri's teakwood decks, chipped and painted, polished bright work, and swabbed all manner of things to keep the Mighty Mo shipshape. We handled lines during ship-to-ship refueling, labored on ship work details, and loaded ammunition for the main and secondary batteries during gunnery exercises. It was hard work.

One day while we were anchored, another midshipman and I were sent to the anchor chain locker on some now forgotten chore. While there, we heard the engines start up to weigh anchor. Each link in the anchor chain was the size of an automobile. We knew we had to get out of there immediately. Somehow, the door to the chain locker had become locked. There was no way to exit other than to climb out through the anchor chain hole to the deck. The other midshipman went first. I was getting ready to get out when there was a jerk in the anchor chain. It was getting out then or never! I barely made it out in time, but in doing so I severely pulled some muscles in my lower abdomen.

I went to sickbay, and the doctor said I would need surgery to repair the damage. The ship's medical staff performed the operation, and I was placed on light duty for the remainder of the cruise. I was able to go ashore at the liberty ports we made, but I was still in discomfort and pain.

When we returned to Annapolis, I reported to the Naval Academy sickbay. The pain had not diminished. It was worse; so, the Academy medical staff decided to operate again to find my problem. In little more than a month, I went under the knife once more. The Academy surgeons found that the Missouri's surgeons had not untied some veins they had stopped off during the first operation, and they had left a small surgical tool inside me. After the second operation, I was in and out of the hospital several more times, and I needed a third operation to repair the damage done by the shipboard surgery. The only satisfaction I got out of the entire miserable affair was knowing that the Missouri's sickbay found their surgical inventory missing one of their tools, and somebody had to explain what happened to it during a Title B survey.

I was supposed to play basketball at the Academy, but my medical problems finished any contact sports for me. Instead, I went out for the rifle team, and played intramural tennis and squash. In hindsight, the injury probably saved my Academy career. I was a very poor student in math and engineering subjects, which were most of the Academy's curriculum. By not participating in a major team sport, I had more time to study. Studies didn't stop me from having some fun though. I did invite young ladies to the Academy from time to time and went to the hops, as did my roommate, Bill Gorski. Ski was also a Marine from NAPS.

I recall one humorous occasion when Ski really fouled up and inadvertently invited two young ladies to the same hop, Academy slang for "dance." Midshipmen called inviting young ladies to hops "dragging" back in those days, and midshipmen called their dates "drags". Dragging was an involved weekend affair that entailed the young lady's arrival Saturday morning in time for luncheon, then going to an athletic event in the early afternoon. Mid-afternoon featured sailing, tennis, sightseeing in Annapolis, or any of a large number of activities until time to dress for dinner and the dance. The dance itself usually lasted from 7:00 p.m. until 10:30 p.m. after which the midshipmen escorted their ladies back to their lodgings so the midshipmen could be back in Bancroft Hall for sign-in muster at 11:30 p.m. Sunday morning usually involved breakfast at a nice restaurant followed by services at the Naval Academy Chapel, and finally escorting the young lady to the bus taking her home. You can see that dragging two young ladies during the same weekend required minute attention to detail, exquisite timing, and nerves of steel . . . much like juggling sharp knives, or perhaps chain saws would be more like it.

On this sorry occasion, one of Ski's two drags was a lovely girl from Baltimore, named Jeanne Brandon. My brother, Tex, and I knew and admired Jeanne, and both of us had dated her several times. In fact, I introduced Jeanne to Ski. She was a wonderful and lovely young lady who deserved nothing but the best. I don't remember the name of the other girl, but certainly neither of them deserved to be part of a juggling act.

With two drags converging upon Annapolis, Ski had a big problem! He should have cancelled one of the invitations, but he didn't want disappoint either of them. Ski made a strategic error. He elected the high-pressure, thrill-packed, but not very smart option of dating them both over the same weekend. To make his wild scheme work, Ski had to enlist at least four or five of his classmates to help.

In those days, midshipmen gave their young ladies dance cards for the hops, which were held in the cavernous Academy armory, Dahlgren Hall. Each young lady's card had every dance listed by number with the names of the midshipmen scheduled to have each dance. The young lady would then know when her escort would dance with her, and who would take his place for other dances. Dahlgren Hall was so large that neither of Ski's drags would likely spot him with the other. This part of the plan could work!

With his classmates helping on the dance card, the hop would be no problem. He could easily get from one girl to the other without having either suspect what was happening. But the real challenge would be the extra-curricular activities and dinner. Ski had to arrange for classmates to escort the two young ladies to athletic events and other activities while he disappeared under the guise of Academy duties in Bancroft Hall. Ski would appear at strategic moments wearing a sword and an armband to make his duties appear to be real; then after a few moments of polite chitchat with one of his drags, he disappeared again. For dinner, he had to plan—and be at—two dinners at two separate restaurants, but at staggered times. He managed to cover his dinner disappearances by including his drags with groups of other classmates and their drags so his young ladies wouldn't be left embarrassingly alone while he attended to the other drag. This became a mammoth operation!

Jeanne Brandon finally understood what was going on, and to her credit took it with good humor. I don't know if the other girl ever knew what was happening, or if she did whether she was a good sport about it. I do know that it was a hectic weekend, and none of us wanted to try it again. Neither young lady ever accepted another invitation for a weekend in Annapolis from Ski. Does that surprise you?

In June 1949, youngster year ended and our second-class summer cruise began. This cruise introduced midshipmen to various career paths in the Navy and Marine Corps. It was a two phased cruise primarily oriented toward Navy and Marine aviation. The first phase was called "Air Cruise." At the end of Air Cruise, some of us went to destroyers and submarines for anti-submarine warfare (ASW) training. The rest joined West Point cadets in a large, mock amphibious assault against aggressor forces to introduce us to Marine Corps operations. This group was stationed at the U.S. Naval Amphibious Base in Little Creek, Virginia. I was in this group, and thoroughly enjoyed it.

Navy Air gave those of us at Little Creek flying lessons in N3N pontoon planes and PB-Y amphibious patrol planes. I had no interest in flying Navy or Marine Air, but I did enjoy my cockpit time in those old planes. I was too tall to sit in the control seat of the PB-Y; so, I was allowed to pilot the plane briefly while standing behind the pilot's seat. For those of us not planning to go into aviation, liberty and parties were our main events.

When we were at the Academy between cruises, my summer roommate was James Wesley Hammond. Wes also wanted a Marine Corps career. One weekend, we had liberty and I invited Wes to my mother's and stepfather's new home in McLean, Virginia. On Sunday, we persuaded Boney to loan us his jeep station wagon so we could get back to the Academy on time.

Although I had no driver's license, I decided to drive back. We had only gone a short distance from the house when a policeman stopped us. I was speeding he said. I began apologizing profusely, explaining the consequences that would befall us if I received a citation from him. Wes jumped into the breach and told the officer he had a driver's license, and that if he would not ticket me, he would drive the car to Annapolis. The officer agreed, and we resumed our journey with Wes at the wheel. The encounter with the police officer took about thirty precious minutes. We had barely enough time to make it back before taps.

When we arrived in Annapolis, there was no time to search for a parking space. Parking in Annapolis was scarce then, and is no better today. We needed to be as close to the main gate as possible. As luck would have it, we found a spot near the main gate on Maryland Avenue. Wes cruised right into it, but just then our luck ran out. Our space was right in front of a Naval Academy professor's house at 215 Hanover Street, and he was sitting on his front porch as we pulled in.

"Hey, you midshipmen, you can't park there," he yelled.

Paying no attention, Wes and I took off. We ran through the main gate and passed the *Jimmy Legs* (the gate's guard), who was a retired Navy Chief Petty Officer. As we ran past the chapel, the officer of the day and his midshipman assistant spotted us and took up the chase. We were now not running, but *flying*, and outdistancing the OOD who was hampered by his clanking sword that we could hear fading into the background.

Our rooms were on the second deck of the second wing of Bancroft Hall. The first deck was at terrace level where there was a room with an open window. One-third of the window was open from the bottom, the other third from the top. Wes dove through the bottom and I proceeded to climb in through the top, landing on Wes as I wiggled through.

Wes said something profane when I landed on him, but there was no time for further discussion. We ran up the ladder, down the hall, and into our room. We had just enough time to take off our shoes and jump into bed and pull the sheets up to our necks.

The door opened and it was the officer of the day. "Did you see two midshipmen running down this hall?" he asked.

"No, sir," we answered.

After the OOD departed, Wes asked, "Pete, we broke the honor code."

"No way," I said. "We could not have *seen* those two midshipmen. We *were* those midshipmen!"

The next morning I woke up at about 5 a.m. Then I woke Wes.

"What's up, Pete?" he asked.

"Wes, what are we going to do about the jeep? They will trace the license plate and find out who owns it, and then we are done for."

"Well," Wes said sleepily, "that's your problem, old buddy, and it doesn't need two to fix it." Wes went back to sleep. I could have killed him!

I decided the best defense is a good offense. So, I quickly dressed and went to the main gate to throw myself on the mercy of the Jimmy Legs. Another retired Navy Chief Petty Officer was on duty at the main gate. I proceeded to tell him what happened, and pleaded with him to give me a few minutes to go out to move the car.

"I'll give you ten minutes, midshipman," he said, and suggested that I might find a spot about two blocks away.

I did and was able to return within the allotted ten minutes. "Thanks, Chief," I said. "It won't happen again."

"Good luck, midshipman." he called as I sprinted back to Bancroft Hall.

After our summer training following Youngster Year, the Academy gave us a month's leave. My mother and Boney lived close by in McLean, Virginia, and I looked forward to going home.

When I arrived home, I learned that my eight-year-old cousin, Lisa Hebo, had been kidnapped. My mother's sister, Aunt Lovie, had been married to a Dane named Halfdan Hebo. After their messy divorce, the court awarded Aunt Lovie custody of Lisa. The court granted Lisa's father visitation rights, but he wanted custody and continued to contest the matter. As required by the terms of the divorce, Lisa went to visit her father in New York City and did not return. Her father took her to Denmark, without authorization, in effect kidnapping Lisa.

When Lisa did not return home, Aunt Lovie called the police, and Halfdan Hebo was charged with kidnapping. He later returned to New York, was arrested, and put in jail. Hebo refused to divulge Lisa's whereabouts; so, remained in jail for refusing to cooperate.

We suspected that Hebo had taken Lisa to Denmark, and placed her with his relatives, who were Danish farmers. We were almost certain that she was living on a farm on one of the many islands that comprise Denmark, but how were we to get her back? We couldn't wait for the diplomatic bureaucracy to locate her and send her home. By the time the courts, police, and diplomats of both countries finished their negotiations and diplomatic mumbo-jumbo, Lisa would be a grown woman. In fact, Hebo was counting on that lack of governmental responsiveness. That way he would have defacto custody without receiving official custody of Lisa by the courts in either Denmark or the United States. We had to act. One of the family had to go to Denmark to search for Lisa, and I drew the assignment.

I was deeply apprehensive, but I agreed to try. I was only twenty years old and had never been outside of the United States other than during my Naval Academy Youngster Cruise. This trip would be a totally different operation. I would be alone in a foreign country searching for one small child, and I didn't speak a word of Danish. This seemed like a fool's errand, but I took the challenge. It was a matter of honor. I couldn't refuse.

Boney Close, made arrangements for me to get passage to Bremerhaven, Germany on a military sea transport service (MSTS) ship. From there I had to travel by train to Copenhagen to join a Danish attorney retained by Aunt Lovie. In early August 1948, I boarded an MSTS transport headed for Bremerhaven. Even if I couldn't locate Lisa, it would be an adventure.

In the Navy, midshipmen are sometimes treated as officers; at other times they are regarded as enlisted men since they are not yet commissioned. I was bunked in the hold with the ship's crew, which was okay with me. They were a good bunch with an impromptu band, and I played the drums. I wasn't worth a damn as a drummer, but I made a lot of noise and it was fun.

After I boarded the train at Bremerhaven, Germany I found myself in a compartment with some Norwegians on their way to Denmark. They were partying fools with lots of good schnapps, and we *ein scholed dien scholed* all the way to Copenhagen. This was my introduction to schnapps; so, I didn't know to treat it with great respect. Nor did I know what *ein schol dien schol* meant, but after saying it we all had to drink our glasses bottoms up, and hold the glass out for a refill. I think the translation means: *I'm either stupid, drunk, brain-dead, or all of the above.* I was not inebriated when I met Aunt Lovie's attorney the next day, but no one would have accused me of being in total control of my faculties. Anyone who thinks you can't get goat-faced on schnapps has a major lesson to learn.

I stayed in a comfortable hotel that served wonderful meals, but I was anxious to get on with the search the day following my arrival in Copenhagen. By the time the attorney picked me up, I had shaken off most of the schnapps cobwebs. He had road maps and phone books, which we studied to decide where to start. The attorney, Erik, called Aunt Lovie, and had a long conversation with her about Halfdan Hebo's family and other things he thought might bear on the search.

After finishing our data collection and analysis, which took the entire first day, we found that the name Hebo is fairly common in Denmark, which is a nation of islands. There seemed to be a concentration of Hebos located in the vicinity of two islands, Zealand and Fyn. Copenhagen, the capital and largest city in Denmark, is located on Zealand, the largest and easternmost island that is closest to Sweden. Fyn, the second largest island is a two-hour drive from Copenhagen that includes traversing a long bridge connecting Zealand and Fyn. Zealand seemed a logical place to start. We spent the afternoon searching the area outside of Copenhagen, going from farm to farm with no luck. We didn't find Lisa, but we got a tip from a Danish farmer who thought we'd do better in our search if we concentrated on Fyn. This seemed to make sense since Hebo would most likely have taken Lisa as far away from Copenhagen as he could, because anyone looking for her would probably start near the most important city in Denmark.

The next day, we decided to reconnoiter Fyn, and began driving from farm to farm asking, "Have you seen a little eight year old American girl with curly blonde hair?" It seemed we were heading for another day of futility and frustration. In early afternoon, we were driving down a rural road when I saw a farmer on a tractor with a little blond-haired girl beside him.

"Stop the car." I said, "I think that child could be Lisa."

We drove up to the farmhouse. Erik asked to speak with the farmer, and requested that he bring the little girl with him. When the farmer appeared

Lisa Hebo: The Day We Found Her

he did not have the little girl with him. Erik asked where she was and the farmer said she was outside near the tractor. We went outside, I saw her and called her name. She ran to me with tears in her eyes and gave me a hug. We had found Lisa!

Erik told the farmer and his family that Hebo was in jail in the United States facing charges for kidnapping. He emphasized that kidnapping was a very serious charge, and that aiding and abetting a kidnapping would bring a long jail sentence. He told the farmer that Lisa could stay with the farmer and his family until the Danish police came for her. Erik told them that Lisa was not to be removed from her present location, and that if they failed to cooperate with the police they would be prosecuted. This got the farmer's attention.

Lisa was so traumatized by being taken from her mother that she temporarily lost her ability to speak. However, we *had* found Lisa! I took a photograph of her to prove it. When I phoned Aunt Lovie with the news, the entire family was relieved and elated. For me, it had been an exciting and rewarding adventure, but I was ready to go home for a bit of decompression and relaxation before returning to the Academy.

This was not the end of the Lisa story, although it was the end of the part I played. The Danish authorities did not want to surrender Lisa to the American embassy for transportation home. Aunt Lovie was not about to be thwarted at this point. As a beautiful and successful Broadway actress, she had many well-placed contacts in diplomatic circles. She called on British friends who responded by forming a covert team to take Lisa from the farm and fly her in a private plane to England. Lisa and Aunt Lovie were reunited in London, and they came home about a year after I found her. Lisa's life returned to normal and she grew up like any other little girl. She still is not comfortable talking about this incident; so, the trauma remains.

In spite of Hebo's villainy, my aunt elected not to prosecute him further, and he was released from jail. Lisa did not visit him again. For our family, Hebo was seldom seen, seldom brought to mind. We did learn some years later that a mugger killed him during a street robbery in New York. Perhaps justice was wrought in a strange way.

My trip home was again via MSTS, but aboard this ship I was treated as a junior officer. To my delight, there was a bevy of college girls on board, which made the long voyage pleasant and at times downright exciting. I had a wonderful time flirting with the young ladies, some of whom wanted me to invite them to the Academy for hops during the forthcoming academic year. Being ever the artful dodger, I escaped at voyage end without any declarations of undying love, promises to write, choked-up farewells, or major commitments encumbering my second-class year.

We had a wonderful Baptist chaplain aboard who had been a professional boxer in his younger years before he entered the ministry. As a wise strategy to keep slap and tickle among the college students to a minimum, he taught boxing to all the male students. I guess he thought that expending that over-abundance of testosterone whaling the daylights out of each other would protect the young ladies from being exposed to the slippery slope of too much time and too much opportunity. Verily, verily, I say unto thee, stamp out wickedness before it can raise its ugly head.

When I reached home, I confess that I was pleased with myself. This was a successful operation. I was a twenty-year old midshipman who had been given a mission with very little direction and a high probability of failure. I didn't fail, and I came home with my mission accomplished. As I look back on it, I am amazed that things worked out so well. I would like to claim that success was the product of my brilliance, but good luck and probably providence made the day. I'm reminded of Napoleon's comment whenever anyone recommended a new general to him, "Don't tell me how good he is. Is he lucky?"

Bill, Pete, and Tex

I returned to the Naval Academy for second class year. This was the toughest academically, a "make or break" year. All I did was study, go to extra instruction and study some more. For the entire year, I had no dates except for the ring dance, when I had a blind date. My only respite from the academic grind was occasionally seeing my brothers, Tex and Bill, who roomed together at Princeton University. Tex became captain of the Princeton fencing team, and Bill became battalion commander for the Princeton NROTC unit, the highest ranking NROTC midshipman.

My worst subject was electrical engineering, which the midshipmen called *juice*. I just did not get it, and believed I would never understand the subject. I feared I was doomed to bilge out! After all this hard work, my goal seemed to be slipping away. I refused to give up. After our midterm exams, the electrical engineering department assigned us to classes by how well we were doing in the subject. I was assigned to what the midshipmen called the "bucket" group. These were midshipmen who were in danger of failing the subject, and needed special attention to help them "pull sat" (midshipman jargon for getting a satisfactory passing grade). After we had taken our seats in the classroom, our new instructor entered. He was an elderly, gray haired gentleman wearing the uniform of a lieutenant commander.

He introduced himself, then said, "Gents, I know why you're here. All of you are having trouble with this course. I think it is important that you learn this material, and not be worried about grades. Therefore, this is what I'm going to do. No matter how poorly you do on the daily quizzes, the lowest grade you'll receive is a 2.5 or 62.5 percent, which is the lowest passing grade. If you make a higher grade on the daily quizzes, you'll receive that grade. You will receive the actual grade you make on the final exam. Your final grade will be the normal combination of grades you received on your daily quizzes and the final exam."

There was an audible sigh of relief from the entire class. It went exactly as he told us, and my final average for the daily quizzes was a 3.2. On the day of the final exam, I was going down the ladder when my friend and self-appointed upper classman tutor, John Niesse, was coming up the ladder.

As we passed, John stopped me and said, "Where are you going, Pete?"

"I'm on my way to take the juice exam."

"Do you know how to solve *this* problem?" he said and proceeded to ask me the question.

"No," I replied. He then gave me the answer.

By a stroke of great luck, that question was the first one on the exam, and the only one I could answer correctly. How John knew this would be on the exam, I'll never know. He was a year ahead of me, and taking different courses. Perhaps he remembered what had been on his juice exam the previous year. Then again, perhaps he was God's messenger, and that God's plan didn't include my bilging out of the Naval Academy. Was I part of God's cosmic plan, or was I just lucky? I would like to think that Divine guidance had taken a hand in my destiny, but more than likely it was dumb luck.

My final grade for the course, after taking the exam, was computed at 2.497, which the Electrical Engineering Department rounded up to a 2.50. Had it not been for my bucket section professor who helped me to build up enough "gravy" at 3.2 on my dailies and John Niesse, I would *never* have graduated from the Naval Academy.

When second class year ended, those of us who advanced to first classmen knew our chances of graduating were good. The government had too much invested in us at that point, and we were needed for the Korean War.

First class year at "Canoe U" was the most enjoyable of my four years there. I was able to handle the academics, and first classmen had more liberty time than the rest of the Brigade. More liberty was a first class rate, and now I had time to do fun things. I was in tall cotton; that is, until our new Superintendent, Vice Admiral Harry W. Hill, USN, reported aboard.

Admiral Hill thought the Naval Academy had become too lax in its discipline. He thought the midshipmen were getting too much time off from the Academy, and were acting like we were at an Ivy League school instead of a military academy. The admiral was convinced that we weren't working hard enough at our academic and professional studies. He thought we had lost the focus on why we were at Navy. Well, the new broom swept clean and our happy days came to an abrupt end. Admiral Hill turned the screw down big time on the class of 1951. Official liberty hours and days were curtailed. Then he made matters worse by requiring first classmen to march to all classes. Proceeding independently to class had always been a coveted first class rate. Now it was gone. We were peons again.

I was a member of the rifle team. Our team captain was my classmate and good friend, Emmons Woolwine, a fun-loving guy from Tennessee. He didn't like the new superintendent's restrictions on our freedom anymore than I did. In our *joie d' vivre*, Emmons and I sometimes pressed the envelope of acceptable behavior.

There was a wonderful beer hall in Eastport, just over the Spa Creek Bridge from the Annapolis Historic Harbor that had country-western music on Friday and Saturday nights. The good music always drew a crowd of "yaller-haired gals" for the young Eastport bucks to dance with. Most of the yellow-haired girls were young, pretty, single, not always blond, but always available. Since they served beer, and because it was against regulations for midshipmen to drink alcoholic beverages inside a ten-mile radius of the Naval Academy chapel dome, the beer hall was off-limits to midshipmen. We also were forbidden to go beyond the ten-mile limit, except when we were on official leave. That was my introduction to logical disconnects that later became famous as "Catch 22," but for us it translated into midshipmen are not allowed to drink adult beverages.

Emmons and I decided to sneak out to the Eastport beer hall one evening to enjoy forbidden pleasures. Having no civilian clothes at the Academy, we went in uniform. We had just been seated in a booth and filled our glasses from a pitcher of beer when disaster loomed.

In walked a Navy lieutenant with his pretty date. This officer was one of our instructors, and knew both of us. We were in big trouble. There was no way we could flee without being seen.

"What are we going to do now?" Emmons asked.

I said, "Let's attack!"

"You mean buy him a pitcher of beer?"

"Yes," I said.

So that's exactly what we did, and instructed the waiter to tell the officer the beer was from us. The waiter delivered the pitcher of beer, and when the officer looked our way, we raised our glasses in a comradely greeting. He raised his in return. With the situation apparently defused, we made a hasty exit leaving our pitcher of beer hardly touched. All the way back to the Academy, we were breathing sighs of relief, but far from sure we were home free.

"Do you think he'll say something to us in class?" I asked.

"I don't think so," said Emmons, "He didn't say anything in the beer hall, probably to avoid upsetting his date. I doubt he'll mention it in class. I suspect he'll forget all about it. Besides, he probably drank beer illegally when he was a mid."

We took aggressive action and won. If we had chosen the less audacious way and tried to sneak out unseen, the officer most likely would have put us on report. Emmons was correct; the incident became history without any further comment from the lieutenant. I think Emmons and I both learned a lesson from that encounter: Be bold! Be audacious! Attack! Attack! Attack!

June week finally arrived. My four years at the Naval Academy had reached its sweet finish—GRADUATION! I couldn't believe I had escaped the *Scylla* and *Charybdis* of the Mathematics and Electrical Engineering Departments. Surely they must be lurking in the shadows with yet another exam for me to take before I could get my diploma.

My mother, Boney Close, grandmother Mimi, and my girlfriend, Frances, attended the graduation ceremony. I received the treasured diploma. John Niesse also came and gave me a beautiful clock.

"This is because you graduated on time," John said. What a great friend!

At dinner that night I gave my mother a gold pin I had specially made for her. It had two gold USNA class crests on it. One was mine, Class of 1951, the other was Boney's, Class of 1924. Mom was thrilled to tears. What a wonderful time of indescribable joy! Its memory still brings me a feeling of warmth from being so happy with those I loved, a sense of release from the ever-present threat of academic catastrophe, and the freedom at last to get on with my life as a Marine Corps officer. I had worked so hard for this day. I had attained my goal. I was ready to move on.

My great grandmother died during my plebe year at the Academy. In her will she left Tex and me her sole remaining property in Fort Worth, Texas. It was a little one-pump gas station near the Fort Worth Zoo. The income from the gas station provided both Tex and me with $25 per month income for the next three years, a fortune for a poor midshipman. Upon graduation, knowing I was going to war, Tex and I agreed to sell the station. With my share of the proceeds, I purchased a Ford Victoria two-door sedan. With the remaining funds, I went to see Mr. Auchincloss, Jackie Bouvier's stepfather, who was chairman of the brokerage house, Auchincloss, Redpath, and Parker. I invested the six hundred dollars remaining from my inheritance as Mr. Auchincloss recommended. I put it in a good mutual fund, and over the years it grew nicely. Because of this financial success, I became interested in the stock market, which led to a second career after I retired from the Marine Corps.

4.0 KOREA

As early as I can remember I wanted to be a soldier, and dreamed of leading troops in battle. I did become a soldier, and I did have my share of leading troops in battle. Of my 24 years in the Marine Corps, I served most of it as an infantry officer, and when I tally it up nearly 4 of those years were in combat and combat zones. My combat record shows that I was successful. I always planned my operations to achieve tactical objectives with the least risk to my troops. Every one of my Marines was like a brother or son to me. I wanted no harm to befall any of them.

Mark Twain said there was nothing like the prospect of a man's imminent hanging to focus his attention. I would add to that: Being shot at by an enemy determined to kill you has that same ability to grab your attention, and make you find the inner strength, skill, and vision to lead yourself and others in the most difficult of situations. Perhaps my tales of Korea and Vietnam will give some future young officer a perspective that he can't find in textbooks or classroom lectures.

Let me begin my recollections of Korea with a talk I gave at the Naval Academy to the midshipmen of the 16th Company on 16 November 2002. I was asked by the 16th Company first classmen to join them at a formal Dining-In to tell about my experiences in going to war in Korea right after graduating because they were soon going to their own war. The audience of over 150 people included the entire 16th Company of the Brigade of Midshipmen and their invited guests.

The Dining-In is a tradition that the British Royal Navy passed on to our Navy. At the Dining-In, the officers of the wardroom mess wear their best formal uniforms with miniature medals, and treat themselves to a first class meal with good wine followed by after dinner cigars and port. The ship's band plays military music and other tunes suitable to the occasion. After dinner, the imbibing continues, and when everyone is properly wetted down, the revelers play games that sometimes get a bit wild. Crockery is often broken, uniforms torn, sometimes bones are broken, but it's great fun for a gathering of high-spirited men with more than their share of testosterone. The purpose is conviviality and shared good times to enhance the comradeship that bonds men who may someday be called upon to fight and die together. The Dining-In is a proven morale builder that improves the combat effectiveness of military organizations. Of course the Naval Academy affair is a more disciplined and decorous event than those usually found in the Fleet. Alcohol is not consumed to excess, nor are crockery or bones broken, but the fun and sense of brotherhood still abounds.

To add a serious tone to the festivities, the wardroom occasionally invites distinguished speakers to attend. With the international situation in Afghanistan and Iraq, the 16th Company first classmen wanted to know about my experiences after graduation from the Naval Academy in 1951, and going to war in Korea. They were in the same situation that I had faced over fifty years before, and they wanted to know what advice I might have for them.

In preparing for this event, I decided to address the following points that I believe every newly commissioned officer should know in anticipation of the possibility of going to war. These points are:

1. Have a sense of humor. Subordinates, peers and seniors will play pranks on you to test you. This is good natured, light mischief that is part of the rights of passage into membership in the club. Lighten up and learn to laugh at yourself. Nobody likes a tight-ass.

2. Continually ask yourself the questions, "Am I hacking it? Am I a good leader? Can I be proud of myself?" To say yes to these simple questions, the young officer must have standards and live by them. Announce those standards to your troops,

and live by them to set an example you expect others to follow. If you live up to your standards, your troops will respect you. Without their respect, you will fail.

3. Keep an open mind and be ready to learn. Understand that although you are wearing the gold sleeve stripe of a Navy ensign or gold bar of a second lieutenant in the Marine Corps, you really are ensigns junior grade USN, and third lieutenants USMC. You must prove yourself to your subordinates, peers, and senior officers. You must earn their respect. You may be a graduate of this fine institution, but respect doesn't come automatically just because you are an Academy graduate. You are still under instruction, and don't forget it.

4. Don't worry about medals. They will come. Keep a cool head and don't needlessly endanger yourself or your troops. Combat entails risk, but always be mindful of the risks that confront you and the options you have to minimize risks to you and your unit. Neither you nor your troops are expendable. It's the highest honor to receive the Medal of Honor or the Navy Cross, but no sane man wants to receive such honors posthumously. Concentrate on doing your job. Do it well and the decorations will come.

I then illustrated these points with the following sea stories.

After graduation from the Naval Academy in 1951, my first duty station was The Basic School at Quantico. The course for new second lieutenants was normally six months long, but for us it had been shortened to four months because of the need for officer replacements in Korea. Upon completion of this course, I was given the basic officer military occupational number 0301 for those assigned to the infantry.

My orders were to report to Camp Pendleton, California for training with a replacement draft of Marines as a platoon leader. I was assigned to lead a platoon of about fifty Marines. All were recent graduates from the recruit training centers at San Diego and Parris Island. The platoon was staffed with the proper number of noncommissioned officers, who were reserve Marines recently activated from civilian life.

Shortly after I became their platoon leader, the senior sergeant came to me with a problem. The problem was with a young Marine named Roberts who couldn't, or wouldn't, do anything right. Roberts was also a troublemaker, and had become a "pain in the ass" to the noncommissioned officers and to this platoon sergeant in particular. I asked the sergeant what he thought we should do with Roberts.

The platoon sergeant replied, "Shoot him!"

After getting this report, I instructed the sergeant to bring Roberts to me. Shortly the sergeant returned with Roberts. Both saluted and I told them to stand at ease.

"Roberts", I said, "the sergeant tells me your conduct is not to the standards of the Marine Corps in general and this platoon in particular. What do you have to say for yourself?" Well, as you might expect, it wasn't much. I then said, "Roberts, do you see this shadow?" pointing to the one I was making in the sun.

"Yes sir," he said.

"Then you move over there and stand in it!" This he did. I then said, "Here's what you are going to do from now on. You will be in my shadow day and night . . . that close! Do you understand?"

"Yes, sir," he said.

Then I said, "Get your bowels adjusted too, because when I go to the head, you'll be going with me. Is that clear?"

"Yes, sir," he said.

So, for the next thirty days Roberts did what he was told. He was with me day and night, and did everything he was instructed to do. After a while, I got so I kind of liked him.

While at Pendleton we received very rigorous combat training. One of our assignments was cold weather training in the mountains to the north of Camp Pendleton. When we arrived at the cold weather training camp, my platoon was assigned a bivouac area, and instructed to defend the perimeter of our encampment against "aggressors." These were Marines trained in mountain warfare and stationed as instructors at the cold weather training camp.

The first night, I established our defensive perimeter and put the troops on a 50% alert. Around midnight the aggressors attacked on skis. They sped down the hill and zoomed through our perimeter, knocking over tents, and generally creating havoc. Shortly after they left, I learned from my platoon sergeant that the aggressors had taken several of my Marines as prisoners. When I heard this, I was mad as hell. This was not a good start for my Marine Corps career!

The next night, the same thing happened. This time the aggressors took about a dozen men prisoner. I really went on a rant when I found out what happened, and told the sergeant to bring one or two of the "prisoners" to me when they returned. When they reported to me, I found out that being captured was a good deal because those taken prisoner received hot chocolate and cookies at the aggressor camp.

Well, I had had enough of this nonsense. "Sergeant," I said, "tonight we are going to give those aggressors a dose of their own medicine. Tonight, after dark and for our defense, we'll have every man in this platoon, including me, standing in front of his tent holding his own canteen cup. We'll all be captured and go over there and get cocoa and cookies."

When the aggressors came through our perimeter that is exactly what they found. Their attack came to a screeching halt. When their leader came over to talk with me, I told him that while cocoa and cookies may be fun, and help to ward off the cold, I didn't believe we would experience this kind of treatment from the enemy in Korea. I stressed that I didn't believe this kind of malarkey would help us learn to fight a war in Korea and suggested that they change their training approach to reflect combat reality. They did change, and the training at cold weather camp proceeded on a constructive basis for the remainder of our time there.

The moral of the story: Take your training seriously. The lessons you learn may help you survive. Don't slack off or take the easy way. That may be tempting and temporarily seem like a good thing to do, but one day you'll have to pay the piper.

In early February 1952, we completed our Camp Pendleton training, and we boarded a troop transport bound for Korea. Several of my Naval Academy classmates who had gone through The Basic School at Quantico with me were also aboard. We all expected to be rifle platoon leaders with one of the Marine infantry battalions. When we landed in Korea, we found that artillery forward observers with frontline Marine units had experienced heavy casualties, and they needed replacements immediately. Because of our Naval Academy gunnery training, we were to be reassigned to Marine artillery units as forward observers. My MOS (Military Occupation Specialty) now became 0801, signifying that I was a basic artillery officer.

I was not happy about this reassignment. I wanted an infantry platoon. In retrospect, though, it probably was a good thing for my career. In 1952 the war became static trench warfare, much like it was in World War I. Our lines opposing Chinese and North Korean lines were dug in facing each other, east to west, across the entire Korean peninsula. In our sector, a large valley lay between the opposing lines. Our Marines operated mostly in small unit patrols supported by artillery fire. Artillery forward observers were actively engaged with the enemy around the clock. It wasn't the infantry, but I liked it.

My first assignment as a forward observer was with a Korean Marine Company located on an outpost forward of the Korean Marine main line of resistance (called the MLR for short). Upon arrival at the outpost, I met the U.S. senior noncommissioned officer, our scout sergeant, who introduced me to my artillery observer team, consisting of two U.S. Marine wiremen, a radio operator, the sergeant, and me. He explained that at mealtime we would all be given boxes of C rations, called "C-rats." Each box contained three assorted meals, plus coffee, cocoa, cigarettes, and toilet paper. The sergeant explained that the meals were usually beans and franks, ham and limas, and corned beef hash. All the rations were okay, except for the corned beef hash, which was barely edible. Each package was supposed to have one of each, he said, but sometimes this didn't always happen.

"You know how those guys in the rear screw things up," he told me.

That night, the sergeant handed out the ration packages, and I received mine last. That was fine, I thought, officers should not be fed before their troops. When I opened my box, I noticed that I had three cans of corn beef hash. I wondered about this, but didn't say anything. I supposed those guys in the rear just goofed up my rations. The next day the same thing happened. Again, I didn't say anything and proceeded to eat three meals of corned beef hash. Then it happened again. Once more my box had three cans of corned beef hash. At this point I began asking questions, and while I did so, I noticed four big grins. Then the light went on, and I realized that my troops had sabotaged my rations.

After we all stopped laughing, I informed the group, that since I *was* the lieutenant, I would receive my box first from then on, and they could have theirs after I had inspected the contents of mine. That was my initiation into the team.

After being relieved on the Korean Marine outpost, I was reassigned as forward observer for a U.S. Marine rifle company. The company was located at an outpost on a hill near Panmunjom, where the peace talks were taking place. The Chinese had similar positions opposing us. Every day both sides sent out small probing patrols supported by artillery. The Chinese artillery shelled us, and in return, we clobbered them with our big guns. Our outpost was a hot spot with enough action to keep us all from getting bored.

Our company was the first U.S. unit to occupy the hill we were on as a permanent position. No defensive positions were in place; so, we had to immediately lay barbed wire, dig fighting positions, and build our observation bunker and team living quarters. After two days of digging, the troopers had created a hole in the ground approximately ten feet long and eight feet wide for our observation bunker. This accommodated two cots, and had room for four men to work. The Marine on watch, a radio operator, the scout sergeant and I were usually those four. The other two Marines were off duty and either sleeping or performing necessary tasks within the sleeping bunker, which was similar in size to the observation bunker.

The observation bunker hole was about five feet deep when Scout Sergeant Henderson came to me and said, "Lieutenant is it deep enough yet, sir?" He was not a tall Marine. He was about five feet six feet inches tall, a good foot shorter than I am, but he was wiry and strong. Henderson was a good, tough Marine warrior who knew his business.

"No," I said, "We need to dig it a couple of feet deeper. I'm not going to stand in the bunker hunched over all day."

With that the men went back to work. Before long they had dug the hole another foot deeper. Henderson approached me again, and instead of asking if the hole were deep enough, he said, "Sir, I think the hole is deep enough now."

"No," I said, it still needs to be deeper."

He then responded, "Sir, the men haven't started on their sleeping bunker yet. I recommend we stop digging on this one now."

"No," I said, "we need to finish the observation bunker, and it's still not deep enough for me."

I could sense this conversation was headed in the wrong direction. It was about midday at that point and I was starting to heat up my midday c-ration.

Henderson then said, "Sir, you want the bunker deep enough so you can stand up and see out of the aperture, right?"

"Yes," I answered.

"Well, we can do that, I have an idea." he said and walked back to talk with the men.

A little while later he returned and said, "Lieutenant, it's fixed, come see. We would like you to get in the bunker and see if it works now."

As soon as I walked in the entryway, I knew the observation bunker wasn't deep enough, but when I entered the bunker pit I saw a hole two feet deep and two feet square.

The sergeant said, "Sir, here's where you'll stand. See if it works for you."

I stepped into the hole, and it worked. I could stand and look out of the aperture without bending over.

Then he proudly announced, "Sir, when you are not in that hole we have a board we can put over it so no one falls in."

That's when I first learned that you can depend on a Marine sergeant to find an innovative solution to any problem. The troops did a great job placing large timbers the size of railroad ties on top of the bunker to build a base for our roof. Under the sergeant's direction, they built a roof on top of the timbers that was twelve sand bag layers thick. It was a fortress! When the enemy shelled us with heavy mortar and artillery fire we withstood numerous direct hits without taking any casualties. My sergeant was a construction genius.

We may have been able to withstand enemy artillery fire, but the Korean rain was another matter. Water has a maddening way of finding weak spots where it can break through. After a while the bunker leaked, and my observation hole always had water in it. I continued to use it without complaint. The men had worked too hard for me to bellyache about my soggy accommodations; so, I had to suck it up and pay no attention to wet feet.

One morning Scout Sergeant Henderson awakened me. "Lieutenant," he said, "look out there . . . coming through that pass."

I looked where he was pointing and saw about eight or ten enemy soldiers moving to their main line in single file. They looked to be carrying radios and small arms. I guessed those with side arms were officers and those carrying radios and rifles were the enlisted troops.

Henderson said, "Sir, can we shoot 'em up?"

"No," I answered, "this may be the lead element of a relief of lines. Let's see what happens tomorrow."

The next morning we observed a larger group of thirty or so enemy moving in. Again all were in single file. I then radioed our artillery battalion, and told them about the troop movement the day before and the enemy activity again today. Before I knew it, I was talking by radio with Colonel Fredrick P. ("Toots") Henderson, the regimental commander. Colonel Henderson was the brother of the Marine aviator hero in World War II for whom the Marine Corps named Henderson Field in the Philippines. The colonel questioned me and asked if I thought this was the beginning of a relief of lines. I told him I did, and that I thought the main body would be coming in tomorrow.

Shortly thereafter, he called me back and said, "Lieutenant, I have notified division headquarters of your observation. We all believe you are onto something. Tomorrow, when the main body comes through, you'll have every gun in the First Marine Division plus some eight-inch guns from the Army to shoot. I hope you are correct on this."

Then Sergeant Henderson turned to me and said, "Lieutenant, we had better be right."

I replied, "I know," and said a silent prayer.

Luck was with me. Early the next morning, sure enough, the main body of Chinese came threading their way through the pass. I notified Regiment and they told me to give the command to fire for effect when the enemy relief troops were most exposed and vulnerable.

When I thought the bulk of the enemy was in our impact zone, I radioed the command, "FIRE FOR EFFECT!" Actually, I shouted it.

All the First Marine Division and supporting Army artillery big guns immediately let loose with devastating results. As the shells landed we saw bodies and body parts fly in the air. The enemy's combat discipline dissolved and pandemonium broke out. Enemy stretcher-bearers ran out of a big cave nearby, and began carrying off their dead and wounded. This went on almost all day. The enemy casualties were over 200. Our troops had none.

This is one of my most memorable moments in the Marine Corps. A second lieutenant made a report to headquarters command. Headquarters accepted the report with my assessment of the situation, and they accorded me the honor of giving the fire command for all the artillery concentrated for my mission. I had learned my Basic School and combat training lessons well, and they paid off. That was the day I knew that I was promoted from third lieutenant to second lieutenant. I also received the Bronze Star with Combat V to add to the glow of pride I felt.

After my tour at the Panmunjom outpost, the Marine rifle company I was supporting moved to an outpost in front of our main line of resistance. The Marines called this place "Bunker Hill," and it was even a more tenuous position than that at Panmunjom. At various places, our lines and the enemy lines were less than fifty yards apart. Talk about being too close for comfort!

I gave up smoking on Bunker Hill. Let me explain . . . A Chinese soldier had been shooting at me all morning long. Every time I lit up a cigarette, he took a shot at me. By late morning I had figured out he was in a foxhole at the top of a hill in front of our position and with a clear line of fire down into our location. My throat was raw and I had a headache from the cigarettes. I wasn't sure which was going to get me first, the Chinese soldier or the unfiltered Camels. Then and there, I decided to give up the evil weed. .

I ran up to one of our forward foxholes that were only about thirty yards from the enemy sniper's foxhole. I slowly snaked through the scrub underbrush on my hands, knees, and belly until I was close to his position. I slid a book of matches into the cigarette pack cellophane, and lobbed the pack into his foxhole. About two minutes later I saw cigarette smoke coming out of the sniper's foxhole. Sure enough he was taking a smoke break from his target practice with my helmet. I followed up my little gift with a hand grenade that I lobbed into his foxhole. After the dirt and debris settled, all was quiet and I made my way back to my position. I never smoked again after that . . . nor did he.

Word of this incident got back to the rear. I then received the order to go down to the right flank of our lines where the enemy position was only about fifty yards from us, and crawl up close to see if we could drop mortar and artillery shells in their trench position. I had no burning desire to go back for another visit to enemy lines, but orders are orders.

Piles of empty C ration cans separated our line from the enemy's on the right flank, and the terrain where I tossed the cigarette pack and grenade to my Chinese friend. Our Marines threw their waste tin ration cans from their foxhole and bunkers into no man's land.

This got rid of the trash and provided a primitive early warning system against enemy soldiers creeping up on our positions. Kicking one of those cans was sure to sound an alarm.

Well, I not only had to crawl forward of our line in broad daylight, but I had to avoid kicking any of those cans and making noise the enemy could hear. After going 10 or 15 yards, I kicked a can. To me the noise was deafening, and I decided to make a hasty retreat. The bad guys had been alerted, and were trying to do me bodily harm. Small arms fire was all around me, but the Almighty and some good USMC rifle fire covering my escape got me safely back to our lines.

Back in friendly territory I saw a bunker and ran to the hole that was the bunker entrance. I might as well have run into a wall of sandbags, because the bunker was full of Marines seeking safety from the incoming fire I had caused. All I could do was sit outside the bunker entrance and hope this would protect me from the hail of small arms fire.

Then I heard a voice call out, "Lieutenant, is that you, Lieutenant Hilgartner?"

"Who are you?" I answered.

"It's me, Corporal Roberts!"

"Well, I'll be damned," I said.

Corporal Roberts came out of the bunker and sat down beside me. We had a nice chat in spite of the bullets whizzing around us like angry hornets. When I left, we shook hands and bid each other a warm goodbye. I later learned he had been wounded, awarded a Bronze Star for gallantry in action, and sent home to recover from his wounds. When I think about it, Corporal Roberts may be the finest thing I did in the Marine Corps; even better than calling in artillery fire on a battalion of Chinese infantry. Corporal Roberts found his own high standards, lived by them, and became a damned fine Marine. I think I had something to do with that.

My thirteen months in Korea finally came to an end. The return voyage to the States was by troopship again. This time I was designated compartment commander for an enlisted berthing area in the bowels of the ship. One day a senior sergeant in the compartment came up to the main deck to see me.

"Lieutenant, you've got to do something about the terrible smell in our compartment," he said.

I immediately followed him down to the compartment, and indeed there was a bad smell there. After further investigation, I determined that it was coming from a sea bag owned by a Marine of American Indian lineage. The troops called him, "Chief."

I asked Chief what was in the sea bag, and he declined to tell me. So I suggested we go topside where we could talk privately on the fantail.

"Chief," I said, "I want to know what's in your sea bag. You know I can go down there and order it opened. If I do this, you might be embarrassed. Let's avoid this hassle. Just tell me what's in the bag!"

"Okay," he said. Then he told me that the customs of his tribe called for a returning warrior to hang the head of his enemy on a pole outside his lodge.

"So, you have a Korean soldier's head in your sea bag?" I asked.

"Yes sir," he said.

Wow, I thought. They didn't teach me how to handle a situation like this in basic school! So, while I was pondering what to do, I engaged him in a long discussion about war and warriors.

"Did the Korean soldier fight you valiantly and with honor?" I asked.

"Yes sir," he said.

"If he had won, would you have wanted him to take your head and put it on a pole," I asked.

"No sir," he said. Chief then proceeded to educate me about good medicine and bad medicine.

I listened, and then suggested that since he was an honorable Marine warrior and the Korean was an honorable warrior too, that maybe we should send his head back to Korea where it belongs.

I noticed the wake created by our ship, and pointed out that if we dropped the head overboard the current would probably take it back to Korea.

"That is the right thing for you to do," I said.

Chief agreed, and went below deck. Shortly, he returned with a bundle, and with dignity dropped the head into the water. I breathed a sigh of relief, and the matter was ended then and there. A few days later the senior sergeant tracked me down, and thanked me.

I finished my talk to the midshipmen with one final comment. "Remember what you heard tonight:

1) To become a real ensign or second lieutenant you'll need to prove your professional competence to your subordinates, peers, and seniors.

2) Establish a standard of conduct, live by that standard yourself, and enforce the standard with your troops.

3) Keep learning, and remember everything you learn won't be a school solution. Sometimes you'll have to improvise. You never know when you'll find a head in a sea bag!

4) Keep a sense of humor.

5) You cannot demand respect from your troops; you must earn it, and once earned you must work hard to preserve it. In the military services, respect from your subordinates, peers, and seniors is the coin of the realm. It reflects your professional competence, your values, and your character.

If you do these things, you'll be fine and have a good career in the service of your country.

Speaking of respect, and how each of us must earn it, I am reminded of Sergeant Macy, my Parris Island drill instructor. I didn't tell this story to the midshipmen, but I should have.

After I had been in Korea for some months, division headquarters pulled our rifle company off Bunker Hill, and directed us to relieve an infantry company on the MLR. Once we had returned to our main lines, we went to an area where we could shower and get clean uniforms before we moved out to relieve the other company. I recall that as our unit moved up the hill, we passed the Marines we were relieving as they came down the hill.

I was the last man in our line of troops going uphill. The last man coming down the hill seemed familiar to me. It was Sergeant Macy, my drill instructor at Parris Island. He was a gunnery sergeant now.

As we passed I said, "Hello, Sergeant Macy."

He was tired, I could tell, and looked at me quizzically. I told him I was Hilgartner, the tall private in his platoon at Parris Island in 1945.

He remembered me and said, "Congratulations, Lieutenant. I'm glad you made it."

We then sat down on a nearby rock and I briefly told him what I'd done since boot camp. As our two columns moved further away, he shook my hand, saluted, and we both moved out on the double to catch up with our units.

I never saw Sergeant Macy again, but that brief encounter reminded me of the great respect I have for him and all Marine drill instructors. What a heavy responsibility they bear in training young Marines! They serve as teachers and role models that their charges will never forget. There is not enough money in this world to buy respect like that. You must earn it!

In my talk to the midshipmen I wish I had told them about lighter things that happened on the outpost near Panmunjom. For example: My harassment of the enemy with my ukulele; the visit from the British Army officer; and of the day I learned I was a new father. These are great memories for me, and make an important part of my Korean tale.

Somewhere in my Korean travels I acquired a ukulele. I thought learning to play it would help pass the time and provide some entertainment. It took a while, but I finally learned to play one, and only one, tune. That was a fumbling, and not very well rendered, version of, *My Bonnie Lies Over the Ocean.*

One day, the Chinese tried to harass us with psychological warfare. They had a sound rig with a loudspeaker they used for "psywar" blasting us with Chinese tunes like *Ah De Dong* and giving us the old harangue: "American GI, go home. You will lose this war, and die." Chinese music may have had wide appeal in their circles, but to us it was God-awful racket. It was an ear-offending, cacophonous combination of weird sounding oriental musical instruments in a steady stream of noise that sounded like fingernails scratching on a blackboard. The musical abomination was punctuated by loud shrieks and wails from a female apparently in great distress. She was the accompanying vocalist, and I use the term loosely. In fact, she might not have been human. She could have been a sow giving birth to a porcupine. It was definitely not music to sooth the savage beast, at least not the round-eye savage beast. The Chinese knew it would get on our nerves.

At the height of the musical onslaught, Sergeant Henderson suggested we counterattack the Chinese psywar effort with my ukulele . . . our own version of Marine psywar.

"Lieutenant, why don't you play the *My Bonnie* tune, and we'll all sing it to the enemy!"

I thought Sergeant Henderson's suggestion was truly diabolical. So, I broke out my uke, began to play, and the troops joined in. Our combined effort was worse than awful. It did, however, raise our spirits, and the Chinese capitulated. They turned off their propaganda harangue and their Chinese music after one last broadcast insult, "GI you no hocking good. You music terrible!"

One day we had a surprise visit from a British Army officer. I was making a batch of hot chocolate when he entered our bunker. After we greeted each other, I invited him to have a seat, and he explained why he had come. Then he eyed the cocoa, sniffed the air, and asked what I was doing. When I told him I was making a batch of cocoa, he exclaimed, "Cocoa mate, even the bloomin' Queen don't have cocoa. I'd be pleased to share some with you."

His comment made me laugh; so, I served him a double ration of hot cocoa. I told him the bloomin' Queen might not have cocoa, but you Brits do serve booze in the wardroom messes of Royal Navy warships. In our Navy not even the bloomin' President gets a tipple in a warship's wardroom. He was a great gent and bloomin' good company, but unfortunately I never had the pleasure of seeing him again.

The 19th of September 1952 was a rainy miserable day, and

our observation bunker was leaking like a sieve. The phone connecting our observation post to the company command post rang. It was our company executive officer, Rudy Trevino.

"Pete, come down to the command post. I have some good news for you, and by the way bring those cigars with you."

Rudy wouldn't detail the news, but I knew it must be about the baby my wife and I were expecting. It was due to be born around this time of the month. So, I dug into my pack for the cigars I'd been carrying with me for some weeks and pulled them out. The cigar package was wet, but I put them in my pocket anyway. When I arrived at the command post, Rudy greeted me and told me I was now a father of a fine baby girl.

"When was she born?" I asked.

"On September 12th," he answered, "and your wife is fine."

A beautiful baby girl, I thought. Now I really have something to look forward to when I get home. Then we warmed the cigars until they were mostly dry, and I passed them around. Seven days had passed after Linda was born before I got the news. I wished I could have been home for this wonderful event.

My unit moved to a new position on top of the mountain behind Bunker Hill. Since I had seen the enemy at close quarters while on Bunker Hill, I thought it would be a good idea to survey the Chinese position from this higher level where we were now located. In short order, I spotted the opening of their observation bunker, which I had been unable to see at the lower elevation. From this observation post, the Chinese could direct fire with devastating effect on our positions in the valley below. We needed to take it out fast.

I notified the company commander of my find, and requested that he send a tank to my location to destroy the enemy observation bunker. The trajectory of a tank gun is flat and just what I needed to put rounds through the bunker aperture to destroy the enemy position. When the tank arrived, I walked in front of it to point out the observation bunker for the tanker sergeant. He then said,

"I see it. You are in a bad place, Lieutenant. You better take cover behind this vehicle."

He then disappeared into the tank, and closed the hatch. I had no sooner taken cover behind the tank when it took a direct hit from a rocket-propelled grenade on the turret. The explosion bowled me over, but I was quickly back on my feet. The tank sergeant immediately trained the tank's gun on the bunker entranced and opened fire. He put four rounds right into the aperture. Scratch one enemy observation post. There was nothing left in there but hamburger meat.

That was one more small victory for us, and with no casualties.

The company I provided artillery support for occasionally sent patrols to a cone shaped mountain that was contested territory about halfway between our lines and the Chinese lines. It was called Hill 229 because it was 229 meters high. One patrol that stands out in my memory was a disaster, and one I was lucky to come through unscathed.

From my lieutenant's perspective, our company commander did a poor job of planning the patrol mission. The platoon commander didn't understand what we were to accomplish; neither did I. If I didn't know it before, I soon found out that poor planning and unclear objectives are a guarantee for disaster. To complicate the platoon commander's job with an additional burden, the company commander assigned three lieutenants to the patrol who were new arrivals in country. This was to give the newcomers experience and practical factors under fire before they got their own platoons.

We moved out for our Hill 229 objective at *o-dark-thirty*, with me along to provide artillery support for the patrol if required. As we moved along in single file, I looked to my right, and in the early morning grayness, just as the first glimmer of dawn was breaking through, I thought I saw an enemy soldier sitting stone-still on the side of a small hill watching us. It looked like we could be walking into a trap the enemy would spring after the last Marine was in it. To my frustration, I was near the end of the column and couldn't get word to the platoon commander about my sighting. My artillery support radio was not on the same frequency as the platoon commander's tactical net radio, and he was too far ahead of me to call out to him, or for me to run up to catch him. Besides, things were about to start happening fast!

When we reached the base of Hill 229, we began to receive small arms fire that was light at first. The platoon commander ordered us to fix bayonets and move into our attack. We found the enemy well dug in on the hill, and as we moved up to engage them they hit us with greatly increased small arms fire and mortar rounds.

I was moving up the hill on a small trail when two Chinese mortar rounds landed on either side of me. They caught me standing upright as they exploded, and filled my face, arms and exposed body with tiny particles that totally blackened me from head to toe. Fortunately, the shrapnel in the rounds had pulverized; so, I was not hurt, but the blast gave me a roaring headache that lasted for several days.

I suddenly realized that my radio operator, who was slightly wounded, and I were out in front of the assault. Before I had time to panic, I saw a potato-masher hand grenade rolling down the hill towards me. I ducked behind a large rock, pulling my radio operator with me. I got a glimpse of the thrower just before the grenade exploded. We were in trouble, and I had no grenades to throw back at the Chinese soldier. I turned and saw a Marine down the hill and a few yards behind me entangled in the enemy's barbed wire.

"Marine," I called, "do you have any grenades?"

"I have two thermite grenades," he shouted back.

"Pitch them to me." The thermite grenades wouldn't spray shrapnel as they exploded, but if any burning phosphorous fragments hit the enemy soldier it would put him out of action. So would the concussion, if I could get the grenade close enough to him.

I threw one of my thermite grenades. It fell a little short of the Chinese soldier's trench and exploded. He threw a second potato-masher at me. It exploded harmlessly in front of my big rock shield. I then threw my last thermite grenade. It was the toss of my life; the longest I've ever thrown anything like a grenade. It went right into the trench, exploded, and either killed the enemy soldier or put him out of action. That ended our grenade exchange.

At this point, I feared the enemy might counterattack. This would have been a disaster for us, because we were strung all over the side of the hill. We had numerous casualties including our platoon leader, who had been killed. One of the new arrival officers sent with us for training had assumed command and ordered us to withdraw, but the enemy had sprung the ambush trapping us in an exposed position on the hill. There was now heavy fighting to our rear, and the enemy counter-attack that I feared was about to happen.

We desperately needed close fire support. I knew my old NAPS sergeant and Naval Academy classmate, Haig Donabedian, was the forward observer on the main line; so, I called him. Haig immediately gave us accurate covering fire, and earned my everlasting gratitude. Because of Haig's effective artillery fire, the Chinese couldn't counterattack, and our platoon beat off the attack on our rear.

When the fighting died down, helicopters came in to evacuate the dead and severely wounded, and our patrol limped back to our lines. The enemy stayed on Hill 229; so, if our mission was to capture the hill, we failed. If we were only to reconnoiter and find out if he was there and harass him . . . well we sure accomplished that mission, but it seemed like a tactically stupid mission not worth the casualties we took. Even if we had chased him off the hill, we weren't logistically prepared to stay, and a platoon didn't provide enough manpower to hold the position. It was dumb, dumb, dumb, and I was pissed! I learned something that day about poor planning and unclear mission objectives. They are a sure route to disaster, and I pledged to myself that I would never get in such a situation again!

Too much happened for me to have just been lucky. Again, the credit must go to Almighty God, my guardian angels, the

Marine in the barbed wire, and good old Haig Donabedian. I had read Psalm 27 before going out on this patrol. After I returned, and my headache went away, I began reflecting on this day. I believed that if I had been the platoon leader, the outcome would have been different. I made another pledge to myself: If I survive Korea, I'll get out of artillery, and return to the infantry.

While it may appear that I spent all of my time in Korea on the front lines or in front of the Main Line of Resistance (MLR) that was not the case. In fact, of my thirteen months in Korea, I spent only ten months on or forward of our MLR. That's enough though, and I came through without a scratch.

My time off the lines was not particularly eventful. After we arrived in Korea, I went to artillery school for a short time. I also got sick from a severe intestinal bug, and went to a hospital in Japan for treatment. While I was in the hospital, my Academy classmates, Bill Holmberg and Jack Grace were in the same hospital with me. Jack and Bill had been wounded in action, and Bill's wounds were quite severe. It was good seeing them, even though none of us were at the top of our game.

Bill Holmberg was recovering from wounds he received while leading his platoon in an attack on Chinese positions that were harassing Marine lines with artillery and mortar fire. Bill took his unit through a heavily mined area covered with intense small arms and automatic weapons fire to attack the enemy entrenchment. Holmberg's unit captured the enemy position, killed 120 of them, and drove the remainder off in retreat. For this action, Bill was awarded the Navy Cross.

I recently asked Jack Grace how he happened to be at the U.S. Naval Hospital in Yokosuka, Japan. This is what he told me.

> As I remember it . . .
> On 7 August 1952 (ten years to the day after the Marines landed on Guadalcanal), I was shaving near the entrance of the command post bunker of Company E,

Second Battalion, Fifth Marines, then occupying a position on the Main Line of Resistance in the right regimental sector of the First Marine Division's front. A Chinese 76mm artillery round came over the hill and impacted near our company supply point, near the bottom of the hill. After the explosion, I stepped out of the bunker to see if anyone was hurt down the hill. Apparently I didn't wait long enough because a nearly spent piece of the round's "tail spray" came back up the hill and stuck in my right arm. I was able to remove it, put a bandage on my arm, and continue my duties as company X.O. (I still have the piece, about the size of a dime, but thicker and ragged around the edge). Later in the day, when things quieted down, the C.O. suggested I go back to the battalion aid station and have the hole in my arm treated properly. The battalion surgeon, concerned about the possibility of infection, sent me farther back to the medical company supporting the Fifth Marines. There my little hole was "debrided," making it longer and deeper. Now I was really wounded!

After an overnight stay with the medical company, I became a "walking wounded," eating in the doctors' mess and listening to their stories, which rivaled the conversations in MASH, years later. I also found Bill Holmberg in the ward, still bedridden from a stomach wound he received in July.

On 9 August the Chicoms attacked a terrain feature in the center regimental sector of the division held by the First Marines that became known as "Bunker Hill." This local engagement lasted from 9 to 16 August and cost 48 Marines KIA, 313 WIA and evacuated. The Chinese had an estimated 3,200 casualties, but in those pre-McNamara days we didn't bother with enemy body counts; so, we didn't have a precise enemy KIA WIA count.

Because of the "spike" in casualties caused by "Bunker Hill," all the less seriously wounded held in the medical companies supporting the division were moved farther to the rear, to make room for the more immediate casualties from the First Marines. Thus, I spent one night on the hospital ship anchored in Inchon harbor, and finally ended up at the U.S. Naval Hospital in Yokosuka, Japan. There I again encountered Bill Holmberg, by now getting around a little better on his own, and Jerry Thomas, who had been wounded in July, in a different sector of the division front. Our "mini-reunion" was complete when Pete Hilgartner arrived, suffering from a stomach infection. In the first week of September I returned to my company and my old job after a month "R&R" in Japan.

So the old Naval Academy song is true: "Whenever two or three shall meet" . . . we have a reunion. Bill, Jack, Jerry, and I had a great Class of 51 reunion at USNH YOKO. None of us were feeling well enough to raise too much hell, but it was great being with old friends, sleeping in clean bunks, and eating reasonable chow. Grunts are easy to please!

I also spent a short time in the rear as battalion personnel officer. My Naval Academy classmate, Pete Wickwire, and I were tent mates. In the evenings we entertained ourselves giving poison to the rats and mice seeking shelter from the cold. We had a pot-bellied stove in the tent and it really put out the heat. It gave us comfort and attracted all sorts of wildlife for our sporting amusement. Grunts are REALLY easy to please!!

During this time the paperwork arrived for me to be upgraded from basic field officer, (0801), to qualified artillery officer, (0802). If this change were made, the 0802 designation would have become my primary MOS, and would have kept me in artillery *forever*.

I wasn't a very good personnel officer. Somebody lost that piece of paper, or by mistake it went into the trash, because I went home at the end of the Korean War still as a basic artillery officer, 0801, and not a qualified artillery officer. I was determined that I would become an infantry officer.

I had survived Korea, and as our plane approached Washington D.C., my stomach was in knots. I had not seen my wife, Frances, in over a year. We had been married in fine style on December 1, 1951. It was now April 1953. We had a baby girl named Linda, whom I had never seen. Would I recognize Frances at the airport? I wasn't sure. The plane landed and as I exited, I spotted her mother. Frances was standing next to her holding the baby. All was well and I was one happy Marine. I had come home safely, been decorated with the Bronze Star medal, and promoted to first lieutenant. It was good to be home!

5.0 BETWEEN WARS

My orders to Camp Lejeune directed me to report to the Second Marine Division for further assignment. I carried my orders and my record book, with instructions to deliver them to the division adjutant at Camp Lejeune. When I reported to division headquarters I delivered my orders. The adjutant asked me where my record book was.

"It wasn't mailed to you, sir?" I asked.

"No," he said, "We haven't received it. Let me take a look at your orders." I gave him the orders.

"You came home with an 0801. Why didn't you get an 0802 MOS?" he asked.

"Well, sir, I didn't have a very good tour in Korea. They kept me in the rear doing personnel work, administrative duties . . . stuff like that. I would really like to be assigned to an infantry regiment so I can get qualified. I had a 0301 when I left Basic School, and I think that 0801 on these orders is a mistake."

"The Eighth Marines could use another lieutenant right now. You report to them right away," the adjutant instructed me. He then told me where the regimental headquarters was located.

I couldn't get over there fast enough. This time when I entered the regimental adjutant's office, I had my orders plus the record book, which for some strange reason I had left in my car when I reported to division headquarters.

The adjutant looked at my orders, record book and then me. "Lieutenant, you're in the wrong place."

"No, sir, I'm in the right place, may I speak with the regimental commander, sir?"

"No lieutenant comes into this office and asks to speak with the C.O.," he barked.

When I had entered, I had seen the colonel at his desk. It was Colonel Leo Dulacki who had commanded the First Battalion, Seventh Marines in Korea when I was a forward artillery observer in his battalion. I knew he would remember me.

The colonel heard me and heard what his adjutant said. The next thing I heard was, "Pete, come on in here."

I then poured my heart out. I told him I never wanted to be in artillery in the first place, and that he wouldn't regret ever giving me the opportunity to become a qualified infantry officer.

After listening to me, he called the adjutant in and said, "I know this lieutenant. Don't we have an opening for a lieutenant in B Company?"

The adjutant replied, "Yes sir, they need an executive officer."

"Well, send Hilgartner down there." Then turning to me, he said, "We'll have to work fast to get you qualified as an 0302. You have 90 days to do it."

I replied, "Thank you, sir, I'll be qualified in 90 days, you can count on that!" And I was. I earned the treasured 0302, (qualified infantry officer) designator, but the 0801, basic artillery officer number stayed tacked on as a secondary MOS. So, I was 0302/0801 in the record books. When I thought about it, both designators said important things about me. Those two designators said: Here is a qualified infantry officer who knows something about supporting arms. That had to be good for my career.

I was only in the Eighth Marines for about six months when I received a new set of orders. In the spring of 1953 I was reassigned from the Eighth Marine Regiment to duty with the newly formed First Infantry Training Regiment at Camp Lejeune. My initial assignment was as company commander for D Company. The staff consisted of five senior noncommissioned officers and me. One noncommissioned officer functioned as first sergeant, the others as platoon leaders. Each platoon had about 40 recent graduates from recruit training at Parris Island, S. C. All of the recruit trainees were slated for assignment to Marine division infantry units upon completion of the advanced infantry training we were to provide. We were to be *bird dogs* for the trainees.

I was company commander for about seven months, during which time all went well . . . and without incident. My happiest times were those evenings when D Company was undergoing field training and in overnight bivouac. My noncommissioned officers would build a nice campfire, and we would sit around it. They always invited me to join the group, and I thoroughly enjoyed hearing their *sea stories* and jokes. I also picked up their scuttlebutt and complaints. In the complaint department, nothing I heard about the two regimental mess halls was good.

One day I received a call to report to the regimental commander, Colonel "Red" Culhane. Colonel Culhane was a no-nonsense veteran of the old school. Nobody wanted to go see him.

When I entered his office, he said gruffly, "Pete, I am not happy, not at all happy with our two mess halls."

I replied, "Yes, sir, my NCOs don't think much of them either."

"That's the reason I called you in," he said, "I want you to become my full time mess officer. Go down there and square them away."

"How long do I have to go down there for?" I asked.

"Until you square them away," he replied.

"Will you back me up on this?" I asked.

"You know that, Hilgartner. Why do you ask?"

"Because I intend to have those mess halls squared away in 30 days," I replied. "I don't intend to be a career Marine Corps mess officer, sir."

"Good enough," he growled. "Get down there ASAP, and get cracking."

There were two mess halls, A and B. They were located directly across the street from each other. A mess sergeant operated each mess, and both of them were master sergeants. My office would be in the rear of mess hall B.

I went from Colonel Culhane's office to mess hall B and immediately summoned both mess sergeants. After introducing myself, I asked them to give me an orientation of their duties, status of their cooks and every detail they could think of. After listening to them and touring the mess halls, I still wasn't sure I had a handle on the problem. They were both operating out of the

Marine Corps master menu book; so, the same meals were being prepared in each mess hall every day.

Early one Saturday morning I received a call that the Marines were rioting in mess hall A. I raced for the place picking up two MPs along the way. When I entered the mess hall the disturbance was still in progress. The troops were having a food fight, and the place was a mess. With the two MPs, I walked down the center aisle and told them to select and arrest three culprit corporals at random on each side of the aisle.

We then marched them out of the mess hall and down the street straight to Colonel Culhane's office. He was there. I told him what had happened, and requested that he convene and conduct "office hours" immediately and "bust" these six corporals on the spot. "Office hours" is Marine Corps jargon for any disciplinary hearing.

This he did. I then had the MPs cut the stripes off the sleeves of the six corporals, and marched them back to the mess hall. When we marched in, there was dead silence. I told the MPs to seat the new privates in the same places they had been in when the fracas started. Then I announced to the entire assembly that I was prepared to march more noncommissioned officers down to the regimental commander's office and get them reduced in rank if they couldn't exercise some leadership to keep things orderly. As you can imagine, things quieted down very fast.

Then I had a meeting with the two mess sergeants. "The reason for this riot was that you are serving lousy food to the Marines in your mess hall," I said to mess sergeant A. "You must be taking short cuts, because the food in mess hall B is better. From here on, both of you will eat your meals in each mess hall daily. I will do the same thing. I will take a half ration in A, and then go to B for the other half of my meal. You will do the same. After the meal, we will meet, and you will tell me who, in your opinion, served the better meal. I will then give you my opinion. I hope we will be able to agree that the meals in both mess halls are equally good. And I mean *good*. Equally bad meals are not acceptable. Do you understand me?"

They clearly understood me, and the plan worked. Getting those mess sergeants to compete with each other produced substantial positive changes almost overnight.

About three weeks later I received a call at home from mess sergeant A that he was having a severe problem with a Marine at his Sunday brunch. At Sunday brunches, which we had recently introduced, the troopers could eat whatever they wanted and as much as they could hold. It took about ten minutes for me to get to mess hall A. When I walked in the mess sergeant was standing in front of a Marine private, a big, well-built, good-looking young man.

"What's the matter?" I asked.

"Sir, this Marine has had firsts, seconds, and thirds and he's back wanting fourths," he said angrily. "We don't have enough food to feed each man this much." The sergeant had a point, I thought.

"Marine," I said, "where are you from?"

"Tennessee," he replied.

"Do you get firsts and seconds at home?"

"Yes, sir, my momma feeds me good. Sometimes I even get thirds."

"She draws the line after you've had thirds, though, right?"

"Yes, sir," he said.

"Well," I said, "we're gong to treat you just like your mother does. I'm glad you like the chow here, but three full servings are enough. I don't like to see fat Marines."

Two weeks later, Colonel Culhane reassigned me as commanding officer of H & S Company. My old buddy, USNA classmate, and former NAPS gunnery sergeant, Gene Balderston, took over as regimental mess officer. Gene was not pleased with this assignment. I think he got the idea that I had something to do with it. I didn't, but I still kept my distance from Gene until he calmed down. Maybe he thought I was still trying to get even for all those work details he assigned me to at NAPS.

These were happy times for my family. On 2 June 1954, my daughter Diana joined our family. She was a cute, roly-poly child who would grow up to be her father's patient sidekick and helper with his carpentry projects. Then a year later, on 28 August 1955, Sharon Dale, whom we call Dale, came along. Dale, our third daughter, was irrepressible. She had a cute smile, winning ways, and penchant for accidents.

In early 1955, the Commandant of the Marine Corps initiated a program whereby all Marine Corps line officers, company grade level, must have a tour in service support. I got my service support tour as an infantry captain detailed for a two-year supply tour at the Marine base in Quantico, Virginia. We moved to Quantico, and with a small nest egg I had accumulated purchased a little house on Tralee Lane. Money was tight, and we had to scrimp in every conceivable way to make ends meet. I began raising chickens and rabbits to help supplement our food budget.

A Warrant officer named Larry Betts introduced me to the savings I could make by purchasing crates of capon chickens and pigs at the livestock auction and slaughterhouse in Fredericksburg. So that is what I did, and I did save money on my family's food budget.

My supply assignment at Quantico was as officer-in-charge of the clothing cash sales unit. Staff Sergeant Mallard was the senior noncommissioned officer in my unit. He was a fine, young, freckle-faced Irishman about six feet tall from New York City. He was smart, diligent, and efficient. He was everything a good noncommissioned officer should be. Mallard was a picture perfect Marine, but definitely a big city boy.

Mallard knew about my trips to the stockyards in Fredericksburg and the crates of live fat capons I had been purchasing at bargain prices. One day he asked if I would pick up a crate of those birds for him on my next trip. I agreed; so, the following Saturday I made the trip to Fredericksburg and purchased two crates of capons. When I returned home I called Mallard and told him to pick up his crate the next day, which he did.

We held muster every morning except Sundays at 0700. At

that time, Marines would be in formation and answer in a loud voice, "Here," or something close to it like, "Yo" when their name was called. The first sergeant or another senior NCO usually held morning roll call.

At 0730 after the unit muster on the Monday morning following my trip to Fredericksburg, the first sergeant notified me that Staff Sergeant Mallard was absent. This puzzled me. Mallard was never late. Something must have occurred. Maybe he had a problem with his car, a flat tire or something. I didn't want to have to put Mallard on report for missing muster. I instructed the first sergeant to give Mallard a little more time, and not to submit the muster report until I told him to.

At about 0800 in walked a most unusual sight. It was a Marine, but his head was bandaged, and all kinds of band-aids and first aid dressings were pasted all over his face and arms. This Marine was a mess! It was Staff Sergeant Mallard.

"Mallard, I said, "what happened to you?"

He replied, "Well, Captain, it's like this. As you know, I'm a city boy. When I returned home with the crate of capons, my wife told me to bring them into the kitchen so we could pluck them. I brought the crate in and reached in to get a chicken. That chicken didn't like being plucked alive. I forgot to close the lid on the crate. Then all them chickens got out. They was flying all over the kitchen. My wife got a broom and began hitting at them. That made matters worse, because then they started pooping. We had chicken shit all over the kitchen, and them birds was still flying around, all twenty of them."

I was laughing so hard that tears were rolling down my cheeks. I managed to ask, "What happened to the chickens?"

He replied, "My wife opened the kitchen door, and flushed them all out the door with her broom."

At this point I was almost rolling on the floor with laughter.

Finally, "Sir, I don't think we want you to get us any more capons. We'll get our chickens from the commissary from now on."

While we were living in Quantico, we joined the local Episcopal Church. The rector was fine young minister and this was his first church. Since I had a role in getting this church started, the minister invited me to serve on the church vestry. About that time, Colonel Fred Henderson, who had been my artillery regimental commander in Korea, joined the congregation.

One Sunday after church services, Colonel Henderson came up to me and said, "Pete, I was visiting Headquarters Marine Corps yesterday, and I took a look at your service record. I noted that you never received an 0802 designation for your artillery service in Korea."

"I know, Colonel, but it is okay by me, I have an infantry primary 0302 now."

He replied, "Yes, I know this but you should have received the 0802 designator too; so, I fixed it!" My knees buckled.

"Don't worry, the 0802 will be a secondary MOS, but it will tell the world that you are a *highly* qualified Marine officer. It will help you in your career."

I thanked him after breathing a sigh of relief.

Church services were held in the gymnasium of our base elementary school. As often as possible we attended the services. To make going to church more fun for our daughters, Linda, Diana, and Dale, we used to sing songs on our way from our house in Triangle to the base school.

We arrived a little late one Sunday morning, and the kids ran ahead of us as we entered the building. With a burst of speed they opened the doors and ran down the center aisle to the seats on the front row, singing a rousing chorus of, "*Rye whiskey, rye whiskey, rye whiskey I cry. If I don't get my whiskey, I think I shall die.*" I wanted to die myself, and tried to find something to crawl under. The entire congregation broke into laughter.

That wasn't the end of it. When time came to pass the offering plate, Linda came running back to us, shouting, "Daddy, Daddy, you forgot to give me my nickel." I felt the entire congregation was looking at me and thinking: What a cheapskate! I died for a second time that day.

In 1957, my supply tour ended. Happily, I had accomplished some things that gave me great satisfaction. One new procedure worked well for the troops. We established an evening work time when the cash sales store would be open so that Marines could make clothing purchases during their off-duty hours. As far as I know this program is still in effect at Quantico. I also helped get the base on a computer system for taking physical inventories of Marine Corps property. This automated system had a number of surprising results including locating a truck engine that had been missing for several years. The system produced major budget reductions and improved financial planning efficiency.

I definitely did not want to become a career Marine Corps supply officer. On 2 July 1957, much to my great pleasure, I was reassigned to the Basic School for Second Lieutenants as an instructor. That was a year that I really enjoyed. The instructors at the Basic School were the best of the best, and I was glad to be part of this quality group.

My initial assignment was to be an instructor in the Leadership Group. This group taught subjects such as hand-to-hand combat, drill and ceremonies, and leadership. After about six months, I was reassigned as platoon commander, C Company to be the *bird dog* for a platoon of about fifty new second lieutenants. I really enjoyed working with them.

The first afternoon with this new platoon, I formed them up behind the officer's club and proceeded to give them their initial indoctrination lecture. I covered a variety of items pertaining to their duties and class schedules. At the end I asked, "Any questions?"

One lieutenant raised his hand and asked, "Sir, how many cuts do we get from class?"

I answered, "Just try taking one, lieutenant, just try taking one."

A most unusual thing occurred on a bright, sunny day when we were conducting field maneuvers. I had my platoon organized in a line of skirmishers. We were moving downhill toward some woods with a streambed running left to right through it. All of a sudden we spooked a flock of turkeys. I had positioned myself a few yards behind the center of the line. As the turkeys flew over, I reached up and grabbed one by the leg. I had never done that, or even shot a turkey before. I was as surprised as the turkey. However, I had one now and thought he might make a good meal. So, I bound up his legs, took him to my car, and then rejoined the lieutenants.

I made a big mistake, however. I didn't leave a car window open so fresh air could enter. When I returned to the car, I found my turkey stone dead and fairly ripe too. I learned a lesson that day, and lost a great dinner.

The lieutenants didn't forget about the great turkey catch either. Just before their basic training ended, we had a happy hour and roast the boss session. They put on a skit teasing me about the turkey catch and a couple of other amusing incidents. They really nailed me, but it was all in good fun, and we had lots of laughs. You can't be thin-skinned and survive in the Corps.

My Basic School tour ended on a good note. My next assignment was to the Junior Amphibious Warfare School, also located at Quantico. It was primarily a school for captains, and one had to be selected to attend. This nine-month assignment told me my career was on the right track. Upon completion of the Junior Amphibious Warfare School, I was assigned to an unaccompanied infantry tour with the Third Marine Division in Okinawa. I hated leaving my family for a year, but it was necessary. The division had to be ready to move out quickly on a combat assignment without the encumbrances of taking care of dependents left in a foreign country.

On 3 November 1958, our troopship landed in Okinawa. I was hoping for, and looked forward to, being an infantry company commander. As I walked down the gangway carrying all my gear, an officer jumped out of a parked jeep and shouted, "Captain Hilgartner, welcome to Okinawa. I sure am glad to see you, because you are to be my relief!"

"Relief, doing what?" I asked.

"You are going to be the new Marine Club Officer on Okinawa."

I almost passed out from shock. I looked around to see if Gene Balderston was lurking somewhere near, getting even for his assignment relieving me as regimental mess officer.

"Not me." I said, "You had better find someone else. I will resign from the Corps before I accept that job."

That evening I was sitting at the bar in the officer's club pondering my situation and trying to figure a way out of it. I was surprised when my Naval Academy roommate during second class summer walked into the bar. Wes Hammond was not only a welcomed sight, but was aide to the commanding general of the Third Marine Division. He greeted me saying that he knew I was coming to the division and had been looking for me. At that moment Wes started growing wings. He was more than a friend, he was an angel sent by God. I told him what had happened, and asked if there was anything he could do. He said there was a lot he could do for me. Wes told me to come to headquarters in the morning.

When I arrived the next morning, not having slept a wink, Wes said, "I've talked with the general, and you are to meet with Colonel McReynolds this morning.

Colonel McReynolds, known as *Blackjack*, was the chief personnel officer in the division, and was responsible for all personnel assignments within the division. I seemed to have found another angel on the scene. Blackjack had been a neighbor in Quantico during my supply and basic school duty. He knew me well.

"Come on in, Pete," he said, "I understand you're not happy with the officer's club assignment."

"That's correct, sir," I said.

"What do you want to do instead of that?"

I answered, "Command a rifle company, sir."

"Well, there is a vacancy in one company in the division, but I'm not sure you will want it. The company has a very bad reputation"

Without hesitation I said, "Sir, I'll take it. What company is it?"

"Company A, First Battalion," he replied

Then he briefed me on Company A's problems. The more he told me the better I liked the prospects of commanding Company A. Not only would I be commanding officer of the company, but I would also be the senior captain; therefore, commanding officer of the two-company base. The base was called, Camp *Awase*, which was the military base in the play, *Teahouse of the August Moon.*

My orders were to square away a Marine unit with a bad conduct record, a large number of venereal disease cases, and a serious lack of leadership. Upon my arrival at Camp *Awase*, I saw a Marine tied to a flagpole. Upon investigation, I learned that he was an A Company Marine who was a total misfit, and had incurred the first sergeant's wrath. I directed that he be untied. I then had a little chat with the first sergeant about this. He told me that he had administered "First Sergeant's Punishment."

I knew about "First Sergeant's Punishment" and had seen it administered effectively by First Sergeant Edgar L. Huff, a black first sergeant and one of the most famous noncommissioned officers in the Marine Corps. When I was at Camp Lejune in 1953, Huff disciplined a black Marine who had just returned to our company from a stint in the brig. The problem Marine was a real troublemaker with a bad attitude. His time in the brig hadn't done anything to improve his behavior. In fact, he was more resentful, and convinced the Corps was picking on him. Huff took the problem Marine behind the barracks and counseled him, as only Huff could do. Our problem Marine got the message, and squared himself away. Huff's method was tough, and not officially sanctioned, but it worked. Sometimes doing it by the book isn't the best way to handle problems, but deviate with great care.

It took me a while to understand the A Company first sergeant was not like Huff. When he threw this same Marine misfit he had tied to the flagpole bodily through the screen door of our Quonset hut office, I notified the battalion commander about the incident, fired the first sergeant for cause, and sent him to the battalion staff. He was not my kind of leader. He had a bad temper, was a bully, and was one of those "do as I say, not as I do" leaders. He had cowed the other noncommissioned officers, and my young lieutenants. His departure proved to be a definite benefit for A Company.

After assuming command and discussing the VD situation with Captain Walt Puller, the other Awase company commander, I decided that with a camp as small as this one, physical fitness and exercise would be the order of the day. There was no drill field, and the camp was located in a small space surrounded by rice paddies. The area had been a school ground before our Marines took it over. The VD problem was out of control because "ladies of the evening" came to the edge of the compound at night to offer their services.

To fix this, I intended to get my Marines so tired they wouldn't want to do anything but go to bed at night. Was I ever wrong on this one! I held reveille at 0400 followed by troop muster and a long, *long* run. I ran my troops until every man threw up. What happened as a result?

We won the division flag football competition, the regimental basketball competition, and won or placed in about every intramural activity. We also stayed in first place in the division "VD competition." One day, the assistant division commander, a Bible carrying one star general paid us a visit. After his inspection, he said to me, "Captain, do you know Company A has the highest VD rate on the island?"

"Yes, sir," I replied.

"Well, you better get it reduced and fast."

I had done everything to reduce the VD rate I could think of. There was one thing I hadn't tried, though. That was to get suggestions from the troopers themselves. I ordered the troops to their Quonset huts, called in the key noncommissioned officers and told them to discuss this matter with the men. Then each Marine was to write on a slip of paper what he thought we could do to solve the problem.

I went back to my office to await the results. As the slips of paper were turned in the First sergeant put them into one of our steel helmets. He then brought the helmet containing all the notes to me, and I began reading the suggestions. They were useless.

I was almost finished when I pulled one out that read, "Captain, I feel sorry as hell for you. I don't know what to do about the problem either." I almost fell out of my chair laughing. This was at least an honest comment.

What A Company needed was to go into the field to get away from Camp *Abase*. To my relief, this happened. The company was in great physical condition; so, I believed we would perform well in the field.

Division had planned an exercise in South Korea, and my battalion was to be a part of it. The Navy transported us to the Pusan area by LST (Landing Ship Tank). Our aggressors were to be Army units, and an Army company would oppose me. This one would be fun. I was determined A Company would make a good showing.

We chased the aggressors around for a few days. One evening my battalion commander told me to expect the Army to attack us during the next twenty-four hours. We went into a defensive posture, and I sent out scouts to see if they could locate the aggressors. About midnight several scouts returned and reported that they had located the Army aggressor unit. The soldiers were bivouacked about two kilometers away.

"Captain," one scout said, "they have no perimeter security. I believe they have all sacked out."

Our battalion commander was not one of my favorite people, and the feeling was mutual. After all we had the highest VD rate in the Third Marine Division. He felt this made him look bad, and he held me accountable.

I radioed battalion and told them we had located the aggressors. I asked for permission to conduct a probing action. The battalion commander granted permission, and strangely enough he didn't request any details about my plans. I could now do something I had always wanted to try, a dawn attack.

After giving my platoon commanders their orders, we moved out. My plan was to surround the Army unit and capture *all* of them. One platoon would move into a blocking position in their rear. The other two would attack from the opposite side of the Army perimeter. I planned the attack for first light, about thirty minutes before sunrise. The attacking platoons would attack from the east so the rising sun would be at their back. The Army soldiers would be looking into the sun as we came in.

We started the attack just before sunrise, and my Marines executed it perfectly. We captured the entire army company! This included all their officers, their first sergeant . . . every single one of them. To embarrass them further, we lined them up, removed their weapons, and stacked them in a big pile.

It would take them quite a while to sort the pile of weapons and return each firearm to the proper soldier. By then we would be long gone from the area. I radioed the battalion and told them what we'd done. I was expecting to receive a well-done and lots of complements. However, the opposite happened. I couldn't believe it. The battalion commander was furious.

I requested that he fly out and see what had happened. He would not. Then I asked if they would send out a helicopter, so I could at least send the army first sergeant back to verify my story. He finally granted that request.

The final words I heard were, "Hilgartner, you've upset the entire exercise!" I was crushed.

Late that afternoon we received orders to march back to Pusan. It would be an all night trek over rugged terrain. We walked for almost eighteen hours before reaching our embarkation point and our Navy LST. My men were so tired some of them began falling asleep while they were walking. I did too. Once I found myself in a ditch lying on my side.

Reaching the LST around midday was like getting to heaven. I'll never forget how the sailors greeted us. The weather was cold and damp. We were tired, cold, and just plain miserable. The ship's captain had stationed sailors with big pots of hot split pea soup near the after brow. As we came aboard, the sailors invited each Marine to dip his canteen into the pot and fill it to brim with hot soup. This really bolstered our spirits and made me proud to be a part of the Navy-Marine team.

After all the troops were aboard and refreshed, the ship's captain invited me to his wardroom. I apologized for my filthy uniform, but he said, "Never mind. Come on in, get some hot soup for yourself, and fill me in on your adventures." I could have hugged that man!

While my battalion commander hadn't appreciated my tactical victory, it proved to be a valuable learning experience for me. I was convinced that if I ever had the good fortune to lead troops in battle, this was a tactic I should use again. When the attacking commander can achieve total surprise, not only is victory almost a given, but casualties to his own troops will be minimal. A good, well-trained Marine is not expendable. Each man in the unit is an integral part of the whole team, and war *is* a team effort.

After about seven months as A Company's commander, I assumed command of the Regimental Headquarters and Service Company. My H & S Company tour was fairly uneventful. I managed to win a set of golf clubs playing bingo at the Kadena Officer's Club. I also purchased a motor scooter, and with Gene Balderston and other good friends, I zoomed around the island on weekends. My Okinawa tour ended with orders to report to the Marine reserve unit in Beaumont, Texas. I was to relieve Captain Dick Kephart as Inspector-Instructor for the Thirty-Third Marine Reserve Rifle Company.

My new unit had about 65 reserve Marines. The Inspector-Instructor (I&I) staff consisted of one officer and about five or six Marine noncommissioned officers. I&I personnel were all active duty, career Marines. The I&I Marines trained the reserve Marines, recruited, and participated in unit public relations. It was an important job, and the first time I had ever worked closely with a civilian community. The district director, a colonel, stressed to me that he wanted me to place a big emphasis on training and recruiting. The size of the Thirty Third Rifle Company was not much larger than a regular Marine platoon, and he wanted me to double the size.

The two years in Beaumont, Texas, were good ones. We started an NRA sponsored Junior Leatherneck Rifle Club. One of my noncommissioned officers, Gunnery Sergeant Russell Polk, was like a pied piper when it came to attracting the youth of the area. I put him in charge of the rifle club. Polk recruited young men and a few young women, supervised shooting instruction, and organized competition matches on the unit's indoor rifle range. It was a huge success and we soon had a waiting list to join the club. Our other Marines joined Sergeant Polk to help him with his rifle club activities, and before long club members were enlisting in the reserve unit. The Junior Leatherneck Rifle Club became an important adjunct to our recruiting effort.

Community activities became a major element of my job. I joined the local Kiwanis Club and served on the Armed Forces Committee of the Beaumont Chamber of Commerce. To help the Kiwanis Club with its annual fundraiser, we brought the Marine Band from Washington, DC to Beaumont for two concert performances. It was a sellout.

The best part of my I&I tour was spending more time with my family. We had three lovely young daughters by then, Linda, Diana and Dale, and I truly found our time together as a family in Beaumont some of the happiest days of my life. One of the benefits of living in Beaumont was visiting my brother Lee and his beautiful wife, Mary, in Yorktown, Texas at my father's ranch. After he graduated from Texas A&M, Lee was commissioned in the U.S. Air Force. Following his service commitment, he worked for my father as ranch manager. Lee was fun to be with, my daughters worshiped him, and I dearly loved Lee and Mary. We had many wonderful times together on the ranch hunting, riding, eating Bar-B-Que, and enjoying each other's company. For excitement, we sometimes went rattlesnake hunting, which I enjoyed more than Lee did. In fact, Lee really didn't much like the whole thing, preferring to leave rattlesnakes alone in their own part of the ranch.

South Texas is a large rural area, and one of its most important features is the magnificent opportunity to see the abundant wildlife that this area supports. One of the less understood, and fear-inspiring creatures are diamondback rattlesnakes. Now make no mistake; I am as afraid of the rattler as the next man is.

Mary and Lee Hilgartner

Lee used to say that everybody who ever came to the ranch wanted to go find a rattlesnake. Everybody but Lee, who found no interest in looking for trouble. He saw enough of snakes and wanted nothing to do with rattlesnake hunting. On one vist with Lee, I became obsessed with a snake hunt. After a few bottles of beer and a little whiskey, finding a rattlesnake became the most important thing in my life. There was nothing more important than rattlesnake huntin'!

I had Diana, Dale and Lee's young son, Louis, get into the back of the pickup truck that still had the cattle sides on. Linda says she was playing with a horned toad in a red ant bed; so, she missed the fun. Lee and I got into the front seat, and we took off with him driving. He went to as many places as he could that he thought would *not* have a snake. Lee wanted nothing to do with this snake hunt, and was doing his best to sabotage the effort. Finally, I called his hand; so, he took us to a big live oak tree that he thought would be a likely location. The tree had a hole at ground level all the way through the trunk, and sure enough, we saw a snake in there. Lee told me to bring him a stick so he could pull the rattlesnake out of its lair. I brought him a stick about two feet long that he threw away telling me that if I could see over it, it was too short. I found part of a dead tree limb that looked to be long enough, and brought it to Lee. He used the long stick to reach in the tree hole carefully and touched the snake. That was more than enough to wake it up with a chorus of rattles as it got ready to strike.

Lee asked for the .22 caliber rifle behind the truck seat, and one of my girls brought it to him. I told him that I wanted to shoot, so he let me. I got into the prone firing position and fired a round, but I didn't kill it. I only shot the lower jaw completely off the snake's head, leaving the fangs and real business parts of the head still intact.

Lee thought he could hit and kill the snake with the stick; so, he squatted down to do hit the creature that was now mad as hell. I had gotten up close behind Lee and was stooped down draped over him trying to see what was going on. Well, when Lee hit the snake, it decided to come out of that tree and attack the source of its misery. Rattlesnakes can crawl faster than you might think, and Lee jumped back to get away from the oncoming rattler. Unfortunately he jumped right into my legs and lower body, knocking us both down. The snake kept coming at us, and we were trying to get untangled so we could protect ourselves. The snake was still coming right at us, and Lee started hitting at the snake with the stick as fast as he could. Lee killed it when it was about six inches from us, and ready to strike one of us. That was and will be our last snake hunt. In August 2002, Lee passed away after losing his battle with pulmonary fibrosis. He spent his last days writing his life's story, which Mary published in December 2002. This story comes from Lee's memoirs.

I was promoted to Major just prior to the end of my tour in Beaumont. The Thirty Third Rifle Company's strength stood at 125 enlisted and 5 reserve officers. We had met our goal of doubling its size.

My family became greatly attached to Beaumont, and we had many friends there. As we drove out of town, I remember turning on the car radio and heard the announcer say, "Major Pete Hilgartner and his family are leaving Beaumont today. He has orders to report to the Commander in Chief Pacific Fleet (CINCPACFLT) in Hawaii for duty. Beaumont will miss Pete and his family. We wish them God speed." We were very touched by this!

It's a long drive from Beaumont, Texas to San Diego, California, where I had to get my military air transport flight to Honolulu. To make the time on pass quickly, we sang songs and played car games like, who will spot the biggest cactus, license plate bingo, and who will be the first to see the next Burma Shave signs. It was a long trip, but I still remember it warmly.

My flight to Oahu, the most important of the Hawaiian Islands, was pleasant and relatively quick. My family followed by ship, which arrived in Honolulu about ten days later. Until they arrived I lived in the bachelor officers' quarters.

After reporting in, CINCPACFLT assigned me to duty as Assistant Assault Forces and Unconventional Warfare Officer. My boss was Commander Bruce Thompson USN, a man whom I came to admire greatly.

There were three Marine officers on the CINCPACFLT staff: Lieutenant Colonel Dayton Robinson, the Marine aviation officer; a communications officer; and me, the Marine infantry officer. Dayton and I became good friends, and later in my tour, we hunted wild boar and feral goats together on Molokai. He became my big brother on the staff, and his counsel was invaluable. The job meant long hours, frequently including weekends. One of my collateral jobs was as a duty officer and the Admiral's briefer.

One weekend, early in my tour when I was the duty officer on watch, I received a frantic call from the White House. The agitated White House staffer said that one of President Lyndon Johnson's daughters was visiting the island, and they didn't know where she was. She had disappeared! The White House staff demanded immediate action in locating her. I figured she had disappeared on purpose to escape LBJ's prying eyes, and was probably at some "No Tell Motel" with a naval aviator. I didn't feel a tragedy unfolding, but the White House staff was in a state of high dudgeon. I notified the command duty officer, a Navy captain, and he came down to the operations center on the double.

It wasn't long before the entire operations center was filled with Navy brass including one admiral. It was actually a very amusing scene from my observation post in a quiet corner of the room. I was far too junior to participate actively in such monumentally important events. The unfolding excitement and air of crisis seemed on the level of Eisenhower's operations center during the D-Day landings at Normandy. Phones were ringing, we had an open line to the White House operations center, and all about us stood senior officers with looks of grave concern on their faces. This was becoming a major emergency. I expected Secretary of Defense McNamara to intercede and personally take charge, as was his wont. Maybe LBJ himself might get on the horn and start giving us directions.

Eventually we located her, and things quieted down. We never did find out where she had been during those lost hours. Maybe she had been in the Christian Science Reading Room and just lost track of time. Whatever! The crisis was over as far as CINCPACFLT was concerned. Any further action was a matter for LBJ and Lady Bird.

There were important aspects to the job that related to operations in Vietnam. CINCPACFLT was responsible for all U.S. Naval forces in the Pacific. These were the Seventh Fleet, the Fleet Marine Force, Pacific, and other Navy commands not directly controlled by Seventh Fleet or the Fleet Marine Force, Pacific. CINCPACFLT's boss was Commander-in-Chief Pacific (CINCPAC) who had overall command of Navy, Marine and Army units in the Pacific. See Appendix C for a summary of Pacific Command organizational relationships.

At the beginning of my tour as a CINCPACFLT staff officer, I was primarily focused on Marine counterinsurgency activities in South Vietnam. Several times I went to Vietnam for an in-country look at what was going on. Once I went on a riverboat patrol with an old friend from the Basic School Leadership Group, Captain Al Smith. Al was a Marine advisor to the South Vietnamese Navy conducting riverboat operations and patrols in the Mekong Delta. This gave me a good look at warfare on rivers and inland waterways, a new and important aspect of combat operations in Vietnam.

Our Navy's primary mission is oriented to open ocean combat. With that focus, the Navy had not been involved in riverine or littoral warfare since the Civil War. Much new doctrine needed to be developed.

Later, when major deployments of Marine forces began, my job included staff work for these deployments. This involved tracking the Marine units deployed, and tallying the actual numbers of Marines in country and being sent to South Vietnam. It was a huge job keeping on top of all the constant changes, and I had to work with the technical staff at CINCPACFLT to develop computer capabilities to track such things.

The CINCPACFLT admirals were not well grounded in the details of Marine Corps force structure, policy, and operations. As time went on, I frequently found myself in the Admiral's office answering questions, or explaining matters about Marine operations. I served Admiral Thomas Moorer for most of my time on the CINCPACFLT staff. Admiral Moorer, who later became Chief of Naval Operations, was a well-known personality in the Department of Defense at that time. He was high profile and made good copy for the press, particularly with things starting to heat up in Vietnam. Admiral Moorer was a good man to work for, and I had the highest respect for him.

Victor (*Brute*) Krulak was the Fleet Marine Force Pacific (FMFPAC) commanding general. General Krulak was called *Brute* because of his diminutive size. He was one of the smallest officers in the Marine Corps, but he was brilliant, and known throughout the Corps as a tough man to work for. His standards and work ethic were of the highest order, and he was uncompromising with those who failed to measure up. Colonel Bob Barrow was on General Krulak's staff, serving as his chief operations officer. Colonel Barrow was also brilliant, and my hero in the Corps. I knew when I was with him that I was with a *real* leader. Colonel Barrow had a most distinguished career. He rose to the rank of four star general and became commandant of the Marine Corps. I was working for, and with, some of the greatest officers the Navy and Marine Corps had during those years.

When it became obvious that the Commander U.S. Military Assistance Command Vietnam (COMUSMACV, or just MACV for short) required more Marine units in Vietnam, the request for those deployments came to CINCPACFLT from CGFMFPAC (Commanding General Fleet Marine Force Pacific), and the first one was a *doozy*. Admiral Moorer called me to his office one day and said, "Hilgartner, General Krulak believes we need more Marine units in Vietnam. He has submitted a request for a Hawk antiaircraft missile battery to be deployed to the Chu Lai and Da Nang area. Why is he asking for a Hawk battery? The North Vietnamese don't have any air power."

Not knowing exactly what to say, I requested permission to go find out. This meant a trip to FMFPAC headquarters for a talk with Colonel Barrow. Colonel Barrow had a twinkle in his eye when he said, "The Admiral wants an explanation? Well, let's go in and see the Brute and tell him about it."

Once inside the General's office, Colonel Barrow explained why I was there. "Admiral Moorer wants to know why we are requesting the Hawk unit."

General Krulak said to me. "Well, I guess I'll have to give him a call and teach him a few things." Then the general focused on me, "Hilgartner, do you know why you are at CINCPACFLT?"

"I hope so, sir."

"Hope so, my foot," he said. "You are over there to be my eyes and ears. You are to help me guide the Admiral properly on Marine Corps matters." The message was clear. General Krulak wanted all his deployment requests approved by CINCPACFLT, no ifs, ands, or buts, about it. My job was to help the general get what he wanted.

I wasn't certain he would like my response, but I decided to give it anyway, "General, I understand, sir, but whatever I advise the Admiral, I will tell him the truth and loyally support his best interests. I am a Marine, but in my present assignment, Admiral Moorer is my boss and I owe him my best effort."

"Fine," General Krulak said noncommittally. Then Colonel Barrow and I left. I wasn't sure whether or not "The Brute" had marked me for later assassination.

Once we were in Colonel Barrow's office, he said, "Pete, this Hawk unit is only going to be the first of many future deployments. I'll keep you clued in so you won't be caught by surprise anymore." This was to become an important and successful relationship between Colonel Barrow and me.

Many times afterwards, when General Krulak called Admiral Moorer, I would be in the room with the admiral listening on his other phone. At key times in the conversation, the admiral would look to me for a thumbs up, a thumbs down, or a side to side wave of my hand meaning, sir, let me explain this to you in more detail. I don't ever recall using the thumbs down, or no, signal, but I was always truthful. I never misrepresented things with Admiral Moorer in order to satisfy General Krulak. It was a clumsy situation that made me feel very uncomfortable. It's never easy serving two bosses.

To this day I do believe that General Krulak put a Marine missile unit in Vietnam because it would need infantry troops to defend it. He was doing this as a subterfuge to get Marine infantry into Vietnam without creating a stir in the press. General Krulak had a good political reason for deploying a Marine Hawk unit in Vietnam, but to my mind there was never a tactical reason for bringing in such a unit. Somehow General Krulak must have given an answer to Admiral Moorer that satisfied the admiral because Marine Hawk units were deployed to South Vietnam, and Marine infantry were deployed to defend them.

The requests for deployment of more Marine units continued and USMC forces ashore grew until two Marine divisions, the First and Third, were deployed in I Corps (called Eye Corps), the northern part of South Vietnam. As the unit deployments grew, so did contact with the enemy. Command and control problems between the Army and Marine combat operations also became more complex. An Army general, COMUSMACV (Commander U.S. Military Assistance Command Vietnam), controlled all Army and Marine forces ashore. COMSEVENTHFLT (Commander Seventh Fleet) controlled the forces afloat. CINCPACFLT (Commander in Chief Pacific Fleet) provided the naval support (including amphibious support) requested by COMUSMACV.

This was a complicated organizational structure that spawned too many command and control difficulties, which became a major issue between COMUSMACV, COMSEVENTHFLT, and CINCPACFLT. To resolve this command problem, CINCPAC called a meeting in Okinawa in the spring of 1965 of representatives from all the commands concerned with this matter. Because amphibious warfare is the Marines warfare specialty, CINCPAC sent one of his top Marines, Colonel John Chaisson, to chair the conference. General Krulak sent Colonel Bob Barrow, and Admiral Moorer sent me. There were Seventh Fleet officers at the meeting, but I don't remember them. Colonel Chaisson and Colonel Barrow dominated the proceedings. I played the minor role of recording secretary, which I was happy to be. I was with those great officers, and I soaked it up like a sponge.

The meeting was a success. There had been much discussion, and we drafted an official agreement called the *Agreement for U. S. Naval Support Operations in the Republic of Vietnam (RVN.)* Several years later, while assigned to Headquarters Marine Corps in Washington, and at the urging of my boss, Colonel Calhoun Killeen, I compiled an article for publication in the *Marine Corps Gazette*, entitled "Amphibious Doctrine in Vietnam." It appeared in the January 1969 issue of the Gazette. I subsequently heard that the article had been incorporated in the officer school curriculum at Quantico. My article also appeared in the 1985 issue of the History and Museums Division, Headquarters Marine Corps *Anthology and Annotated Bibliography* and was cited by them as one of the best writings relative to the Vietnam War. I was, and still am, honored by this recognition.

While I worked hard and diligently at CINCPACFLT, I had a few lighter moments for recreation. We often made family outings to the many wonderful beaches on Oahu. I was also able to hunt goat, sheep, deer and pheasant, which is a passion for me. And certainly the highlight of that great tour in Honolulu was the birth of my son David on 21 February 1964.

Honolulu is a magnet for visitors, and it drew my father and stepmother. My father and I were never close, and we hadn't seen much of each other since he sent me away from his Texas ranch when I was in high school. In spite of the cool feelings, I felt that since he was making an effort, we would make the visit enjoyable for them.

My good friend and former boss on the CINCPACFLT staff, Commander Bruce Thompson USN, had been reassigned, and was skipper of a destroyer with its home-port at the U.S. Naval Base in Pearl Harbor. I contacted Bruce to tell him of my parents' visit, and he invited all of us to have lunch in the officers' wardroom mess aboard his ship. I accepted with great pleasure.

Bruce planned to have his captain's gig pick us up at the USS Arizona Memorial after our visit. My father and stepmother were very excited and impressed with the arrangements. We boarded the ferry for the trip to the Arizona Memorial, then disaster! The ferry ran aground. We were stuck in the mud in Pearl Harbor, and there was no way to contact Bruce about our mishap. It looked like we weren't going to make the noon luncheon aboard his ship that we had all been looking forward to with great anticipation.

About 1 p.m., we saw a launch headed our way. It was from Bruce's ship. Bruce rescued us, and to his credit, he had a special late luncheon and ship tour prepared for us. My father told this story to his friends at every opportunity. The "shipwreck" and shipboard luncheon made their day.

My CINCPACFLT tour ended in September 1966. I was ordered to Vietnam for duty with the Seventh Marine Regiment. This was a fine assignment, and I was one happy Marine. My new job would introduce me to combat operations in Vietnam, and might eventually lead to a battalion command during my tour. Combat command is what I had spent years preparing myself for, and battalion command was the next goal I set for myself.

I hated to leave my family, but we decided that they should remain in Honolulu. This would be pleasant for them, and better than moving to a new location, and then moving again upon my leaving Vietnam in about twelve months.

I knew from my own childhood experience how disruptive changing places to live and entering new schools could be. It had set my education back to where I had to struggle to catch up with my peers, and I vowed not to subject my children to the same unsettling experience. My family was comfortable in their Honolulu surroundings, and it made no sense to change it. Besides, living in "Paradise" ain't all bad.

6.0 VIETNAM

The flight from Honolulu took about eight hours. When we landed at Da Nang on 17 September 1966, it was a standard day in Vietnam—hot, about 95 degrees and humid. Da Nang is about 10 miles inland from the coast and gets no ocean breeze. As I disembarked from the air conditioned plane, the heat hit me like a blast from a furnace. After two days of in-processing with the First Marine Division, I received my orders and caught a flight to Chu Lai Air Field about 90 miles south of Da Nang. Marines in a regimental jeep met me at the Chu Lai airport and took me to the Seventh Marine Regiment Headquarters. Colonel Larry Snowden, an outstanding officer who later became a lieutenant general, commanded the Seventh Regiment.

The Seventh Marines were located west of the Chu Lai airstrip on the western side of Route One. I looked forward to joining the Seventh Marines again, having been attached to them as a forward observer during the Korean War. The base was large, sprawling, and full of activity.

The Seventh Marine Regiment was a proud organization when I was with it in Korea during the early fifties, and it had not changed in the intervening years. The commanding officer, Colonel Larry Snowden, had an outstanding reputation as a combat and staff officer. He later rose to the rank of lieutenant general and served as the chief of staff of the Marine Corps.

After reporting in, I learned that I was to be the regimental operations officer (S-3). My duties were to plan field and battle operations for the regiment and its battalions, which I would then submit to the regimental commander for approval. Once an operation was underway, my staff and I kept the colonel informed of ongoing events, and provided tactical recommendations as we saw fit.

The regimental staff had two officers I knew, and both were first-rate. They would be invaluable in helping support the regiment's operations. Major Dick Alger, a 1953 Naval Academy graduate, was the S-2, (Intelligence) officer. Alger had been in my battalion at the Naval Academy; so, I had known him for quite some time. He was extremely bright and hard working. Major Gerald Turley was the S-4 (Logistics) officer. Gerry and I had been company commanders in the Third Marines on Okinawa. He too, was very bright and an aggressive warrior. Both officers greeted me warmly upon my arrival.

We ate our meals in a regimental mess, where Colonel Snowden had a table for his key staff officers and occasional guests. Some of our visitors were well-known entertainment personalities with the USO. Cowboy actor, Roy Rogers and his actress wife, Dale Evans, once honored us with a visit at noon meal. I sat next to Mrs. Rogers. Their visit was enjoyable, and we were kept busy answering their questions concerning the Marines, the war, and our duties in particular. I was talking with Mrs. Rogers when one of my staff assistants came in to tell me that one of our battalions was engaged with the enemy. I reported this to Colonel Snowden, and excused myself to get back to work. As I departed, Mrs. Rogers said, "You dear boy, I will keep you in my prayers."

Near the end of October 1966, Colonel Snowden took operational control of the First Battalion from the Fifth Marine Regiment (First Battalion, Fifth Marines). We planned an operation for this battalion to make an extended sweep of an area west of Chu Lai with the objective of engaging the enemy in a search and destroy mission. We gave the battalion clear operational objectives, and they moved out as ordered on 2 November. Early that evening, First Battalion notified us that they had reached their initial objective, and would establish a defensive perimeter for the night. Shortly thereafter I learned that the battalion commander had ordered his unit to return to the combat base, and that they were moving out to come back. I couldn't believe what I heard. I radioed for a position report, and plotted it on the map. They were indeed coming back to base. I then notified Colonel Snowden.

When he received the report that the battalion was heading home, Snowden went into a rage and stormed out of the operations tent. I had never heard of a Marine unit taking an action like this. I began to think I had done something wrong. Did the battalion commander not understand his orders? Had I not been clear? I was one upset Marine S-3.

The next morning Colonel Snowden asked me to step outside of the operations tent. "Pete, I need to talk with you," he said. As I went out of the tent, I was thinking, well, you blew it; your career is over.

"Pete," he said, "you've done a good job here and I hate to lose you. As you may know, First Battalion, Fifth Marines presently has the worst reputation of any battalion in the First Marine Division. I will not tolerate what happened last night. I relieved the battalion commander, and I'm offering you command of this historically fine unit. It won't be an easy assignment. You'll have to go down there and clean house. What do you say? Do you want the job or not?"

My knees buckled. This was the answer to my dream. However, he was right, cleaning house had to be my first task, and I couldn't do this without strong help. A leader's success is largely the result of the quality of people working for him. I had to get rid of the deadwood, and bring in top quality officers and senior noncommissioned officers. I had been silent long enough. The colonel was waiting for my reply.

"Colonel, it's been an honor to work for you," I said. "I gladly accept your offer; however, I'll need help. I'd like to take a couple of the staff officers to assist me."

"Who were you thinking of, Pete?"

"Colonel, I request that Majors Alger and Turley go with me."

"What!" he exploded. "I'm losing you and you want to take both Alger and Turley? They are key to my operation here."

I just stood there and said nothing. After a pause, Colonel Snowden laughed and said, "Okay, you can take Alger with you.

He'll follow you there tomorrow. Now, pack your gear and get moving."

"Thank you, sir," I said. If there weren't tears of joy in my eyes there should have been.

On the Fourth of November 1966, Major Peter L. Hilgartner USMC became commanding officer of the First Battalion, Fifth Marines. The battalion had temporarily fallen on hard times, but the First Battalion was the premier combat battalion in the most decorated regiment in Marine Corps history. Shortly thereafter I was selected for Lieutenant Colonel, but I initially assumed command while I was still a major. This was a high honor!

During the helicopter flight to the First Battalion, Fifth Marines combat base my head was full of thoughts about how to turn the battalion around quickly and make it a first-rate fighting organization. Weeding out the deadwood had to be an immediate and priority task, and I knew the regimental commander would support me in what I had to do. I was fortunate that during my command of First Battalion, I worked for some of the finest colonels in the Marine Corps, and most of them became general officers. Colonel Snowden, Colonel Widdecke, Colonel Haynes, Colonel Houghton, and Colonel Davis were all outstanding Marines. They all guided me, and supported me in everything I had to do to make my battalion an effective fighting unit.

During the flight, I also thought about the leadership principles I had to set for myself and the battalion. Initially, I had too many items on my list. After some agonizing over the subject, I realized the list was cumbersome. I started combining, paring, and simplifying until I narrowed it down to the following:

(a) always accomplish the mission assigned;
(b) take care of my troops and minimize casualties; and
(c) keep my trust in God and my guardian angels.

And I did keep faith with these principles the entire time I commanded the battalion. This was not just another list; it was a set of principles I lived by.

The battalion commander's tent was located near the top of Hill 54, just down from the helicopter landing pad, which was at the very top of the hill. Compared to what the troops had, the commanding officer's tent was a very comfortable place.

At "zero-dark-thirty" that first night, I awoke and went outdoors to find the "head" (Marine and Navy term for toilet). I hadn't gone far when I collided with a young Marine. Both of us were surprised and the Marine came to the "ready" instantly.

"Halt! Who goes there?" He commanded.

"Who are you?" I asked. He knew who I was.

"I'm your sentry, sir. My job is to guard your tent while you are sleeping."

"Son, the entire perimeter of this position is full of Marines at the ready. If the bad guys get this close to me, we're all done for. Marine, I hereby relieve you of duty on this post. Report to your sergeant, tell him this, then go back and stay with your squad. They need you more than I do."

"Thank you sir," he said and departed.

That Marine was the first one I relieved in my new job as battalion commander. From then on, I could go unchallenged to the head at night anytime I needed to.

Before taking bold action in my new command, I wanted to make a thorough evaluation of the relations between the officers, noncommissioned officers, and troopers. I also planned a thorough "recon" of the combat base. After making these first assessments, I intended to go on a patrol or two with my company commanders. Then when I had a good evaluation of the situation, I could take informed, forceful action.

As I had planned, I began making sweeping changes in the battalion's officers and senior enlisted personnel. I suppose everybody was waiting for the axe to fall. One day shortly after my arrival, I called First Lieutenant Art Blades (now a retired Lieutenant General) to my hooch. Art was the executive officer of Charley Company. I asked Art if he knew why I called him in. Having seen so many called in before him with an unpleasant aftermath, most recently a company commander, Art was reluctant to speculate openly. I interrupted his hemming and hawing with a chuckle and told him that he had nothing to worry about. Based on Buck Darling's strong endorsement and Art's excellent reputation I made him Alpha Company commander effective immediately.

I had great confidence in Buck's judgment. He was Charlie Company's commander, a superb Marine, an aggressive warrior, and had been with the battalion for almost a year. Buck had seen all of First Battalion's officers perform under fire, and knew who was good and whom we could do without. He made a good choice in recommending Art for commanding Alpha Company.

Art kept his company until February 1967, when he went to the hospital in Chu Lai with malaria and a staph infection from leeches. Shortly after his hospitalization, I learned the full extent of Art's illness, and that he could not soon come back to the battalion. I reluctantly had to replace him because it was an operational necessity. I went to the hospital in Chu Lai to tell Art what I had to do. He took the bad news gracefully, and understood that it was in the best interest of the company and the battalion. I then made him my battalion logistics officer (S-4), to assume his new assignment as soon as he could return to duty. Art later told me he always appreciated the way I handled the situation.

The troops give every battalion commanding officer nicknames that they use when talking about their C.O. Some are funny, some not so flattering, but all are right on the mark. Nothing escapes the critical eye of a Marine trooper. Blades and Darling, later told me that my troops first gave me the moniker of "Big Pete," which became "High Pockets." The name could have been worse, and I'm sure at times it was. In fact, I later found out that my officers called me "The Dragon." Buck Darling, who had a sense of humor coupled with a monumental mischievous streak, tagged me with "The Dragon" moniker. I wonder how I earned that.

When Alger reported in, we met in my tent, and I explained the situation to him. The current executive officer was partially responsible for the First Battalion's problems, but I needed him because he knew the battalion and I needed his experience. I wanted Alger to officially assume duties as operations officer (S-3), but in reality he was to be my executive officer (X.O.) as well.

"You'll have to be eyes and ears for me, Dick. Can you handle it?"

Dick gave me his wonderful big grin and replied, "You bet! I know you, Pete. You're going to be a hands-on operational commander; so, I'll need the X.O. job to help keep me busy."

Dick was right about my hands-on approach. Battalion intelligence (S-2) and operations (S-3) reported directly to me. Personnel (S-1), logistics (S-4), and civil affairs (S-5) reported to the executive officer. That way I could focus my attention on combat operations and leave the battalion administrative business to my X.O. I knew Dick was going to work his butt off, and I was confident that we would work well together.

After getting Alger started, I began to explore the battalion's internal perimeter. I found most of the battalion combat base located on a cone shaped hill that the maps designated Hill 54. The companies were in fighting positions dug in a circle around the base of the hill. A large rice paddy flanked our east side, with the main road running north and south on the far side of the paddy. Delta Company, commanded by Captain John J. Carty, had combat positions on Hill 10, about a quarter of a mile away from the main firebase on Hill 54. Although my battalion's companies were not concentrated within the same defensive perimeter, I had no problems with the deployment. There wasn't enough room to group all companies on Hill 54, and supporting fire from Hill 54 could cover Carty's position on Hill 10.

When a unit has problems, I knew from experience that the food might have something to do with it. The previous battalion commander had set up large tents over stand up tables where the troops ate. About 15 yards away he had established an officers' mess tent. The tent's ceiling was lined with a white silk parachute that also provided extra insulation. The officer's mess tent was a very cushy place by Vietnamese bush standards.

There was a horrible pigsty smell where the troops ate. It came from the mess tents, and was sickening. I called for the mess sergeant, and discussed the foul odor with him. He agreed with me that this was a bad place for the men to eat. The stench came from rotting scraps of food the troopers dropped on the ground while they ate standing up. They stepped on the scraps grinding them into the earthen floor of the tent, where the food scraps decayed. With little or no air circulation inside the mess tent, the odor of decay accumulated, festered, compounded, and the stench became overwhelming. Compared to the mess tent, the battalion latrine was a bouquet. I then called Sergeant Major Aiken for consultation.

"Sergeant major," I said, "We are a combat infantry unit. In the Marine Corps the officers share the same hardships with the men. I want *all* mess tents torn down. Until we build a proper place for both officers and men in this battalion we'll all sit on stumps or whatever is available and eat in the open, rain or shine. Is that clear?"

He nodded.

"Then tear those tents down now, and get that cook who's been cooking special meals for the officers out of here. He's fired!"

Sergeant majors in the Marine Corps are a very elite group. They are the highest ranking noncommissioned officers in the Corps. Strangely enough, at the battalion level their duties are not specifically defined. In general, they are the enlisted men's liaison to the battalion commander. However, they do much more than that. A good sergeant major is an indispensable part of a well-run battalion, and my sergeant major, "Pappy" Aiken was top of the line. The troops called him "Pappy" because they looked upon him as a father figure. I looked on him as a man whose counsel I could trust. Sergeant Major Aiken was the first noncommissioned officer I met upon taking over the battalion. We became close associates, and I relied upon him heavily.

After Pappy Aiken left, I was very fortunate in having several more excellent sergeant majors during my ten and a half months in command. All were outstanding Marine warriors and great noncommissioned officers.

The sergeant major supervised tearing down the mess tents, and led the effort to build the new mess hall, quarters, and showers for the troops. I leaned hard on my staff to get, officially or unofficially, the necessities such as plywood from Regiment, a well digger to dig a well for the shower, and a water tower from the Seventh Marines. We became excellent scroungers and cumshaw artists.

In building the new mess hall, we first had to obtain construction materials and haul them into the site. The sergeant major suggested that the Seabees had the materials and the necessary construction expertise we needed. My friend and Naval Academy classmate, Commander Ward de Groot, USN, commanded a Seabee battalion stationed in our area; so, I contacted Ward about my problem. Like a good classmate, he immediately responded. Ward provided the engineering advice and materials to complete the mess hall project. It helps to be well connected, even in the Vietnamese bush.

Infantry battalions in Vietnam did not own trucks, and we needed one. The sergeant major and I had a serious discussion about our little motor-transport problem.

"Sir, we need a truck to haul in the building materials," Sergeant Major Aiken said.

"That we do Sergeant Major. Do you know where we can get one?"

"I believe so, sir. It may take a couple of evenings to see if we can borrow one."

"Do I need to know more?" We both knew what had to be done, but I left the challenge of how it was to be done to the sergeant major.

"No sir, just leave it to me."

"Make sure it has the proper Marine Corps and Battalion insignia on it." I added.

"Yes sir, you won't have to worry about a thing," the sergeant major replied.

A few days passed and the sergeant major came to me and said, "Sir, I don't believe you've inspected the motor-pool yet." He was correct. It was the next thing on my list. "Today would be a good day if you care to go down there."

"Fine, Sergeant Major, let's go now," I answered.

When we arrived at the motor pool lot, the sergeant-in-charge was standing proudly next to a big, newly painted truck with all the appropriate insignia.

"She's a beauty!" I enthusiastically exclaimed. The sergeant-in-charge of the motor pool beamed with pride over his new acquisition. "It really is grand, Sergeant Major. How much did it cost?"

"Not much, sir, the Army gave it to us for a case of scotch and two cases of beer."

I didn't ask him where the booze came from. We had our truck. We had the Seabee support, and before long, we had a beautiful, new mess hall. The roof had a few holes in it, but the deck was slatted so that water fell through to the ground. The sides were screened to keep the flies away. Our new mess hall was the Taj Mahal of mess halls in the Vietnam bush. And the pigsty smell was gone!

The mess hall was divided inside so that three quarters of its length was for the troops. The other fourth was partitioned off for the officers and the staff noncommissioned officers. We all ate the same food.

When I walked in for our first meal, the sergeant major pointed to a large round table. "Sir, that's your table. We put a Lazy Susan in the center for you. It's the biggest and best in the regiment."

I went over and pushed the Lazy Susan with my hand and it turned beautifully without any noise at all. It was almost as if it were mounted on the axle of a jeep, which in fact it was.

One morning I walked down the hill from my command post to the mess hall for breakfast. There was a huge sinkhole in the road about ten feet in diameter and four or five feet deep. The mess sergeant was standing there looking dismayed at this development.

"How will we get our supplies in and around to the back of the mess hall?" he asked.

We had to get this hole filled, and fast! Our battalion truck wasn't suited for the job, and we had no other vehicles for hauling rocks and dirt fill. I certainly didn't want to take an infantry platoon out of action to fill it using shovels. If I did that, the platoon designated for the job would believe it was punishment. There was only one other way to meet this new challenge. With all of our manpower, we could quickly fill it if every man carried a rock to the hole and dropped it in as he came to eat.

We had about 1,000 men in the battalion. Multiplying that by three times a day meant we could get a lot of rocks moved in short order. So, that's exactly what we did. The sergeant major took charge of this and posted two noncommissioned officers to enforce the new rule. No one, officer or trooper, could eat until he had dropped a rock in the hole.

"That includes me," I said.

It soon became a game. Troopers and officers began bringing not one but several rocks with them to put into the hole. In five days we filled the hole and provided a better surface for trucks than before.

One day, Lieutenant General Victor Krulak, Commanding General Fleet Marine Force Pacific (CGFMFPAC) selected our battalion's encampment on Hill 54 as one of the stops in his regular rounds of visiting his troops in the field. Art Blades recalled General Krulak's visit, and reminded me of the following humorous account.

I had selected the battalion's reception committee for the general to consist of First Lieutenant Art Blades, Captain Buck Darling, Captain Jerry McKay, and myself. All of us are well over six feet, and General Krulak stands about five feet five inches when he stretches out to his full height. Art relates that I was so concerned about making the general feel comfortable that I didn't want any of us towering over him. As Art tells it, I directed that our troopers dig a small trench at the helo landing pad that was lower than the area where General Krulak was to debark from the helo. This reduced our height by six or seven inches, and was designed to make the general feel he didn't have to look up at anybody. According to Art, I further instructed each of my reception group not to look down at the general when shaking hands with him. Well, Blades forgot. He looked down at General Krulak and got a strong, blistering glare from him. "The Brute" may not have been a giant, but he knew how to make you feel he was.

After we greeted the general, we gave him a quick tour of the Hill 54 complex. We then retired to the chapel, the largest building that we had, to brief the general on our local situation and combat operations. After our briefings, General Krulak gave us his comments and observations. The general gave us his remarks while sitting on a table in the back of the room. It was hard to see him, but we sure heard his strong command voice. The booming, disembodied voice sounded like Jehovah Himself ringing throughout our chapel. It was hard keeping a straight face. I bit my lip so hard that I could taste blood.

All in all, the general's visit went well. We made him an honorary member of the First Battalion, Fifth Marines, and he sent me a memorable thank-you letter that I have to this day.

Many years later Lieutenant General Art Blades recalled the helo landing pad trench and Jehovah's voice in the chapel with retired General Victor "The Brute" Krulak and his son General Charles Krulak, who later became Commandant of the Marine Corps. All had a good laugh about my attempt to make the general feel at home on Hill 54.

When I first assumed command of First Battalion, Colonel Charles Widdecke, a tough ol' bird, was the Fifth Marines Regimental Commander responsible for Marine operations in the Que Son Valley. I was, in his eyes, a green battalion commander; so, he gave First Battalion minor patrol and combat assignments. At the time, I chaffed with impatience because I wanted a bigger combat challenge, but in retrospect, Colonel Widdecke was right. I *was* inexperienced, and needed to be brought along with care. Preparing combat commanders is in many ways like preparing promising prizefighters. The smart boxing manager picks the opponents with care to give ever-increasing challenge to his fighter so that skills consistently improve. But the smart manager also makes certain his fighter isn't over-matched and dealt a crushing blow that might destroy confidence. With Marine combat commanders, regiment and division commanders must be concerned with the battalion commander's self-confidence and the confidence the troops have in their commander. The regimental commander has a daunting task as boss and teacher. I was fortunate to have superb regimental commanders the entire time I commanded First Battalion.

On 26 December 1966, Colonel Fred Haynes a fine officer and now a retired major general took command of the Fifth

Regiment. Although Colonel Haynes was my regimental commander for only a short period, I really learned my job during that time. He was a good mentor and brought this new battalion commander along with care and good advice. I was sorry to see him reassigned as Operations Officer (G-3), Third Marine Amphibious Force (III MAF) in Da Nang, the senior Marine headquarters in Vietnam that controlled all Marine units in country. The assignment recognized his superb abilities as a strategist and tactician.

I continued to clean house in the battalion, and bring in excellent officers and noncommissioned officers. We also began to get meaningful combat assignments. I was pleased with the progress we were making.

On one battalion sweep we were helo-lifted into an area. Just after we landed, Alger came over to me and said, as any good battalion operations officer would, "Sir, here is my recommended plan of action."

I brushed him off saying, "I'm not ready to talk about that yet."

He moved a few steps away, just as a radio call from Colonel Haynes came in. "Cottage Six," that was my radio designation, "I understand that you have landed. What's your plan of action?"

Well, the truth is, I had not yet come up with my plan. I also knew I couldn't tell that to Colonel Haynes, nor could I fumble with extemporizing something on the fly. Haynes would have relieved me on the spot if I had said I didn't know what I was going to do now that I was in hostile territory, or if I had sounded uncertain about how I intended to engage the enemy. Colonel Haynes could detect bullshit a mile away!

"Dislodge Six, my plan is . . .," and I gave him Dick Alger's plan exactly as he had written it.

Dick, looked at me wide-eyed, and said, "That's the plan I just gave you. I thought you didn't like it!"

"I didn't say I didn't like it," I replied with a smile. "I said I wasn't ready to talk about it. Now I am; let's get on with it." I don't know if I ever thanked Dick for saving the day for me. He certainly anticipated my needs and came through for me. He was a damn fine officer, but that's why I worked so hard to get him in my battalion.

Since the Civil War, officers in the U.S. Military have adorned their uniforms with side arms. First it was a sword, and then the revolver replaced that ancient weapon. Later, the semi-automatic became the weapon of choice. I don't know why Marine field grade officers, (i.e. majors through colonel) feel that they need a sidearm, but all carry or wear one in combat zones despite their being surrounded by the best bodyguards in the world, United States Marines.

My sidearm, a standard issue M 1911 .45 caliber semi-automatic pistol, was more of a cross to bear than a blessing. It always embarrassed me when Corporal Billy Long, my driver, asked if I'd cleaned it lately. He knew that I hadn't. He would then ask for it so that he could take care of that chore for me.

On one operation, we had to cross a large, rapidly flowing river. It had been raining most of the day; so, the current was very strong. Our objective was on the other side of the river, and I was worried that men and equipment would be swept downstream if we didn't get a rope across first.

I was accompanying Delta Company, and asked Captain John Carty, the company commander, to bring me his strongest swimmer. John produced a fine-looking young sergeant named Gerald Clore. After explaining the situation to him, I asked if he thought he could make it across.

"Yes, sir," he answered without hesitation. He then entered the water and began to cross the river. The swift current required that he use both hands to swim a breaststroke as he struggled to keep his head above the fast rushing water. Clore was indeed a strong swimmer, but he struggled against the current with his rifle strapped to his back and the safety line strapped around his waist. After he had crossed, in an amazing feat of strength, and tied the safety line to a tree on the far bank, I wasn't sure all my Marines could make it across safely, even holding on to the line.

"It's my turn now," I said as I entered the water.

Without hesitation, Captain Carty protested. So did the sergeant major and several others. I told them that I wasn't the strongest Marine in the battalion. If this old man could make it across, then we all could. So with pistol held high in the air with one hand and the other gripping the safety line, the "old man" proceeded to transit the fast rushing river. I got about half way across when my grip on the line gave way. I went under and the river carried me quickly downstream. I still had my steel helmet on, and tried to hold my pistol up with my left arm while swimming with my right. I was more under water than on the surface, and for a moment I thought this was it. I'm going to "Buy the Farm" in Nam in a swimming accident! Not in combat, but a dumb-assed S-W-I-M-M-I-N-G accident! God was with me and upon rounding a bend I saw an overhanging tree branch. I grabbed it, and pulled myself onto the bank.

John Carty, the sergeant major, and others came running down alongside the river yelling at me. After scrambling ashore and standing there soaking wet, I found myself surrounded by my officers and noncommissioned officers all chewing me out.

"What if we lost you, Colonel?" Carty yelled. "My career would be ruined because I lost my battalion commander in a dip-shit accident!" Then he smiled at me to emphasize his humor while retaining the seriousness of the event.

I started to laugh.

I knew then that this battalion had come together. We were one, and I didn't need that pistol any more. They would look out for me as I would for them. After that incident, I carried a walking stick instead of a firearm. The stick was all I needed. It would be handy for fighting snakes, but not much use against the VC or NVA. My battalion was ready to fight!

As I stood on the riverbank dripping wet, I was pleased with the reaction of my troops. I had a great feeling about my battalion's cohesiveness and readiness to tangle with the enemy. Yet something told me the entire situation didn't seem right. I had a sense of apprehension that made me very uneasy. I was mixed with happiness and foreboding, and I didn't know why.

I now knew the river current was too strong to get men and equipment across without high, and needless, risk to both. Neither did I have good reconnaissance about the terrain and situation on the far side of the river. *High risk. Unnecessary risk.* Poorly defined objectives characteristic of clear and sweep operations. *Inadequate intelligence.* My antennae were up! I had seen this before in Korea, and knew the consequences. It wasn't my nature to avoid tangling with the enemy, but I wanted to fight on my own terms. I wanted a better sense for where the enemy was, and what might happen. I wanted to feel I wasn't leading my troops into a possible ambush that could be a massacre.

Reluctantly I radioed Dislodge Six recommending that we abandon crossing the river and pursuing clear and sweep operations on the other side. My sense of apprehension about what lay in wait for us proved to be right. I later learned the enemy was dug in and waiting for us on the far bank. The NVA would have cut us down in an ambush while we were reorganizing on the far bank after the crossing. We would have been in disarray, and most likely have lost men and equipment in the swift river current. This was just what the enemy wanted. We would have fought him on his terms, in a situation that he had carefully set up. It would have been a disaster!

We would find him and fight him on another day.

February 1967 was a miserable month. For days it rained, rained, and rained some more. Down south in Quang Ngai Province, the Viet Cong, also affectionately known as Victor Charlie, VC, or just plain Charlie, were giving the Seventh Regiment Marines fits. Quang Ngai is a large rice producing area, noted also for salt production. Rice and salt were important food staples for both the South Vietnamese and the VC forces. The Thirty Eighth VC Battalion launched a series of offensive actions to secure their access to, and control of, rice harvesting and salt production in Quang Ngai.

Lieutenant General Louis Walt USMC, I Corps Commanding General, initiated Operation De Soto, also known as Deckhouse VI, to deal with this VC activity. The regimental commander gave Lieutenant Colonel Ed Bronars, USMC (USNA '50), commanding the Third Battalion Marines, operational command of De Soto. As part of the operation, Regiment selected my battalion, First Battalion, Fifth Marines and two South Vietnamese, Army of the Republic of Vietnam (ARVN) battalions to engage the Thirty Eighth VC Battalion in support of Ed Bronars' Third Battalion. I greatly admired Bronars and considered him to be a good friend. I was pleased to be part of Ed's operation.

On the morning of February twenty sixth we were helo-lifted about 75 miles south to an area just northwest of the town of Duc Pho. Our orders were to sweep in a wide northeasterly arc in what would be my first major operation as battalion commander. I looked forward to the operation and believed it would be a good test for us. We had worked hard to make this battalion a strong combat team; what we used to call, with a bit of tongue in cheek, "a lean, mean, green, fighting machine." Over the months, the battalion had come together. I had noticed in many small ways that the troops were no longer focused on self-interest and individual differences. We were all Marines with a mission; nothing was to get in the way of that. Green was the color of our uniforms and green was the color of our skins. That was the way it was.

After landing in the Duc Pho operating area, I formed the battalion into the planned battle formation and we began moving out. In less than thirty minutes we made contact with VC snipers. Fortunately, the VC were poor shots, and succeeded only in revealing their positions. After determining their location, we returned fire with rifles, machine guns, and grenades. When our heavy fire began to take its toll, the snipers abandoned their positions and fled with our Marines in hot pursuit.

One of my sergeants in the lead company spotted two fleeing VC, and took off after them with several members of his squad. The sergeant was in excellent physical condition and soon out-distanced his squad while closing the gap with the fleeing enemy, who were starting to tire.

After he returned with two prisoners, he reported to me with this account, "Sir, as I was chasing them gooks I saw both of them jump into a large pond. When I reached the place where they jumped in I saw nothing. As I walked around the edge of the pond, I saw two straws sticking up out of the water. Since there was no other vegetation around, I had a hunch it might be them. I threw a few rocks in the water near the straws. It didn't take long for them two to stand and put their hands up. I got 'em out of the pond and marched them back to where my squad was. And you know what I found out a little while ago, Colonel?"

"What?" I answered.

"My rifle was unloaded."

All soldiers sooner or later find out that good training is essential to success in battle . . . a bit of luck also helps!

The next day we moved farther to the north and crossed over a range of small mountains into a lush green valley with a large village. All the "hooches" were made of bamboo and had straw thatched roofs. It looked peaceful and comfortable enough, but when we closed on it we took heavy fire, and had a stiff firefight before we gained complete control of the place.

We took a few casualties. Sadly, one of my Marines was killed and several were wounded, including Captain John W. Peterson, my Bravo Company commander. John's wound wasn't serious, but it required medical attention we couldn't give him in the field. As much as I hated to do it, we medevaced him by helicopter. John would be out of action for only a short time, and would return to resume his command, but I was not happy.

This village was the base for the Thirty Eighth VC Battalion. They had lived in relative comfort here. They were out of our artillery range, but still close enough to cause substantial problems for Ed Bronars. *And* they had killed one of my Marines, and shot one of my company commanders. If that village weren't there, the VC would have to base themselves in the next mountain range to the west, which was about ten miles away, too far for easy access to the area. I made a decision that I believed necessary to save Marine lives in Bronars' area of operations. There were no Viet Cong or civilians in the village; so, I gave the command, "Torch this fucking place!"

Soon huge plumes of black smoke billowed into the air. I felt absolutely no remorse. These were enemy barracks, not civilian homes. This was a VC base of operations, not a peaceful village of Vietnamese farmers.

After the firefight, evacuating the wounded, and torching the village, it was late in the afternoon. Just as I was about to relax a bit, we received a new mission to attack a village on the east side of the mountain the next morning. That meant leaving the valley immediately and re-crossing the mountain range. I would have to make my attack plans, fire support plans and related matters after we crossed the mountains and set up our new position. To complicate matters, it would be dark by the time we made the transit to our new area and set up for our morning attack.

The rain started again, first as a slow drizzle, then it came down hard. Fortunately, the helos arrived and evacuated my casualties before the rain started. The Vietnamese rain was good for rice, but tough on troopers.

After we crossed the mountains and completed our preparations for the first light attack, I began looking for a place to sleep. We had traveled light for this operation. One extra pair of socks, one pair of skivvies, a poncho, and two full three packs of C-rations were all the luxuries we carried. My pack contained the same items that all my troopers carried. I had no luxury items for the battalion C.O.

While I was inspecting the bivouac, I spotted my sergeant major and asked him what he was doing.

"Looking for a place to catch a snooze," he replied.

"Got a tent mate?" I asked.

"No sir," he replied.

"Well, you have one now," I said.

It was still raining and turning into a penetrating cold, as only a damp cold can be. We pooled our meager resources to make a small shelter with one poncho; the other we used for ground cover. When I awoke a few hours later, I found that we both had been sleeping on the soggy ground. We had pulled the ground cover poncho over both of us because it was so cold, and we were snuggled back to back for warmth. Let it be known that this was the first, and last time I ever snuggled with a sergeant major!

Intelligence—and I use the word loosely—told us the village we were to attack was an important enemy base camp that would be strongly defended. The attack plan called for our early morning infantry assault to commence after a heavy bombardment by air, naval gunfire, and artillery support to soften up the village defense. The coordinated support fire covering us would be the first time that all three elements—aviation, naval gunfire, and ground artillery support—would be used in an operation in which I was involved. This would be quite a show.

The air-artillery bombardment began and decimated everything in sight. It was hard to believe anything could live through that. As soon as the barrage ceased, my Marines moved in on the double. Our "line of departure" was the railroad tracks running north to south just to the west of the village. Everything was going according to plan, and we were taking no enemy fire. I was pleased that the pre-attack bombardment had been so effective, and our attack plan so well executed. We quickly moved into the village and secured it. A perfect operation . . . right?

Wrong, the village was empty!

As we moved in, I noticed a haystack that was on fire. Most of the houses had been leveled by the bombardment, but there were no bodies. There were no signs that the enemy, or anybody else for that matter, occupied the village. As we were searching the village, a chopper landed and two senior officers disembarked. One was Brigadier General "Willie" Stiles who commanded the operation's task force. The other was Major General Lew Walt from Headquarters, U.S. Marine Forces, Vietnam. I moved quickly to greet them. General Walt acknowledged my salute perfunctorily and moved quickly past me. He was focused on the burning haystack. I positioned myself on his right side, one pace to his rear, as is the military custom.

He stopped and turned to me, growling, "You see this haystack, Colonel?"

"Yes sir," I answered.

"Who set this haystack on fire?"

"I don't know, sir, it might have been a hot piece of shrapnel from the bombardment preceding our attack."

"How do you know it wasn't one of your men, Colonel?"

"Because, General, I was in the center of the attack formation and so is this haystack. This is the first thing I saw as we entered the village. None of my men were near this haystack?" As I said, this, I was wondering, what's so important about this haystack? I would have been in really deep *kim chee* if he'd been out here yesterday and seen the village I'd ordered torched?

"Did you set fire to this haystack?" he asked again.

Now, I was starting to get angry. What's bothering this general? He's questioning my truthfulness, and he's focused on the trivial. My response must have showed this when I emphatically answered, "No sir, I *did not* set fire to this haystack".

Without further conversation, General Walt abruptly left, leaving General Stiles with me. As the two of us began walking the battlefield, General Stiles motioned to me and said, "Pete, let's go over to that tree where we can talk in the shade."

The sun had come out, and it was beginning to get hot as hell. We walked over to the tree and Stiles began in, a nice way, to tell me to be less testy and more respectful to the commanding general. Stiles told me how lucky I was that General Walt hadn't relieved me.

As I was about to respond, I heard, "Sirs, don't move, freeze!"

A Marine was standing to my right with his arm pointing up at the tree branches. "Look up there," he said as he moved towards me. We did. A deadfall booby trap was in the tree branches. It was a rake-like object, a long rectangular beam with sharply pointed stakes driven through it. Had General Stiles and I moved a few inches closer to the tree trunk we would have hit the trigger release and that would have been it for us. That Marine had just saved our lives. Everything else—burning haystacks and my short-tempered remarks to the commanding general—was forgotten. I think I said a quick thank you prayer and probably even smiled a little.

Our participation in Operation De Soto ended on March third. The results were disappointing. We had accounted for only 17 enemy killed and captured 11. Our casualties were two Marines KIA and a dozen wounded, including Captain John Peterson of my Bravo Company. Happily, John returned in a few days. I was glad to see him.

Operation De Soto was a disappointment, but I learned from it. I saw, once again, how poor intelligence can destroy an otherwise well executed attack. Our well-planned and coordinated use of air, artillery, and naval gunfire followed by a quick infantry attack on an empty village was a failure because the enemy had better intelligence about the operation than we did.

The VC provided us with a clear example of a problem that would plague our future operations if we couldn't fix it—poor intelligence! Or perhaps it was poor security on our part and superb intelligence on the VC's part. Either way, something was seriously wrong in our operations, and it had to be fixed by senior leadership. I couldn't help but think that General Walt should have focused his attention on the empty village and not a burning haystack. Our problems lay with poor intelligence and unsat security, not burning haystacks. Besides, after the air strikes and artillery bombardment flattened everything in the village, why had a smoldering haystack assumed monumental proportions? Somebody's perspective was seriously askew.

On 28 February, Colonel Kenneth Houghton took command of the Fifth Marines. Kenny was a renowned Marine warrior and a feisty one at that. He needed two things: a good S-3 and a Roman Catholic Chaplain. I had both. So Dick Alger became the Regimental S-3 and my battalion chaplain, Chaplain Vincent Capodanno, went with him. I hated to lose them, but it was not my call. Chaplain Capodanno was initially assigned to the regiment, and later went to the Third Battalion. We could still have Catholic services, but only when Capodanno was helo-lifted in for that purpose.

In March and early April 1967, we began to conduct battalion-sized operations. One of these I remember to this day because of the unique way we totally defeated a Vietnamese guerrilla unit.

Regiment had directed my battalion to conduct a sweep of

the Que Son Valley and take a platoon of tanks with us. I did not ask for, nor did I need the tanks. I saw no mission for them. We were ordered to take tanks with us anyway because Regiment felt that the tank crews needed some combat activity. So, the tanks went with us. I made them follow behind the troops who were walking. Tanks normally lead the infantry, not follow, but the tankers didn't complain.

Our mission was to seek and destroy a guerrilla unit that had been harassing the village of Que Son. The village was located near two mountain ranges that ran approximately east to west. There was a valley in between the two mountain ranges, and the road from Hill 54 to Que Son ran generally north to south passing the valley entrance on the east side.

Intelligence told us the guerrillas had a base camp on a plateau to the north of our right flank as we entered the valley. When we arrived at the entrance to the valley, I halted the column, and studied my map. I could see the plateau with the guerrilla encampment to our right, sitting high above the valley. The wall from the floor of the valley to the plateau was almost vertical. A frontal attack would be extremely difficult, and would mean heavy casualties. While studying the escarpment with my binoculars, I noticed a narrow cut filled with trees and vines in the nose of the mountain that seemed to lead to the plateau.

I had a flash of inspiration. What if we brought the tanks up, put them in a V formation, and staged a parade-like troop movement through the valley? This would be something those guerrillas had never seen before. They might just come out to the edge of the plateau to watch those crazy Americans do this dumb thing. If they did, my troops could climb through the narrow cut leading to the plateau unnoticed by the enemy. Our Marines could then come in from the Viet Cong's rear and totally surprise them.

When I told my company commanders about the idea of using the tanks as a decoy and taking the guerrillas by surprise from behind, they agreed it might work. A key part of the attack plan was to send the toughest platoon leader we had up that steep cut with a platoon that mirrored this platoon commander's tenacity. I asked the Charlie Company commander, Captain Jim Caswell, to send me a platoon commanded by his toughest platoon commander. Caswell picked Sergeant Hillous York, a descendant of the famous Sergeant York of World War I fame, and also from Tennessee.

The plan was simple. Sergeant York and his platoon would very quietly make the hazardous climb up the cut to the top of the ridge, and attack the enemy from behind. The risk was enormous. All thirty men would have to climb from one bush or tree to another without making a sound. They would be totally vulnerable and essentially defenseless while making their way up the steep incline. If the enemy discovered them in the process, the entire platoon could be wiped out.

When he reached the top and was ready with his men deployed, Sergeant York was to radio me. I would then set the parade in motion. With the tanks leading, the rest of us would make as much noise as possible . . . sing, yell, blow bugles, and generally make a ruckus.

While York and his men were climbing up the gorge, we were busy. I brought up and deployed the tanks, and formed the two rifle companies in a spread column with the men four abreast. The whole scheme took about an hour to organize.

Soon after we had our parade tanks and troops in place, we received Sergeant York's radio call. He was ready! I gave the command for the parade to commence and the First Battalion, Fifth Marines moved into the valley behind the tanks as we had planned. Our parade formation was completely in the valley when we heard shooting up on the plateau. Then all was quiet.

Sergeant York had completely surprised the enemy and wiped them out. This is what he told me.

> After we received your order Colonel, we began climbing up the ravine. I was leading followed by my radio operator, PFC Edge, the machine gunner, his ammo carriers, and with the rest of the platoon following. About three quarters of the way up Edge handed me the speaker set and said, "Listen to this!" Someone in Charlie Company had spotted

us and thought we were the enemy. They were calling for rocket fire on us. I growled back into the speaker, "Knock it off you S.O.B.s, you're seeing us, the Third Platoon. Don't shoot!" They got the message and didn't shoot, and we continued our ascent.

As I reached the crest of the ravine, I saw a flat meadow about an acre in size. It had a number of large boulders, and the flat land extended to the edge of the plateau on the left side with woods on the right side. I didn't see anybody; so, I stood up. PFC Edge was right behind me. Then I saw them! Six armed VC were only about ten yards away, and facing in the opposite direction. They were looking towards a group of about twenty more VC further away who were looking into the valley where you were conducting the parade with tanks and all.

One of the VC in the center of the nearest group must have sensed our presence, because he turned around and looked right at me. His eyes opened wide. I believe he was in total shock. I fired my AR-15, and he went down, dropping his weapon. I tried to fire again at the others, but my freaking rifle jammed. This was not uncommon, and Edge and I had a procedure for dealing with it. I pulled the bolt back to open the chamber. Like lightening, Edge pulled out his ramrod, shoved it down my barrel, and knocked the jammed round out. I then closed the bolt to chamber a new round. By this time the other five VC had turned around to see what was happening. Less than a minute and a half had elapsed since I had shot the first VC. When they saw us, they were also paralyzed by shock and surprise. Before they could act, I shot the two on the right side, but not before they shot at us and missed. The other three turned and ran, but by then the rest of my platoon had reached the crest. They fired and dropped the three who were trying to escape.

As I turned to instruct my machine gunner and his team to sweep the area and cut down those who were looking out into the valley, the man I shot first got up, leaving his weapon and ammo on the ground. He stumbled towards the edge of the cliff, and jumped over the side. I could tell he was badly wounded. If he survived the fall over the side of the cliff, I doubt if he survived the wound.

By this time my machine gunner was sweeping the area, his bullets traveling about six to eight inches above the ground. My troopers were following up with heavy volleys from their M-16s, and chasing survivors into the woods on the far right side of the meadow. Except for the VC who jumped over the edge of the precipice, there were no enemy survivors. We got them all, and had no casualties of our own. My men returned loaded down with captured weapons that included AR-15s, AKC-47s, U.S. Garand M-1 rifles, and assorted pistols.

After York gave me his report and I saw the large number of weapons his troopers had captured, I told him, "Well Done!" and that he could have his pick of the enemy's weapons to take home when he rotated back.

And that was indeed well done Sergeant York! Even after all these years I still marvel at how well that mission was accomplished, and the bravery shown by York and every member of his platoon.

Shortly after the firing on the plateau stopped, our parade came to a little village on the valley floor. We stopped there to wait for York and his men to rejoin us. The only people in the village were an old woman, who had been shot in both wrists by the enemy, and a small child. We called for a chopper to take them out.

We put the captured weapons and the small boy on the chopper to take them back to a secure area, but the old woman refused to get on the chopper. Our corpsman treated her wounds, bandaged her wrists, and did the best that he could to care for her wounds. My Vietnamese interpreter was unable to convince her to go with the child, so we moved out.

I asked the interpreter what would happen to the old woman. He replied sadly, "She will die."

I learned two valuable lessons that day. First, it is hard to over-emphasize the value of surprise in combat operations. It helped us to achieve our objective without casualties of our own. This engagement forcefully demonstrated the value of innovation and surprise in a battle plan. Those may appear to be obvious virtues, but when you witness the devastating results that innovation and surprise can bring in combat, the lesson becomes a powerful one. The second lesson: Always honor the chain of command. I violated one of the cardinal rules of military leadership when I gave a combat attack mission directly to the platoon commander, Sergeant York, without apprising his company commander of the mission. After Jim Caswell brought Sergeant York to me, he didn't tarry. He quickly returned to his company, which was proper. I broke the chain of command when I failed to inform Caswell of my plan for his platoon. Even though Jim had immediately returned to his company without participating in the attack plan, that didn't release me from my obligation to keep him informed of what I was doing with his troops. This could have led to a tragedy if Caswell's Charley Company had mistaken York's platoon for the enemy, and fired on them as they were climbing up the ravine. Not only would our own fire have caused casualties, but it would have destroyed the surprise. The VC at the top of the plateau would have had an easy time picking off York's vulnerable platoon still part-way up their climb. I never made the error again of giving orders to a platoon without the full knowledge of the company commander.

To this day, I marvel at the professional manner in which Sergeant York executed his mission. He certainly lived up to his famous name. We killed the entire enemy unit, and *not one Marine was hurt*. I prayed that we could achieve those kinds of results in every battle we fought.

From time to time, units from my battalion were detached for special missions. On one such mission we were called upon to provide security for a downed CH-34 helicopter and to support evacuation of its crew. The rescue operation began on 11 April

1967 when we deployed troops from Company A to support the helicopter rescue operation code named BALD EAGLE. The rescue force jumped off from a point approximately 10 miles northwest of the city of Tam Ky.

The plan was to bring two infantry platoons plus support elements to the rescue site using nine CH-46 helicopters for the insertion. The planned insertion began at approximately 1800 with Lieutenant Rick Zell aboard the first CH-46 entering the landing zone. The enemy was waiting and immediately brought our Marines under intense small arms fire as the first wave of four CH-46s came into the landing zone. The situation quickly became critical.

Lieutenant Zell was the only officer that made it into the landing zone with the first wave. He immediately directed his men into firing positions to secure the landing zone for the remaining A Company Marines to land. Zell contacted the on-station HUGHEY gunships and requested strafing passes. Despite the gunship support, the enemy fire was so heavy that we could make no further troop insertions, and the rest of the airborne reaction force had to return to the combat base at Hill 54.

The pilot and co-pilot of the downed CH-34 left the area on one of the four rescue CH-46s that brought in the reaction force first wave. Zell, at the time was a newly commissioned second lieutenant with about one month of combat experience. He assumed that one of the two pilots would take command of the recovery operation since both were senior to him. One was a Marine Corps major and the other a Marine captain. As Captain Queeg said, "You can't assume a god-damned thing in the Navy!" Or in the Marine Corps either. Both of those pilots hauled ass out of there on the CH-46 that dropped Zell and his troopers into the hotspot. Their parting instruction to Zell was, "Do not remove the machine gun from the helicopter." Zell gave them a crisp salute and a cheery aye-aye as their helo lifted them off to safety. After they were out of sight, Zell's first action was to remove the machine gun to use in his defensive perimeter.

Our two battalion S-2 scouts, Corporal Tom Manion and Lance Corporal Jack Kennedy, were passengers on the downed chopper. They could have helo-lifted out with the two pilots, but elected to stay with their brother grunt Marines to help defend the perimeter. Manion and Kennedy truly reflected our motto of *Semper Fidelis*. They knew Zell was seriously outnumbered by NVA troops that were closing in on his position. He needed all the help he could get.

Zell's reaction force on the ground was less than a platoon in strength. It consisted of Marines mostly from Alpha Company's first platoon and a 60mm mortar team. Zell quickly deployed them in a defensive perimeter around the downed CH-34. The crash site was very exposed with little cover except for a shallow ravine, where they found the downed helicopter. Lieutenant Zell gave his small group instructions to remain in a defensive perimeter around the downed CH-34, and stayed in constant touch with me over the single radio they had on the battalion tactical net.

As evening came, a C-47 "Puff" (for *Puff the Magic Dragon*, a popular folk song of the day) dropped illumination flares and provided suppressing fire on a regimental size enemy force closing in on Zell's defensive positions. The enemy started laying on heavy mortar, automatic weapons, rifle grenade, and small arms fire from the high ground west of Zell's position. Our troopers were dug into fighting positions in a perimeter around the downed CH-34, and were effectively keeping the enemy away from the helicopter. Lieutenant Zell constantly moved from position to position despite the heavy incoming fire to set the direction of return fire for each defensive position while stressing the conservation of ammunition, and assuring his men that he would be able to call in supporting fire all night if necessary.

Rick called on the battalion tactical net to request permission to withdraw to more defensible positions. I could not approve his request, as much as I wanted to, because our mission was to provide security for the CH-34, and that we could not do in a more defensible position. I also had to inform Zell that we probably would not be able to extract him that night because of the heavy incoming fire. Further, our helicopter reconnaissance indicated that a regimental size enemy force was moving in to attack his position. I elected to use HUEY gunships and C-47 Puffs to provide suppressing fire to relieve the pressure.

Zell continued to move from position to position instructing his men to remain in their foxholes and assume that anything moving was the enemy. He told each position not to expend ammunition unless they had a clear target. To avoid being shot by his own men, Zell had to shout at each position that he was coming their way. Under cover of darkness, the enemy tried to infiltrate Zell's defensive perimeter. His Marines repulsed them, but enemy fire continued all night.

B-52s pounded the enemy in the hills to the west of our reaction force position and C-47 Puffs provided effective suppressing fire as close as possible to Zells' perimeter. The action continued until daylight when the enemy broke contact and withdrew. With the enemy out of the picture, a recovery helicopter lifted the downed CH-34 out. We evacuated our reaction force by helicopters at 0930 on 12 April 1967 to rejoin the remainder of A Company.

The results of the action were recovery of the C-34 helo and its crew, and two confirmed enemy killed in our defensive position at the cost of two Marines wounded. An estimate of enemy casualties in the heavily wooded hills that surrounded the western side of our defensive perimeter was not possible; so, we submitted no count of enemy KIA beyond the two confirmed in the after action report. For his heroic action in defending the downed helicopter and its crew, Lieutenant Zell was awarded the Silver Star medal.

To illustrate that even the tensest moments in combat have their bizarre humor, Rick Zell told me the following story, which I pass on to you.

> As our position was becoming very tenuous and it appeared we would be overrun, Corporal Carl Sulik (one of my fire team leaders) crawled over to my position and said, "Lieutenant Zell, who will make my car payments if I'm killed or captured?" This helped break the tension for me. I laughed and said, "Corporal Sulik, car payments are the least of your problems. Forget about it. Go lead your fire team like I know you are capable of and we'll all get through the night safely." Carl and I still laugh at this incident, even now.

All good things eventually come to an end. So do the bad things, but they seem to take so much longer. In May 1967, the First Battalion moved off Hill 54 to Tam Ky enroute to the Que Son Valley to support on-going operations. As we moved out, I'm sure every man in the battalion looked over his shoulder at the mess hall, our quarters, and the showers. I know I did. It would be a long time before we had luxury like that again. I also knew that when the Army came to Hill 54 to relieve the Marines, they would get their truck back. Of course, it would look like a First Battalion, Fifth Marines Marine Corps truck, but it was in top shape and ran like the general's limousine.

There were two Union operations in the Que Son Valley against the Viet Cong and North Vietnamese Army (NVA). These two operations, in the southern part of I Corps (See map of South Vietnam in Appendix E), involved some of the heaviest fighting in the Vietnam War, and my battalion was in the thick of it. The Viet Cong and North Vietnamese Army had controlled the agriculturally rich Que Son Basin for almost twenty years. The objective of the Union operations was to break that control, and we did.

The Marine Command determined that controlling this region was important to dominating the five northern provinces of Vietnam, which were key to defeating the NVA and VC.[1] The enemy needed this agriculturally rich and populous area to support their operations in the Vietnam Delta and coastal regions, and continually controlled the Que Son Basin despite a number of operations in the area by Marine and ARVN forces. We would push the enemy out, then retire to our base areas of operations, and the enemy would immediately return to reestablish their control over the valley.

Intelligence reports confirmed that the principal enemy units operating in the Que Son Basin were the Second NVA Division reinforced by the Third VC Regiment, which joined them after

---

[1]   Gary L. Telfer, Lane Rogers, V. Keith Fleming, Jr.; *U.S. Marines In Vietnam, Fighting the North Vietnamese* (History and Museums Division, Headquarters U.S. Marine Corps, Washington D.C., 1984) p 63.

moving north into the region from Quang Ngai Province. The Marine's three principal goals in the area were to (1) deny access to the basin and its resources to NVA and VC, (2) provide the security for establishing civil action programs, and (3) force the Second NVA Division into open battle so we could decisively crush them. Operation Union I was the beginning of the fierce fighting for control of the Que Son Basin that raged throughout the spring and summer of 1967.[2]

Before discussing the Union Operations, let me take a minute to tell you something about the Que Son Valley where we operated. It was a visually beautiful, but dangerous place. The First Battalion's Corporal Brad Silliman eloquently captures the essence of the place in the following excerpt from a letter he wrote.[3]

> Que Son Valley, to the NVA, was a corridor from the Ho Chi Minh trail to Highway One on the east coast—a path to rich targets such as Da Nang to the north and Chu Lai and Tarn Ky to the south. Que Son was as beautiful as an orchid but as deadly as a flytrap. Many of us made friends with the natives there. Que Son village had a Methodist Church, and I remember meeting the pastor. Much of the valley was cultivated in rice, but I remember eating bananas, pineapple, coconuts, vegetables and fruits I can no longer identify. There were waterfalls, creeks, rivers and wells with cool, clear water. There were ancient pagodas surrounded by cemeteries where the dead were once buried in large rice urn-jars, which I heard the Plain of Jars in Laos was named for, but later heard it was for the strange rock formations.
>
> In Que Son there was still evidence of the French Indochina War. The colonial road system that ran from the coast to Que Son village had been wrecked years before. Many bridges were gone, and there were countless barriers

---

[2]   Ibid.

[3]   Brad Silliman, *Letter to Eric Hammel*, 1 August 1994, unpublished.

like pits and tank traps dug across the roadway and steel beams driven into it at road junctions. A footpath ran along this route with bamboo footbridges over some of the streams and irrigation canals. Within a kilometer of Que Son village was the biggest trench line I ever saw in Vietnam. It was 20 or more feet deep and about 25 feet vide. It was close to a click long and appeared to have been dug to conceal troop movements across an open area of the valley. It was big enough to put a truck convoy in. Who dug it, we weren't sure. Que Son was pockmarked with bomb and shell craters. Booby traps and mines were everywhere. These included Russian, Chinese and American mines like the Bouncing Betty—stolen or bought from South Vietnamese troops—improvised booby traps using anything from a 7.6 mm bullet (toe buster) to a 155 shell or a 750-pound bomb.

Sometime prior to our operations in Que Son, the Air Force had sewn parts of the valley with butterfly mines. Designed to slow movement on the Ho Chi Minh Trail, butterflies were dropped from airplanes and imbedded themselves in the ground on a metal spike. Butterflies were seismically detonated. Ground vibrations caused by someone walking would detonate the butterfly. These devices were designed to render themselves harmless over a period of time through corrosion. Many of these things remained active and caused casualties regularly. Inactive butterflies were gathered by the enemy and turned into booby traps. One day a combat engineer and a rifleman were inspecting a cluster of three rusty butterflies about 50 meters from me. The mines exploded causing the detonators and the C-4 in the engineer's pack and the rifleman's grenades to detonate.

In addition to all this we still ran into crude punji pits with bamboo spikes in the bottom. The NVA was the main enemy, but there was also a strong Viet Cong presence in Que Son.

Que Son was a solid source of military conscripts. Rural people make good soldiers. Every man under 30 was either

an ARVN, PF, communist or a deserter. Young men out of
uniform, which was uncommon in Que Son, were routinely
taken into custody for questioning.

Well said Corporal Silliman, and beautifully written. Anybody
who ever spent time in the Que Son Valley will recognize of what
you speak.

The Union I battles and tactical operations are chronicled in
the Headquarters Marine Corps, History and Museum Division
publication, *U. S. Marines in Vietnam, 1967,* published in 1984.
My account of these operations is based both on my recollections
and official records such as our First Battalion, Fifth Marines combat
after action reports. I hope this account will give further insight
into what took place. I didn't know exactly what each Marine was
doing at every moment in this battle, but I sure knew what was
going on from where I was. From my limited view, there was
uncertainty and chaos. I knew we were in a scrap and all our
Marines were fighting like grunts. That was all I could ever want.
In several places I have included the recollections of other Marines
who were also there. I want to broaden the account and add new
dimensions to the story that deserve to be part of Union I history.

By March 1967, I had a superb group of officers in the First
Battalion, Fifth Marines. From the standpoint of personnel, we
had completely turned the battalion around. Captain John Carty,
a Naval Academy graduate, had commanded Delta Company with
distinction. He was bright, and I had great confidence in him. I
promoted him to Battalion S-3 from his position as Dick Alger's
assistant when Dick moved up to regimental headquarters as
regimental S-3. Carty proved to be an able replacement for Alger.

Captain Buck Darling, a fierce warrior and superb leader, was
my commander of the Headquarters and Service Company. He
coordinated the defenses for the command group and was available
to take over any rifle company if necessary. This kept him out of
our daily firefights. Buck was due to go home soon. I wanted to

send him safely home to his family, but truthfully, I needed him just where I assigned him. His opinion and counsel were always very valuable to me.

Captain Jim Caswell reported in and took command of Charlie Company. Caswell was John Carty's Naval Academy classmate, but Dick Alger, who also knew Jim, brought him to my attention. We requested Jim and Regiment approved our request. Caswell was as fine an officer as I could have hoped for.

Captain J. W. Peterson commanded Bravo Company for a short time, and First Lieutenant David "Mack" McInturff commanded Delta Company. Mack was a great officer. He was my "utility infielder." He excelled in every assignment I gave him. We had just lost our Alpha Company commander in combat, and I replaced him temporarily with Second Lieutenant William P. Vacca until I could get another captain for Alpha Company. Because of high casualties with infantry company commanders, replacement captains to command rifle companies were hard to come by.

For the Union I operation, I needed a seasoned commander for Alpha Company; so, I gave Captain Jerry McKay, my battalion communications officer, the battle command of Alpha Company. Jerry was an outstanding officer with excellent leadership qualities. With Caswell, McInturff, and McKay I now had a strong company command team. After the Union I battle I replaced Jerry with Captain Ronald G. Babich, a new arrival in-country, and brought Jerry back to his battalion communications job where I needed his communications skills. Captain Babich was later killed during Operation Union II on 2 June 1967.

These command changes in Company A were tough on the troops, but I had confidence the new commanders could do the job. When Lieutenant Vacca was in command, John Carty became his mentor, to make sure that he had no problems he couldn't handle. If he did, Carty was to help him solve the problem. This in no way reflected upon Bill Vacca's competence as a fine Marine. He just had not yet had the seasoning, training, or rank required for permanent company command.

Buck Darling was a strong advocate for snipers. Because of his influence, all of my company commanders began employing Marines from the regimental sniper unit with great effectiveness. We used snipers for long-range (over 1,000 yards) protection of our patrols and platoon-sized deployments. Buck's sniper innovation was a solid contribution to our battalion's effectiveness and safety by sowing fear and a feeling of defeat in the enemy's ranks. I became a believer in sniper teams, and saw them as a valuable force multiplier.

Corporal Tom Manion and several other able NCOs assigned to the S-2 section of the H&S Company assisted Buck with the sniper teams. They helped coordinate the efforts of scouts and snipers for the battalion. Darling's insight and Manion's scout-sniper team coordination were critical to making the sniper program a success.

Sergeant John J. Culbertson's book, *13 Cent Killers, The 5th Marine Snipers in Vietnam*[4] gives a wonderful account of how we used sniper teams to support search and destroy patrols. The snipers carried M-14 rifles and Remington 700 sniper rifles with a high-intensity, range-finding telescope. Both were accurate and had tremendous impact energy that hit with over three times the force of the newly issued M-16 with its .223 caliber rounds. We lost too many Marines assaulting a well camouflaged and dug in enemy with a puny 22-caliber weapon that was poorly made, wasn't deadly beyond 300 meters, and that easily jammed.[5] Here's what one of my Marine troopers said about the M-16.

> We were having problems with the recently issued M-16 rifle, and there were incidents of people dying while trying to clear their weapons. There were incidents of Marines killing NVA soldiers with entrenching tools, knives, and fists. It got uglier than what was reported.[6]

---

[4]   John J. Culbertson, *13 Cent Killers: The 5th Marine Snipers in Vietnam* (New York: Presidio Press, Ballantine Book Group, 2003), Chapter 20.

[5]   Ibid, p20.

[6]   Silliman.

The M-14 and Remington 700 were deadly and hit like a freight train past 500 meters. The Marine .308 caliber bullets could tear through the thatch and wood huts of VC villages causing great damage, and turn superficial wounds into injuries that could put enemy soldiers out of action.

My grunts were ready to fight, and that included me! I was not certain, however, that Colonel Houghton, our regimental commander, felt the same way. Like Lieutenant Vacca, I was fairly new to my battalion, having been in command only four months. I believed Colonel Houghton considered me "untested"; so, I was worried that we wouldn't be included in the forthcoming Union operation. Colonel Houghton had already committed Lieutenant Colonel Dean E. Esslinger's Third Battalion, Fifth Marines. Who else would be assigned, my battalion or Lieutenant Colonel Mallet C. Jackson's Second Battalion? Mal had assumed his command on 1 February; so, I hoped I might have the edge in Houghton's decision since I had been in command a few months longer than Mal.

My battalion operations thus far had been against small-sized VC guerrilla units, not against regular NVA troops. Kipling called these "penny fights," and that's what they were. We had not yet deployed on battalion operations that would have challenged us and proved our ability to handle large-scale operations effectively. I felt this lack of battalion hardcore operations might have given Colonel Houghton the impression that we were still not ready for coordinated battalion operations at the regimental level.

A week had passed and we were still on Hill 54. Finally I could stand it no longer. I called for my driver, young Corporal Billy Long, to bring up the jeep. I instructed him to get a case of beer and put it on the back seat. I hopped in the jeep and away we went to Regimental Headquarters. Colonel Houghton was sitting behind his field desk when I stormed into the operations tent with the case of beer under my arm.

"Colonel," I blurted out, "the First Battalion is ready to fight, Sir! In fact the men are on the landing pad now, packed and ready to go. I don't know what it's going to take to get us committed, but if it's a case of beer, here it is!"

I then slammed the case on Houghton's desk. His eyes opened wide and he looked at me with a startled expression. I thought, well here it comes; I'm fired. Instead he started to chuckle and said, "Cool down, Hilgartner, I'm glad to hear you're ready. You'll be on your way shortly."

During the first weeks of April, elements of the First Division Marines noticed increasing enemy movement in the hills to the west and south of the Que Son Basin. On 15 April we became convinced that at least two NVA regiments were infiltrating into the valley floor. Rather than wait for the enemy to take the initiative and attack, Major General Herman Nickerson, the First Division Commanding General, decided to strike first with a heliborne assault on the enemy positions east of our outpost on the summit of Nui Lac Son. This would keep the enemy from initiating an assault against our troops on the Nui Lac Son outpost, and would further prevent them from seeking sanctuary in the mountains to the south and east. To meet these objectives, Union I began early in the morning of 21 April 1967.

The attack plan called for the First Marines, Second Battalion's Foxtrot Company, which was already in the area, to make contact from its forward position. Artillery in Que Son and the First Marine Aircraft Wing would provide artillery and close air support. Elements of the Third Battalion, First Marines would follow up Foxtrot's probe with a helicopter borne assault into the operational area, followed by the First Battalion, First Marines, and another battalion from Chu Lai to act as regimental reserve. Artillery from Battery F, Second Battalion, Eleventh Marines, and Battery M from the First Battalion, Eleventh Marines would move to Que Son Village to provide direct fire support to the units in the operation.

Early on the morning of 21 April, Foxtrot made contact with small NVA elements, and spotted a large enemy force moving into the village of Binh Son. Foxtrot moved against the village and immediately came under heavy fire. Despite repeated artillery and air strikes on the NVA positions, the volume of enemy fire did not let up. F Company was unable to maneuver.

Lieutenant Colonel Hillmer DeAtley's Third Battalion, First Marines was helolifted into a hotly contested landing zone and fought its way in to help F Company. In mid-afternoon, Dean Esslinger's Third Battalion, Fifth Marines from Chu Lai began landing east of the battlefield. Esslinger moved through scattered resistance to link up with DeAtley. That night, Lieutenant Colonel Van D. Bell's First Battalion, First Marines landed in the darkness near the First Marines command post at Nui Lac Son and moved out immediately to join the fight.

On 22 April the Marines drove the enemy soldiers out of their positions, and forced them to retreat northward exposing them to artillery and air strikes, which took a heavy toll. Bell's and Esslinger's battalions attacked northeast while the ARVN First Ranger Group, consisting of three battalions, moved southwest from Thanh Binh to catch the retreating enemy.

On 25 April, additional elements of Colonel Kenneth J. Houghton's Fifth Marines arrived from Chu Lai and moved into the valley. With the Fifth Marines in place, the First Marines returned to Da Nang, less Foxtrot Company, which remained at the Nui Lac Son outpost. The Fifth Marines made a thorough search of the area meeting only light resistance. It appeared the enemy had escaped again, but reliable intelligence reports indicated that major enemy forces were still in the area. Colonel Houghton, an experienced combat commander, sensed the enemy had not withdrawn. This new intelligence information and his combat intuition must have convinced Colonel Houghton to bring my First Battalion, Fifth Marines into the area of operations. The Second Battalion, Fifth Marines was guarding our regimental base at An Aoa against enemy attack, which kept them out of the Union I operation. This proved to be a tactical error, which I will discuss later in this account. Colonel Houghton's Fifth Marines command group controlled the operation from the Nui Lac Son outpost.

On 30 April 1967, my First Battalion, Fifth Marines went to Tam Ky for helolifting into the mountains 13 kilometers east of Hiep Duc. At last, we were going to get into a major fight!

After my First Battalion landed in our tactical area of operations, we initially encountered only light opposition. As we swept west along Song Chang we had a sharp increase in the number of engagements, which indicated the NVA were still in the area in force. Then on 5 May, Mack McInturff's Delta Company found a regimental storage area three kilometers north of Hiep Duc that contained recoilless rifle ammunition, shoes, over 8,000 uniforms, 3 complete surgical kits, maps, and other assorted equipment. If the enemy had left the area, it certainly looked as if he planned to come back. We removed as much of the enemy equipment as we could by helicopter. What was left, we burned. Then to destroy the enemy's works, our engineers closed the entrances to caves the enemy used as bunkers and command posts.

Esslinger and I continued to sweep north looking for the main body of the Second NVA Division that the First Marines had engaged in the opening days of the Union operation. The First Battalion, Third Marines, part of Special Landing Force (SLF) Alpha stationed aboard ships operating with the Seventh Fleet, was helolifted into the Que Son area to reinforce my battalion. Together we were to sweep northeast of Que Son village in a search and destroy mission.

The SLF was committed to Union I under the operational control of Colonel Houghton to substitute for his Second Battalion, Fifth Marines, which had been left to guard the regimental base at An Aoa. In retrospect, I believe committing SLF troops to the Union fight was motivated by the desire to give them an opportunity to engage the enemy in major combat operations to demonstrate the validity of the SLF concept. The SLF purpose may have merit, but the result in Vietnam was a command and control nightmare.[7]

The SLF concept was conceived as a quick reaction, afloat assault force available for contingency operations. The concept immediately took hold, and both CINCPACFLT and CINCLANTFLT maintained

---

[7]   See Appendix C for the organizational relationships between Marine ground forces in Vietnam and the SLF.

special assault forces. By 1966, the Marine Corps had a major commitment of two divisions reinforced with air, engineers, and tanks to the SLF supporting MACV operations in South Vietnam. The principal Marine Corps involvement in Vietnam centered in I Corps; so, to support the major SLF commitment by senior leadership, I believe that CGFMFPAC and CINCPACFLT created missions for this force to justify its presence in the Seventh Fleet. The resulting SLF contingency operations often placed SLF troops in missions under conditions for which they were not prepared.

SLF officers and troops lived aboard ship. They ate their meals in ship's messes, slept in bunks in air-conditioned quarters, had hot showers, and enjoyed many of the amenities of home. They were not acclimated to living in the extreme discomfort of the South Vietnamese bush with its energy sapping intense heat and humidity. Nor were they prepared to handle the unique command and control problems of operating as integral parts of Marine infantry battalions attached to commands ashore. For an additional disconnect, SLF operational planners also worked aboard ship with little direct, sustained contact with Marine forces ashore. This isolation led to grave environment misunderstanding and operations miscalculations. The SLF was simply not prepared for what they encountered in I Corps combat operations. This may sound like a harsh comment, but the events of the Union operations, particularly Union I, support this assessment.

As the sweep progressed, all three Fifth Marines Battalions— Esslinger's Third, my First, and the SLF—had brief contact with the enemy. The firefights were short, and in each case the NVA withdrew. Things had not yet begun to heat up.

At about 10:30 a.m. on 10 May, Jim Caswell's Charlie Company, while conducting assigned search and destroy operations as part of my First Battalion's sweeping operation, received heavy automatic small arms, and mortar fire from an estimated NVA battalion located in the vicinity of Hill 110. The enemy was wearing khaki uniforms and carrying backpacks, which indicated they were regular NVA troops, not VC guerrillas. They were well entrenched on and around the hill.

At approximately 10:40 a.m., Company C, following an air strike, assaulted Hill 110 and seized it. During the firefight, Company C returned fire with small arms, M-79 rocket rounds, 3.5 inch rocket rounds, and 60mm mortar rounds.[8] Once in control of the hill, Charlie Company called for artillery and air support, but received neither. Captain Warren Walters, commander Delta Battery, Eleventh Marines, could not provide Caswell with artillery support because the battery was relocating to another position in the Que Son Valley. As we learned later, air support could not be provided because of the confusion resulting from an errant air strike on Alpha Company. I'll say quite a bit about this terrible fiasco later.

In addition to the problems delaying artillery and air support, there was a serious communications disconnect within my First Battalion staff in our failure to relay Caswell's call for air strikes on the NVA troops at the base of Hill 110. This was an error that placed Caswell's Marines in great jeopardy, and one for which I take full responsibility. Caswell did not receive artillery or close air support until 1600 that afternoon. By that time, the enemy had begun to withdraw, leaving Caswell in full control of Hill 110.

There were many acts of heroism in Charlie Company's assault on and capture of Hill 110. Lance Corporal John E. Rusth led his fire team to secure the crest on the northeastern slope of Hill 110. Rusth and his team came under intense enemy fire from positions concealed on the hill and in the valley below in hedgerows, tree lines, and cane fields at the base of the hill. The enemy fire inflicted heavy casualties, and Rusth, continuously exposed to hostile fire on the bare hillside, moved among his wounded to ensure that all received proper care. After the hill was secured he led his men in a grenade and bayonet assault down the hills against the NVA positions, routing the enemy and forcing them to flee.

Although Rusth drove the NVA troops from their positions at the base of Hill 110, the enemy remained hidden in positions

---

[8]   Headquarters 1st Battalion, 5th Marines, 1st Marine Division (Rein) FMF; *Combat After Action Report, Operation UNION,* 29 May 1967.

where they could continue to bring the slopes of Hill 110 under
fire. Completely disregarding his own safety, Rusth moved down
the hillside on nine occasions to assist casualties sustained in his
assault. Although painfully wounded in his thigh from an enemy
round when he started his tenth trip to rescue a wounded Marine,
he quickly bound his wound and assisted the wounded man to
safety before collapsing from the effects of the painful wound and
heat exhaustion. Lance Corporal Rusth was a fine Marine who
demonstrated courage and selfless dedication to his fellow Marines.
For his heroic action on Hill 110, Corporal Rusth received the
Navy Cross.

Jim Caswell reports that Charlie Company's success in taking
and defending Hill 110 was directly attributable to the foresight
of Sergeant Sanchez, the Weapons Platoon Commander and Platoon
Sergeant. Charley Company's Marines, as did all of the troops in
Vietnam, had trouble with their M-16 rifles double feeding and
jamming. To offset this problem, Sergeant Sanchez made sure that
all crew-served weapons were serviced, inspected, and made fully
functioning prior to moving out of Fire Base 54. He further made
sure that all C Company troopers had extra ammunition to sustain
them through a prolonged fight.

Caswell later told me, "One of my company policies was that
every single man in the company, except machine gunners and
corpsmen, had to carry a block of TNT or C-4 plus a 60mm mortar
round or a 3.5" rocket round. That way, if push came to shove we
would have enough reserve ammo to see us through most problems.
Sergeant Sanchez also made all of our machine gunners carry
considerably more ammo than standard procedure called for.
Thanks to Sanchez, when I called for a 60mm mortar barrage prior
to assaulting Hill 110, and during the assault, Sanchez put more
than 60 rounds on enemy positions on the hill. Then he ordered
his platoon machine gun teams and rocket teams to direct their
fire on caves and crew-served weapons until he had knocked out
enemy positions that had us under heavy fire. The fact that Sanchez
kept six M-60 machine guns firing all day was a major reason that
we repulsed all the NVA counter-attacks on our position."

Caswell didn't know what he was facing, but he knew he was badly outnumbered and called me for help. At the time, I was at the south side base of Nui Nong Ham, a long "J" shape mountain that curved around the valley battlefield. I was accompanied by elements of my Headquarters and Service Company, which included my command group, our 81mm mortar platoon, and Delta Company commanded by Mack McInturff. Caswell's situation was critical. There was no time to develop a neat and precise attack plan. We had to act immediately!

I sent Mack McInturff's Delta Company to reinforce and support Charlie Company. Mack had to take Delta Company up the south face of Nui Nong Ham, over the crest, and down the other side of a thickly wooded, steep-sloped mountain. Because of the difficult terrain and problems getting down Nui Nong Ham, Delta Company never made the link-up with Charlie Company while the battle for Hill 110 was in progress. This caused Caswell serious problems. However, with Caswell's tenacity and outstanding leadership he succeeded in holding Hill 110 despite being seriously outnumbered.[9]

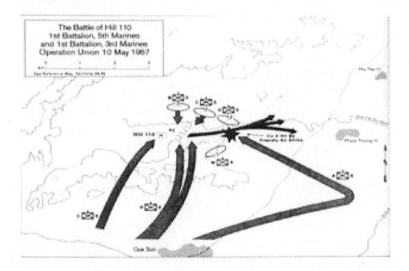

---

[9]   See Appendix B for explanation of map symbols.

I proceeded to the crest of Nui Nong Ham with my command group and 81mm mortars. When I arrived at the crest of Nui Nong Ham, I found the SLF battalion commander already there. He apparently felt the position gave him a better view of the battlefield to assist him in maneuvering his troops. Shortly after my arrival at the crest, Colonel Houghton called me and directed me to take operational control of the SLF Battalion. This surprised me and I gave the receiver to the SLF Battalion commander so he could hear the change of operational control directly from the regimental commander. Colonel Houghton shifted Companies Bravo, Charlie, and Delta of the SLF's First Battalion, Third Marines to my operational control because of command and control difficulties between Houghton's Fifth Regiment and the SLF command group. Colonel Houghton could not find out where the SLF companies were, or what they were trying to accomplish. He thought I could better determine SLF force deployment and objectives through direct contact with the SLF battalion commander. He therefore relinquished control of the SLF passing it to me temporarily.[10] This gave me operational control of six companies to command on the battlefield, which constituted a "regiment minus" (i.e. less one company and one battalion of four companies).

The geography of the battle for Hill 110 is interesting. As you can see from the map[11] (Union I and the Battle for Hill 110), the NVA occupied the middle of a rectangular shaped valley. The valley was approximately 1,500 meters in the north-south direction, and 3,500 meters in the east-west direction. The northern boundary of the valley was the sheer mountain wall that Sergeant York had scaled earlier in his great victory over the VC guerrilla unit. The NVA troops were entrenched in defensive positions around the village of Nghi Thuong, which they were using as a base of operations.

---

[10]   Alger, Richard; personal memorandum to P.L Hilgartner; September 2003.

[11]   Telfer et.al., op. cit., p.

Hill 110 with Jim Caswell's Charlie Company was on the western edge of the valley approximately 750 meters from my command post on the crest of Nui Nong Ham. I figured that McInturff's Delta Company could reinforce Charley Company to relieve the pressure Caswell was getting from the NVA attack.

After I assumed operational control of the SLF battalion, I asked the battalion commander to give me the position of his troops. He led me to believe that his three SLF companies were directly below us in the woods at the base of Nui Nong Ham. Since he was on the crest for better battlefield visibility, it made sense that his troops would be at the base of Nui Nong Ham where he could control them and easily rejoin them. I had no reason to doubt this reported troop disposition; however, it was wrong. As you can see from the map, the SLF units were actually about 1,500 meters northeast of Hill 110. Had I known this, and known that Delta Company had been delayed in their link-up, I could have called on SLF units to render support to Caswell's beleaguered Charlie Company. I also wouldn't have called for the battle plan that I put in place.

With the troops that I had under my operational control, I planned to support Caswell on Hill 110 and to crush the enemy troops in the valley. First, we had to position our forces to hit the NVA on two sides in a coordinated attack, from the south side of the valley and the east side while blocking their retreat to the west around Caswell on Hill 110. I planned to block the enemy on the west side of the valley with Caswell's Charley Company reinforced with McInturff's Delta Company. The SLF battalion was covering the southern flank, so I thought, from their position in the woods at the base of Nui Nong Ham. The enemy was blocked to the north by Hillous York's high, almost vertical mountain wall. We only needed to cover the eastern side of the valley, and then we would be ready to attack.

With our troops in position, we would first hammer the NVA positions with artillery and air strikes, then execute a two pronged attack from the south, with the SLF battalion, and the east with McKay's Alpha Company and Esslinger's Third Battalion. McKay was approaching the combat zone from the east, and Esslinger, who was south of my position on Nui Nong Ham, was proceeding around my rear to take positions on the east side of the valley. I had requested Colonel Houghton to send Dean's Third Battalion to the eastern flank to give strength to the attack and to block any NVA retreat to the east. With our units in position, we would have the enemy surrounded and blocked from escape. We could have annihilated him. It seemed too good to be true . . . and it was.

I didn't know it at the time, but not only had McInturff's Delta Company not been able to link-up with Charley Company on Hill 110 because of terrain problems, but Esslinger had made heavy contact with the enemy as he was moving to cover the eastern flank. The Third Battalion had been delayed and was not in its blocking position. This was not the end of the bad news.

The NVA had captured two of Charlie Company's Marines with some communications gear, which the enemy used to jam the company radio frequencies.[12] The NVA jamming blocked my communications with the three SLF companies and my own First Battalion companies. I also didn't have reliable communications with the Fifth Marines regimental staff. I advised Colonel Houghton of this command and control nightmare, but his communications at the time were no better than mine, and I had the advantage of being on the scene. This breakdown in command and control seriously impeded the battle for Hill 110, and kept us from inflicting a punishing defeat on the enemy. Major Dick Alger (then Regimental S-3) recently said:[13]

> Colonel Houghton and I constantly looked for ways to
> influence *any* combat action that our subordinate battalions
> were engaged in—consistent with USMC doctrine and

---

[12]   One of these Marines later escaped and returned to the First Marine Division's lines.

[13]   Alger, Dick; Informal Memo, September 2003

tactics. We continually examined our options of: (1) changing the supporting arms mix; (2) committing the regimental reserve; and (3) the personal presence of the regimental commander at a battalion's location to influence a favorable outcome. We invariably selected option (1) to shift or increase artillery and close air support. At Regiment, we did not know of Company C's needs, and I believe the problem was caused by inaction of First Battalion's operations section in responding to support requests. It is now apparent that Hilgartner was not advised of this situation by his S-3.

The SLF battalion, which was actually to the northeast of Hill 110 and not in the woods at the base of Nui Nong Ham, began receiving heavy fire from NVA troops in the valley. The SLF battalion requested reinforcements, not from Colonel Houghton, the Fifth Marines commander, or me. Instead, they requested support from the SLF group commander, who was physically remote from Houghton and me. The SLF group commander attempted to helolift his Alpha Company into the area without Colonel Houghton's or my knowledge, and the helicopters met such fierce resistance while attempting to land that only one platoon made it in. Further troop insertions via helicopter to support the SLF troops on the ground were impossible.

On noon of 10 May, Jerry McKay's Alpha Company, which had completed a search and destroy operation to the east in the vicinity of the village of Phuoc Duc (2), was moving rapidly into the valley to take up positions to attack the enemy's eastern flank. On their way into their positions on the east side of the valley, Alpha Company began receiving automatic and small arms fire from well-entrenched NVA units. Company A deployed and was closing with the NVA positions when a HUEY gunship marked the center of McKay's command post with rockets. A flight of F-4 aircraft rolled in and immediately strafed and bombed Alpha Company's command post and surrounding area. The errant strike killed five Marines and wounded 24, which put A Company out of action.

I did not clear the strike, nor did any units of my First Battalion request it. This disaster caused Company A to break contact with the enemy in order to establish a security zone for helicopters to evacuate our wounded and dead. We now know that one of the SLF companies called in the air strike to counter the heavy fire they were receiving from the enemy, and they did it through the SLF group commander. The SLF did not coordinate the air strike with Colonel Houghton or me. The result was a tactical disaster! Even worse was the personal sense of despair I felt for the futile loss of so many of my fine Marines because of a mistake that should have been avoided. I still feel anger and despair to this day whenever I think about it.

Here is an account of that air strike from PFC Robert J. Pine USMC, who was part of Alpha Company during Union I. It is a good account of what this Marine private experienced, and what that gross error did to Alpha Company.

> I was a rifleman with the Second Platoon, Alpha Company, First Battalion Fifth Marines, First Marine Division on 10 May 1967. I was directly involved in the unfortunate air attack, and want to recount what happened from my perspective.
>
> Alpha Company was headed approximately due west on what was a main dirt road leading to the village of Que Son. It seemed that we were headed back to our firebase, which was on a hill some distance beyond the vil.
>
> The company took a right turn off the main road along a narrow dirt side road, and the head of the column came under fire from a hill to our left. Under covering fire from our machine guns, we crossed open ground while taking machine gun and automatic weapons fire from the hill. Alpha Company divided into two groups to assault the hill. The 2nd Platoon arrived at the base of the hill, and closed in to form an assault line.

I was laying rifle fire on the hill from a position behind the dike of dry terraced rice paddies, which extended from the base of the hill. My buddy, Louis Viscusi, was nearby, the very next man to my right, laying rifle fire on the hill from his cover behind a cement well enclosure. Other Marines were changing positions, and taking cover while under fire from the hill.

A Phantom jet arrived unexpectedly, and made an observation pass of the hill. As it reappeared on the left to begin its first attack run, I immediately determined that it was on the wrong angle and too low to hit the hill. I dove fully behind cover, instinctively clasping my hands to my ears and opening my mouth to prepare for concussion. To say that I could have hit the jet with a stone would be to exaggerate only my accuracy and timing. I was actually able to see moving control surfaces of the Phantom. I saw the bombs leave the racks and the drag fins expand to their fully opened position. My final view before I cleared cover was that of one bomb at about shoulder height and the other closer to the ground—with a Marine caught in the open in the same view.

The first effect at detonation was overlapping waves of hissing—very close and directly above me. Virtually simultaneously, the ground transmitted the detonations, and I was crushed by incredibly thunderous overlapping shockwaves. I thought that my body was dead and that my brain would soon follow. When my lungs were able to fill, the air was clear of the smoke and debris that usually accompanied close air strikes. It is not possible for me to know if I had been temporarily unconscious. The air might have been clear because the explosions were so close.

My next rational thought was of napalm. The next strike would be napalm. My body and mind stunned, I moved as quickly as possible away from the hill toward the sugar cane fields. Others were also moving toward the cane fields. I could hear, but it was as if I were hearing underwater. There were muffled shouts—warnings to get clear of the next strike. A green star cluster was fired to identify us as friendly troops, and the Phantom made a low pass of recognition without dropping ordnance.

Those of us who had moved to the cane field immediately rejoined the chaotic scene of destruction at the base of the hill where the enemy had been. There was reduced enemy fire coming from the hill. The NVA had apparently shifted its positions when the Phantom arrived.

The sequence of events after the Phantom's attack is not entirely clear to me. The dead and wounded were eventually dealt with, and the extra equipment they left behind was burned near a cement structure at the base of the hill.

There was further fighting. The platoon leader and others were wounded or killed. Unable to dig foxholes in the stony soil, we spent a tense night on the hill awaiting a counterattack. Our remaining force of about a dozen men then moved into the valley, linked-up with other Marines, and retired from the field.

A moment for Marines who fell . . . .

Semper Fidelis,
Robert J. Pine

I also received a recent note from Rick Zell, who was at the time of the air strike on Alpha, a Second Lieutenant in Alpha Company. Rick was temporarily attached to Dick Alger's S-3 at Regimental Headquarters while he was recovering from a gunshot wound he received on 1 May 1967 during the early part of Union I. Rick was the Regimental watch officer that day. Here are Rick's words.

One of the most indelible memories I have of the war occurred on 10 May 1967. I was monitoring the Battalion Tactical Net when at approximately 1200 hours I heard with horror that a friendly air strike was hitting Company

A. I never felt as helpless in my life. My God, how could this be happening?

Each event as it unfolded, the HUEY gunship marking A Company with rockets, the F-4s strafing the company, the reports of KIAs and WIAs coming in and the company continuing to get hit as they tried to set up an LZ to medevac the WIAs. I couldn't believe what was happening. I realized how much I loved my Marines and wanted to be with them, but all I could do was rage inside at the unfairness of war. No amount of training or leadership could change the confusion of battle. I knew that I had to return to my platoon. Being in the rear was unbearable.

That says something about the feeling of brotherhood that Marines feel for each other. Even though that note was written almost forty years after the event, you can still feel the pain in Rick's words for what he felt for his Marines who were being killed and wounded in a tragic mistake.

I immediately notified Colonel Houghton, the regimental commander, about this disaster. Houghton responded promptly by passing operational control of Company M, Third Battalion, Fifth Marines to me, and concurrently transferred operational control of my A Company to Dean Esslinger's Third Battalion. This was the right thing to do, but it didn't solve my immediate problem of replacing my lost A Company. M Company was not in the area, and it would be some time before they arrived on the scene. Consequently, I couldn't execute my plan to attack the enemy from the south and east sides of the valley.

Caswell's Marines were now fighting against great odds at close quarters with the NVA. He needed help! My mortar platoon on the crest of Nui Nong Ham had a clear line of sight on the enemy in the valley below. The mortar crews started firing with deadly effect, and fired so rapidly that their tubes got too hot to touch. With a clear line of sight they directed their fire right onto clustered NVA troops, and with each direct hit our mortar crews let out a loud cheer. The enemy was taking great punishment from our mortars and Caswell's Charley Company on Hill 110. We could see them falling back in disarray from their defensive positions leaving he valley floor littered with enemy bodies.

The disastrous mistaken air strike on Alpha Company and the delay of Esslinger's battalion in reinforcing McKay ruined my plan for an attack from the eastern flank. Also, the fact that the SLF Battalion was well north of Nui Nong Ham and on the other side of the valley made my attack from the south impossible. The tactical situation was further aggravated by Delta Company's inability to link-up with Charley Company to close off the enemy's western escape route.

Even though we didn't execute the crushing blow to the enemy that I had envisioned, we did badly maul him. The remnants of the NVA Second Division managed to make an end run around Caswell's left flank and escape our trap through a small northern corridor on the west side of the valley between Caswell on Hill 110 and the SLF Battalion. This is different from what is shown in the battle map above, which is the official record of the battle.

I could not believe so much bad luck had happened all at one time. A friendly air strike that decimated Alpha Company, failure of the Delta Company and Third Battalion reinforcements to arrive in time, and the error in SLF location had turned what could have been a "one-for-the-books" major victory into just another engagement with a good outcome. Everything that could go wrong did go wrong.

At 1530, Dean Esslinger's M Company joined my position on Nui Nong Ham, and we continued to provide covering fire for our Marines below and on Hill 110. The air strikes that began at 1600, plus our mortar fire from Nui Nong Ham kept the enemy from launching effective counter-attacks. By evening the Marines drove the enemy force from their positions around the village.

We kept contact with the NVA through the night as they withdrew to the northwest. Our artillery and air strikes followed their withdrawal, and caused further damage to the retreating enemy. Our Marine infantry, artillery, and air strikes had punished them, but we could have crushed them. Therein is the big disappointment for me in Union I. The enemy left at least 116 of his dead in the field. We have no valid estimate of his wounded, but his WIA must have been substantial. We lost 34 killed in action and 120 wounded and evacuated.

In looking back at Union I, the major lesson is the proper use of SLF troops to support forces ashore. It is a mistake to integrate SLF forces into regimental combat operations unless it is absolutely necessary; use them as support troops. It would have been better to assign the SLF units to relieve Colonel Houghton's Second Battalion in providing rear area security around the regimental base at An Aoa. This would have given the Fifth Marines Regimental Commander use of all three of his battalions to fight the enemy. It is always better for any commander to work with his own troops; troops he knows—platoons, companies, and battalions he has trained and commanded.

I absolutely believe the botched air strike on Alpha Company that was called in by the SLF Delta Company would not have happened if the Second Battalion, Fifth Marines had been committed to the fight, and the SLF sent to An Aoa to relieve them. I'm also convinced the Second Battalion commander would have known where his troops were located in the battle for Hill 110, and would have been able to convey that information to me and Colonel Houghton so that they could have been effectively employed when the battle was in a critical stage. As it was, the SLF units were never effectively used in the fight.

If it is necessary to insert SLF troops into the regimental force, the SLF command group should become resident with the regimental headquarters staff. The SLF command group must not remain aboard ship, or in a location remote from the regimental commander responsible for tactical operations. It invites command, control, and communications breakdown to isolate the SLF command group from the regimental staff that has operational control of the battle.

The SLF suffered over 50 heat casualties during Union I. This high number indicates that they were not properly conditioned physically for the rigors of combat in the South Vietnamese bush. The SLF and the Fifth Marines both suffered from the decision to integrate SLF battalions into the Fifth Marines regimental combat operations. General Houghton agrees in this assessment.

Another lesson from Union I is that even the best-laid plans will go awry. That can be the subject of countless classroom lectures, but the lectures don't have the impact of actual combat experience. A lesson from the field gets your attention like a smack over the head with a two-by-four. It gives you a deeper perspective of self-evident truths that makes the difference between a combat veteran and a well-trained replacement from The Basic School. This means that combat leaders must be able to adapt quickly to changes in the tactical situation. To do this, the commander must know where his units are, must have communications with them all and with his superior command group, and there must be a clear line of responsibility in the command and control chain. This is not news. We all knew these fundamental principals at Union I, but never the less, each of these self-evident truths broke down during the battle.

The real purpose of training is to make Marine Corps officers battlefield problem-solvers. The set piece school solutions to tactical problems teach sound fundamentals, but officers must be prepared for the unexpected. Friendly fire goes astray. Units don't link up on time. Communications between units in the field are not always reliable. The infamous "fog of war" is a reality, and it's always there. *Being ready for the unexpected is what Marine officers are paid to do, fight and win no matter what the odds or how many things do not go according to plan.*

In the battle for Hill 110, Captain Jim Caswell was the epitome of what we expect from a Marine Corps officer. He overcame a multitude of problems in a situation that did not go according to plan. He lost a key noncommissioned officer, Gunnery Sergeant Marcelino Rivera-Cruz who was killed early in the fight for Hill 110. Charley Company did not have the supporting arms Caswell needed from artillery and air strikes, and Delta Company did not linkup with his C Company as planned. Any one of these could have meant disaster, but Caswell overcame these obstacles, and prevailed in battle against great numerical odds. This is why Captain

James Caswell is *the* hero among heroes in Union I. For his conspicuous gallantry in action, he was awarded the Silver Star medal.

Before leaving the subject of Charley Company's superb performance in Union I, I want to pass on to you what Jim Caswell told me about Gunnery Sergeant Rivera-Cruz. Jim said, "Marcelino Rivera-Cruz had been the company gunny for me and Buck Darling. Occasionally, when manpower problems demanded, he would assume command of his old platoon—the Third Platoon. A few days before 10 May 1967 we received some replacements, including a new gunnery sergeant. I gave the new replacement the Third Platoon. Rivera-Cruz later came to me and told me that the new gunny leading the Third Platoon wasn't in shape and couldn't keep up. Rivera-Cruz wanted the best for his troopers; so, he asked to switch places with the new gunnery sergeant until the new man became acclimated and conditioned well enough to lead his platoon. The troops loved Rivera-Cruz. He always put his men first. The next day Rivera-Cruz was killed in action. The entire company sorely felt his loss."

Lieutenant General Walt, Commanding General III MAF, and Colonel Houghton came out to the field to view the battle damage. As he walked around the field, General Walt told one of the Charlie Company Marines to give him his rifle. The Marine refused. Captain Caswell had to intercede, and the Marine handed his rifle to the general. I don't know why General Walt did this. I wasn't carrying a firearm, and I felt very safe with our Marines. "Marine Green" provided all the protection I needed. In my judgment, General Walt should have shown the same confidence in our grunts that I had. They were a better safety shield than an M-16, and our gunny sergeants taught our troopers that the only way to get their rifle is to pry it out of their dead fingers. And if the situation was such that General Walt needed the trooper's rifle for his security, what was the Marine to use for his?

After the battle, the Seventh Fleet's Special Landing Force returned to their afloat base. Dean Esslinger's Third Battalion stayed in the area searching for NVA remnants. To assist in the operation, Colonel Houghton assigned McInturff's Delta Company to Dean's operational control on 12 May in the vicinity of the village of Phuoc Duc (1). Hank Stackpole, Esslinger's S-3, assigned Delta as the lead company in a sweep to the southeast, and during the late afternoon, in the vicinity of Phuoc Duc (2), Delta had a major firefight with NVA units that had not yet withdrawn from the area. Mack lost two Marines MIA and 17 KIA in the engagement. The enemy left 68 dead on the battlefield as he disengaged and retreated.

The rest of my First Battalion Fifth Marines went to a new home on a hill located about 1,000 meters to the southwest of Que Son Village. "I want you to become the 'Mayor of Que Son Valley'," Colonel Houghton told me. Before we could move into our new home, we had to kill a few guerrillas and chase the survivors away. After I reported to Dick Alger at regimental headquarters that the hill was secured, he said, "By the way, Cottage Six, our map doesn't show a numerical designation for that hill."

"It doesn't?" I commented, "Well, mine does." Here was my chance for the history books. My high school football jersey number was 51 and I was in the class of '51 from the Naval Academy. Now I commanded First Battalion, Fifth Marines. "The hill designator is Five-One," I said, meaning Fifth Marines, First Battalion.

"Thanks," Alger said.

The number stuck, and in the official Marine Corps history the hill is called Hill 51, meaning it is 51 meters high and is so designated on the map. In reality it was probably only about half that high. Immediately after capturing the hill, we built gun emplacements, bunkers, and other defensive works. We allowed no Vietnamese labor to be used nor did we permit Vietnamese within the defensive fortifications. I knew there were extensive NVA covert operations within the surrounding villages, and I had no intention of letting NVA spies disguised as laborers inside our Hill 51 fortifications to reconnoiter our defenses.

I want to make a slight detour again into the recollections of Corporal Brad Silliman of the Third Platoon, Charlie Company.

He gives a vivid picture of One-Five's patrolling operations from our base at Hill 51.[14]

> We had one under-strength battalion to patrol not just the western end of the valley, but the mountains on three sides of us. The NVA often hid from us high in the mountains and also established supply dumps, hospitals rest camps, training facilities and radio intercept sites there. Also they could see everything going on for 20 miles. One day we were climbing a mountain when we walked into what turned out to be an NVA R&R center. We captured this odd group of Vietnamese men and women who were either a propaganda team or a troupe of entertainers. Personally, I liked being in the mountains because it was cooler and the water was better.
>
> We operated out of a primitive firebase called Hill 51, located adjacent to the village of Que Son. At any one time, at least one of four rifle companies were required at Hill 51 to help man the perimeter with the H&S company, a tank company and an artillery battery. Some personnel from H&S, tanks or artillery, at any time, were scattered around the valley on operations or at Nui Lac Son.
>
> Nui Lac Son was a small but very steep mountain— easy to defend with a small force—that served as an observation post for air and artillery strikes, as a radio booster station for recon teams operating to the west and in Laos, and contained a 4.2-inch mortar used to bombard any enemy troops spotted in the surrounding area. Because it was high, the top of Nui Lac Son enjoyed a steady breeze day and night. It afforded a breath-taking vista. You could see the faint lights of Da Nang, Chu Lai and Tam Ky from there and the moon reflecting on the South China Sea. You could see mountain peaks in Laos, and one late afternoon I

---

[14]   Silliman.

watched, from Nui Lac Son, Hill 51 get mortared. It was a neat place.

At least two rifle platoons, and sometimes an entire company was needed at Nui Lac Son to man the perimeter and mount patrols and ambushes. Considering the constant security requirements of Nui Lac Son and Hill 51, there were two rifle companies, usually totaling about 130 men each, free to patrol aggressively hundreds of square kilometers. At times, most of the battalion would move east to conduct operations with 2/5, 3/5, ARVNs and others outside our own tactical area of responsibility.

Since there was no real road between Highway One and Que Son village, all logistics relied on helicopters. Because of the expense, only essential materials were brought to us. This made living conditions primitive. This led to a battalion that became even more casualty riddled due to an increase in maladies such as malaria, amoebic dysentery, boils, trench foot, scurvy, heat stroke and various skin diseases.

Foot patrol was the only type of patrolling we did. We walked everywhere. The average rifle company grunt spent the day patrolling, or manning an observation post outside the wire. We spent the night either lying in an ambush, manning the perimeter, or working a listening post. If we were on the base we worked for 10 hours at a time, stringing barbed wire or building bunkers. We averaged four hours of sleep a day. I can remember the whole company going 36 hours without sleep during an operation. This was common. I went from 155 to 120 pounds. I can remember single rifle squads tangling with NVA units two or more clicks from Hill 51. Sometimes, if they needed rescuing, a rifle platoon, or more with an M-60 tank would go tearing out into the bush.

The point is that we patrolled as aggressively as anyone could under the circumstances. After Union II, most of the NVA were gone from the valley until a new NVA division came out of the mountains and collided with Delta in early

September. Two platoons of Charlie Company were on Nui
Lac Son at the time, which is where I was. We saw the NVA
coming down from the hills at night using flashlights. We
believed these to be farmers coming out of the hills to vote
in the elections, which were going on at the time because we
could not believe that communist soldiers, infiltrating in
from Laos, would be audacious enough to use flashlights.

In 1969 MACV renamed Hill 51 Fire Support Base (FSB)
Ross. By this time, the First Battalion, Seventh Marine Regiment
of the First Division had assumed operational control of FSB Ross,
and continued to use it to counter enemy operations in the Que
Son Valley. This caused the NVA serious problems because they
still wanted to control the valley for its rice and salt production,
and because the populace provided recruits for their NVA and VC
organizations. FSB Ross sat astride the enemy's main supply route,
making it a major problem obstructing the enemy's attempt to
influence life in the valley. On the night of 6 January 1970, two
NVA battalions hit FSB Ross in a well-planed attack with the
objective of destroying the base and driving the Marines from the
position. In the initial phase of the assault, the enemy succeeded
in penetrating the defensive perimeter. After a furious counterattack
with hand-to-hand fighting, the Marines forced the enemy to
retreat, and abandon the attack.[15]

In early 1999, one of my First Battalion, Fifth Marine troopers,
Sergeant Steven Wilson, in a travel group, which included his son
Andrew, found Hill 51 with the aid of a Global Positioning System
(GPS) device. Sergeant Wilson had been in D Company, as a
corporal, during the Union Operations and Swift. In fact, he was
Captain Morgan's company radio operator when Bob Morgan was
killed during Swift. Steve Wilson was well aware of the significance

---

[15]   Charles G. Cooper, *Cheers and Tears* (Reno, Nevada: Wesley Press, 2002),
pp. 152-154.

and history of Hill 51, and visited our Que Son Valley combat operations base for old time sake. To his surprise, Steve found that the North Vietnamese had erected a memorial statue on our hill commemorating their great victory over the Americans in Que Son. The memorial stands on a large concrete mound, and depicts a man, a woman and a child marching off into some heroic "peoples' future" under the benevolent leadership of Chairman Ho Chi Minh. Steve's son took the photograph of the monument, which Steve recently sent to me. I asked the owner of my favorite neighborhood Vietnamese restaurant, to translated the memorial's inscription *Tuong Dai, Chien Thang Que Son*. It reads: "Statue of the Victory at Que Son."

I don't know what victory they were referring to, because we kicked their butts every time we found the NVA or VC in *our* Que Son Valley. If they erected such a monument on Hill 51, the hill must have been a significant place for the enemy just as it was to our Marine troopers. Let the history books show that the North Vietnamese Army did not take Hill 51 from the United States Marine Corps through military action. We lost our hill because our political leadership lost its will, and those political battles were fought in our nation's media and counter-culture street demonstrations.

For a few days after the first Union operation, I had to handle the usual administrative matters that are a battalion commander's responsibility. Some were pleasant, like awarding promotions and recommending certain Marines for medals. I also had the profoundly painful task of writing letters to the parents and wives of Marines killed in action. They would not be coming home, and it fell to me to tell their loved ones why.

Writing these letters gave me pause to think of the heroic valor of *all* my Marines. It was impossible to decorate each of them with medals, although they all should have been. I was so concerned with this that when Dick Alger became my battalion X.O., I gave him Temporary Additional Duty (TAD) orders to the Division Headquarters in Da Nang for the express purpose of coordination with the division's awards office to ensure that deserving First Battalion Marines received the recognition they deserved. Major Alger continued this valuable effort, and influenced the awards recognition process throughout the Fifth Regiment when he later joined Colonel Houghton's staff as both his operations officer and X.O. in the field.

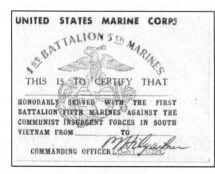

I also wanted each Marine, who fought, survived, and would be going home to have something that he could show to his family. To establish that he had served honorably in the First Battalion, Fifth Marines in Vietnam, we designed a wallet card for each of us to carry. I believe all hands liked the idea. I still carry mine.

Discipline was another matter I had to deal with. From the standpoint of discipline, I really never had any severe problems while I commanded First Battalion, Fifth Marines, especially after we relocated to the Que Son Valley. Once we became established on Hill 51, and got down to the business of carrying out our assigned mission to drive the enemy out of Que Son Valley, we had only minor problems. I dealt with any major problems or offenses swiftly, and removed the offenders from the battalion immediately. I believe our success in having few problems was due, in part, to the initial briefing we gave each replacement when he joined the battalion. Either my battalion executive officer or I gave the briefing. My executive officers were J.P. (Frank) White and later Ernie Cheatham. Both were outstanding officers. Ernie later rose to the rank of Lieutenant General, and became Commanding General, Fleet Marine Force, Pacific (CGFMFPAC). The welcome aboard briefing went something like this:

> Welcome to the First Battalion, Fifth Marine Regiment. You have joined the most combat committed battalion in the First Marine Division. We fight the enemy every day, seven days a week. In this battalion every Marine is important. Just as you will depend on me to make the correct military decisions, so will the Marines to your right and left, as will I, depend on you to do your jobs to the best of your ability. We all depend on each other.
>
> We do not have a drug problem in this battalion. If you are doing drugs of any kind, go down to the supply tent and get measured for your casket, because that is how you will be going home. If I find out you are doing drugs, you will be the point man on every patrol, and you will be sent forward of the lines every night on a one man all night listening post until you are killed.

Do you understand this?

They always answered, "Yes, sir."

"Do any of you not believe me? If you don't, then just test me and find out."

No one ever tested me!

We did have some minor infractions. I recall one minor incident that could have blown into something big. Hill 51 was bordered

on the south and west side of our defensive perimeter by the Song
Ly Ly (River Ly Ly). Where it changed direction from west to south,
it had created a large pool about five or six feet deep. We used this
pool to bathe.

One day I went down to take a bath. I was wearing my soft
cap with rank insignia pinned on it. I had wrapped a towel around
my waist and had my boots on without socks.

There were two Marines in the pool taking a bath, and they
began horsing around as young guys do. They were splashing water
on each other, and trying to dunk each other under the water. One
Marine was black and the other was white. One of them couldn't
swim and he panicked at being pushed underwater. Then they
began to fight.

I saw the fight begin, and feared that with these two I could
have the beginnings of a larger racial problem. I ordered them to
stop fighting and report to me. The two Marines exited the water
and stood before me buck-naked. Except for my towel, I was buck-
naked, too. I put my hat on and reminded them who I was. I then
told them office hours would now begin. I charged them both
with disorderly conduct and prejudice to good order and discipline.

"And you are both guilty," I said. "Get dressed and report to
the sergeant major. He will bring you to my command post for
sentencing."

When they showed up I noted they were both corporals. I
told them they were forthwith reduced in rank to lance corporal,
but the sentence would be suspended after they had filled 100
sandbags. This would take several hours.

I had two reasons for filling the sandbags: First, we needed
them for our defenses; and second, you can't easily fill a sandbag
by yourself. One man needs to hold the bag while the other fills it.
These two Marines would *have* to work together.

When they had finished, they were both hot and tired. The
sergeant major brought them back to my command post, and we
had one final discussion about working together. My last words
were, "Your sentence is suspended. Now report to your platoons
and remember this: We have only one color in this battalion and it

is Marine green. We're fighting a war out here, and it's the enemy we fight, not each other. Is that clear?"

"Yes, sir," they replied, saluted and went back to their platoons. This matter was resolved.

We had hurt the enemy in Union I, but he was still a force with extensive combat capabilities. We thought we had broken the VC and NVA control of the Hiep Duc-Que Son-Thang Binh corridor and dealt the enemy a major psychological blow. To a large extent we had; however, the enemy never fully left. The VC and NVA continued to exert pressure on the populace and influence Vietnamese life in the region even though it was on a greatly reduced level.

After Union I, my First Battalion, Fifth Marines assumed responsibility for the Nui Lac Son outpost and control of the valley from our command post on Hill 51 west of the village of Que Son. I was Colonel Houghton's "Mayor of Que Son Valley." In daily skirmishes with enemy forces left in the area, we lost Marines and we killed more enemy, but it was never high intensity conflict. I suspect this was mostly contact with VC guerrilla units rather than regular NVA troops. The NVA regulars were most likely out of the area regrouping and repairing the serious damage we had inflicted on them in Union I.

This continuing low-level activity together with later intelligence reports that the Third and Twenty First NVA Regiments were moving back into the area demanded prompt action. Colonel Houghton appraised Major General Herman Nickerson, our Division Commanding General of the situation. The Fifth Marines regimental staff then commenced planning Union II as our response to the new NVA incursion.

Union II, like Union I, involved coordinated operations with the Sixth ARVN Regiment and the First ARVN Ranger Group. Colonel Houghton and Dick Alger planned to use my First Battalion with Dean Esslinger's Third Battalion as maneuver elements for the Marine Corps part of this operation. I was pleased with this. I liked Dean and we worked well together. I felt confident that we would have even better results this time with Union II.

The initial regimental battle plan called for my First Battalion to be in a blocking position in the western part of the valley. The three RVN Ranger Group Battalions were to attack southwest from Thang Binh, while the Sixth ARVN Regiment was to attack northwest from a position near Tam Ky. Dean Esslinger's Third Battalion would move by helicopters into the southern part of the basin and sweep northeast. This way, the Third Battalion with the two South Vietnamese regiments would drive the enemy towards me. My First Battalion would block their retreat. Regimental intelligence reported an estimated NVA strength to be about 2,000 highly trained and well-disciplined troops of the Third NVA Regiment.[16]

The Union II operation began on 26 May 1967. After three days of light contact the South Vietnamese withdrew, convinced that we had bad intelligence and that the enemy was not in the area. Colonel Houghton thought otherwise, and implemented a new action plan on 30 May. We found the enemy soon enough, and the Union II battle developed into a fierce one.

Our bad luck started immediately after the operation began. Dean Esslinger's Marines made a heliborne assault into an area east of the Nui Loc San outpost and immediately became engaged with the enemy. They received heavy small arms and mortar fire, and during the subsequent engagement Lieutenant Colonel Esslinger was wounded in the eye. Lieutenant Colonel Charles B. Webster, an officer I had never before met or worked with, assumed command of the Third Battalion.

On 30 May, (D + 4 days into the operation), my battalion helolifted into a landing zone designated by the code name Robin. We were a substantial distance to the south and slightly east of our ultimate objective. Our mission was to begin a sweep in what

---

16   Combat After Action Report, Operation Union II, Headquarters 1st Battalion, 5th Marines, 1st Marine Division, 16 June 1967.

ultimately would take us in a reverse C shaped route. My three companies were Alpha, Delta, and Foxtrot Company from the Second Battalion, which Colonel Houghton attached to us for this operation.

Captain Ron Babich, commanding Alpha Company, had formerly been Colonel Houghton's Regimental Headquarters and Service Company commander. Houghton sent Ron to me with high praise, and I was pleased to get him. First Lieutenant David McInturff commanded Delta Company, and Captain James Graham commanded Foxtrot Company. I knew my own company commanders very well, and had great confidence in them. We all knew Captain Graham to be a fine and exceptionally aggressive officer, but we had not worked with him before.

After landing and getting organized, we moved out in a basic sweep type formation with Foxtrot and Alpha abreast and Delta following in reserve with my command group. We began encountering sniper fire that the enemy used as a delaying tactic.

On 31 May (D+5), Colonel Houghton arrived by chopper to talk with me and learn how things were going. I was pleased to see him, and we had a good discussion. He believed that the enemy was here in force and more likely located to my left. I had placed Alpha and Delta abreast with Foxtrot centered in reserve behind the lead companies.

As Colonel Houghton departed, he said, "Good hunting Pete. And you might want to keep an eye on your left flank." I paid attention to that advice, and it turned out to be sound counsel.

On 1 June, I moved Foxtrot Company from reserve status abreast of Delta Company on Delta's left flank with Alpha in reserve behind Foxtrot. I did this because I knew the A Company commander and believed he would be more responsive to any change in mission. My command group would be with the lead elements of Alpha Company. My main strength was now on the left side of our formation. This switch proved to be of great benefit in the battle to come. Our contact with the enemy slowly increased as we continued the search and destroy mission. On the early morning of 2 June, First Battalion continued its sweep. Our objective was the villages of Vinh Huy. These villages were about six thousand meters southeast of our Hill 51 combat base. What we did not know then was that the Third NVA Regiment had decided to stand and fight us. We also didn't know they were dug into a defensive position I call a "lazy L." This positioned them to attack Foxtrot's left flank when we hit the long horizontal leg of the L with Foxtrot and Delta Companies. However, I had positioned Alpha Company 200 yards directly behind Foxtrot Company so that when the enemy attacked Foxtrot's left flank, Alpha immediately moved up to oppose their attack. Even with Alpha positioned close to and directly behind Foxtrot, the enemy nearly broke through the gap between the two companies. Had I positioned Alpha in the middle between Foxtrot and Delta, the NVA may very well have broken through. That could have been disastrous. To this day I'm thankful for Colonel Houghton's counsel to watch my left flank.

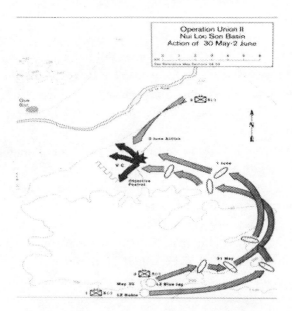

A very large rice paddy varying from 500 to 1000 meters in width bordered the eastern side of the village, and a group of small hills flanked the eastern edge of the paddy. Our battalion moved due west towards Vinh Huy, designated Objective Foxtrot. At 1100 hours First Battalion's Foxtrot and Delta Companies cleared the small hill mass flanking the eastern edge of the paddy, and began crossing the rice field when they came under enemy fire. Delta was slightly out in front of Foxtrot and began taking heavy rifle fire from well-entrenched NVA. McInturff knew his company was near the enemy's left flank, and was trying to get at least a portion of his company, his Third Platoon, on the enemy's flank. Had this worked, Jim Graham's Foxtrot Company could have moved forward.

Consider the unfolding events from Mack McInturff's observations. Mack gives us his perspective, with the admonition that there are one hundred plus Marines still alive that were part of Delta Company's action in Union II, and that each formed a vision in his own mind of this action. Mack says his vision and recollection is only one of one hundred plus. True, but I think it is a good one. Here is Mack's account.

As usual, the morning of 2 June started about 0400 for Delta Company. Its mission was to secure a battalion objective in the Vinh Huy area. The area consisted of three Vinh Huy villages. Delta's axis of advance was toward the west and Vinh Huy 1. Jim Graham and Foxtrot (2/5) were on Delta's left flank. Foxtrot's assigned objective was in the area of Vinh Huy 2, and a little further west-southwest of Delta.

The First Battalion attack formation was basically a "two up, one back" formation with the battalion command post behind the first two attacking companies. Alpha Company was "tail-end Charlie" and the battalion reserve.

The initial advance to our objectives was basically uneventful. As Delta secured the first battalion objective of the day, Lt. Col. Hilgartner called a break (rest stop) on our securing of the first objective and brought Alpha Company up to secure a temporary defensive position with Delta and the battalion CP group. Foxtrot Company was still out of sight on the left flank moving toward its battalion objective.

During the rest stop and consolidation, members of Delta Company observed two uniformed enemy with weapons transiting the open rice paddy to our front area coming from the direction of Foxtrot Company's axis of advance on our left flank. The enemy was taken under fire at a range of 150 to 200 meters with rifle and machine gun fire. Both NVA were later found dead in the middle of the rice paddies to Delta's immediate front. Delta's route to the next objective included the same wide-open area of rice paddies where the two NVA were dropped.

I had given the order of our advance as a "two up, one back" formation with the 1st Platoon left and the 2d Platoon on the right, and they were spread out laterally in order to cover the rice paddy area that we had to traverse. Third Platoon was to follow in trace of the company CP located behind center of 1st and 2d platoons. This formation placed the company CP group in the middle of the rice paddy area.

As I recall, the continuation of the attack commenced early afternoon on 2 June. During the sweep across the paddy area and approximately two-thirds of the distance to the next piece of "high ground," Delta 2 found the bodies of the two NVA taken under fire earlier. I called a halt of the advance in order to have the NVA bodies searched. Weapons and intelligence information were taken from the dead NVA and forwarded back to the Battalion CP. I then ordered the attack advance to continue through the remainder of the rice paddy area.

Shortly after we began moving, Delta 1 and 2, the CP group, and 3d Platoon came under intense small arms and automatic weapons fire from a very substantial enemy force in concealed positions across our front.

It didn't take me but a nanosecond to determine that Delta Company was in a real "shit sandwich." I had two platoons and the CP group in the middle of what began as a two hundred fifty meter-wide rice paddy and now it seemed that it was "two and a half clicks wide." I immediately radioed 1st and 2d platoons to keep their heads down behind the rice paddy dikes, then for the 81 mortar FO, forward air controller, and artillery forward observer to get moving on getting rounds on the target. I didn't need to give coordinates. They knew where the enemy was located, about 50 meters to the front of 1st and 2d platoons and another 75 meters from the CP group.

Sadly, the 1st Platoon radio operator reported that Lt Chmiel had been killed instantly with the first volley of enemy fire along with SSgt Dixon, the platoon sergeant.

My second decision was to try and maneuver the CP group and Lt Bill Link with his 3d Platoon to the right flank into a wooded area. I hoped he and his Marines would be able to provide covering fire that would allow the CP group to move in their direction for cover on the right flank. 1st and 2d platoons were again instructed to stay put. If any of them were to try and move, they would have been wounded or killed. At this time the enemy was a very viable force to be dealt with. Delta Company didn't need any more wounded or killed Marines at this time. Lt Bill Link and his "Third Herd" would suffer their share of casualties in the not-to-distant future.

Initially, the 81mm mortars were doing their best to support two companies in contact, and in fairly short order depleted their ammo. This did not become a problem because our direct support artillery (D Battery, 2/11) began providing some relief to our company front.

I passed word to the company rear for everyone to try to maneuver into cover on our right flank. By late afternoon the company CP group and Link's platoon had maneuvered to cover, consolidated, and continued our engagement with the enemy in an effort to relieve the pressure on 1st and 2d Platoons that were still in the rice paddy.

I really needed to get my troops out of the paddies, and made a decision to deploy 3d Platoon and try out-flanking the enemy's left flank. Bill Link had good situational awareness of the battlefield and understood the "what, when, and where" of this maneuver.

First Lieutenant John Updyke, my forward air controller, was a stellar performer from the start of the engagement until the enemy began their withdrawal somewhere around 0330 or 0400 on 3 June. John became my fire support coordinator, and was able to expertly manage close air support, "Spooky" fire, and close artillery support continuously for five to six hours. Much of his time was spent exposing himself to the enemy in an effort to observe and provide fire accurately on their positions.

Bill Link's effort to flank the enemy was valiant, but unsuccessful because the enemy took the platoon under heavy fire from its front and right flank. The platoon was in a no-win situation, and I ordered him to return to the company CP area. Under the cover of darkness, he was able to bring most of his men out of another "shit sandwich." Remarkably, he extricated the platoon without the aid of radio contact with me. His radio operator was killed and the radio was damaged beyond repair shortly after I had called him back to the CP.

Lt Updyke continued his masterful work of providing close fire support coordinated with Link's extrication and our guys still in the paddies.

Mack's account reminds me of the extraordinary heroism of Private First Class William H. Myers, who was an assistant gunner in D Company's first machine-gun team. His unit, while moving to make an aggressive attack on the enemy, came under heavy automatic and semi-automatic small arms, grenade, and mortar fire. Myers' platoon maneuvered into position to provide flanking fire against the entrenched NVA soldiers. The platoon came under intense small arms fire from a range of about 200 yards, which killed the machine-gun team's gunner. Without hesitation, Myers picked up the machine gun and boldly advanced through withering fire across 150 yards of open rice paddy to get into a position to deliver enfilade fire on the NVA trench works. With enemy bullets and grenades tearing up the earth around him, Bill Myers raked the enemy with deadly fire that caused numerous NVA casualties and confusion in their ranks. When he ran out of ammunition, he fearlessly ran back across the open paddy to the body of his fallen gunner and retrieved the machine-gun ammunition that the gunner had been carrying. In the face of almost certain death, Myers again crossed the open paddy to return to his machine-gun position. He again opened fire on the enemy with deadly effect until an enemy sniper mortally wounded him. Delta Company then rallied and drove the NVA from their entrenched position.

How can you not be in awe of such heroism? He was posthumously awarded the Navy Cross, but the medal can't possibly reflect the admiration and love his fellow Marines have for Bill Myers. The courage, the dedication to duty, the instinctive reaction to do the right thing is what makes a good combat soldier. Bill Myers was one of the best of the best. May God bless him!

While Delta Company was heavily engaged with the enemy, Foxtrot began receiving concentrated enemy fire as they continued down into the rice paddy. The NVA were concealed in pits covered with rice mats. We called these camouflaged positions spider traps, and the enemy used them frequently. Our "Kit Carson" scout (a repatriated Viet Cong soldier) spotted the spider traps and began firing into the mats.

My two lead companies were now heavily engaged. We called for close air support and artillery to assist in the battle. The heavy fire from the NVA defenses stalled our advance, and both Delta and Foxtrot stayed put waiting for the air strikes and artillery support to soften up the enemy.

About 1400 hours, I had to commit Alpha Company to the battle to ward off an enemy attack on Foxtrot's left flank. In the process of moving up to relieve the pressure on Foxtrot's left flank, Captain Ron Babich moved to close the gap between his Alpha Company and Foxtrot Company. While moving to link-up with Foxtrot, Alpha took heavy small arms and automatic weapons fire from an enemy platoon well concealed in brush and vegetation on a small hill on the left flank. Captain Babich attacked the trench position, and in the assault was killed, along with his radio operator, and several other A Company troopers. Alpha secured the hill and blocked the enemy's attempt to break Foxtrot's left flank, but we paid a heavy price with the loss of a superb Marine officer and four of my fine warriors. The NVA losses were six times greater, but that doesn't even the score for me. I deeply felt those losses then, and still do. Paul Kellogg, then a Second Lieutenant commanding Alpha Company's Third Platoon, gave the following account of Ron's death.

> When the NVA hit the Second Battalion's Foxtrot Company, Colonel Hilgartner sent the First Battalion's Alpha Company to attack the NVA positions to relieve the pressure on Foxtrot. Captain Babich, commanding Alpha, moved the company out to attack the enemy aggressively and without hesitation. Captain Babich led the company into terrain covered with extremely high bushes that made it virtually impossible for the attacking Marines to see the concealed enemy. When we made contact, we engaged more than a platoon of the enemy in a heavy firefight and scattered them. The Third Platoon's lead fire team encountered a lone NVA soldier hidden in a huge rock crevice at ground level who shot and wounded the point Marine. The NVA soldier tried to drag the wounded Marine back to his hiding place, causing the wounded man to cry out. The NVA soldier shot and killed two more Marines following the point, who came to assist the wounded Marine. The remaining squad members took cover. Captain Babich arrived on the scene, and began organizing the Marines for an attack on the NVA's entrenched position. The intensity of the fight and rifle fire probably caused him not to hear Marines warning him of the sniper in the area who was still in the fight. While on his feet and yelling encouragement to his troops, the enemy sniper shot and killed Captain Babich. A short time later a Marine flanked the NVA soldier and killed him. I will always

remember Captain Babich's courage and inspiration for those Marines who fought with him. He was an aggressive fighter and a fine Marine.

Once again I called on my reliable communications officer, Captain Jerry McKay, to come to my assistance. Jerry stepped into the breach and assumed temporary command of Alpha Company to replace the fallen Ron Babich. Ron's troops remember him as a fine combat leader and an exceptionally brave Marine.

At 1430 hours, I moved my command group to a higher position nearer the center of our line of battle so we could better observe the action around us. After assuming our new position, we immediately came under heavy mortar fire. Fortunately, there was a huge crater at the location. My entire command group jumped into the crater to take shelter, which kept us from getting any casualties from the incoming mortar rounds.

My First Battalion of less than 500 Marines was taking on a regimental size enemy force of over 2,000 highly trained and well-disciplined NVA troops willing to defend Vinh Huy aggressively because this village was the headquarters of their Third NVA Regiment.[17] As McInturff said, Delta and Foxtrot Companies were now fully engaged with the enemy as we tried to move around the enemy's left flank without success.

About an hour later, at roughly 1530, I received a radio call from Captain Graham. While his Foxtrot Company was crossing an open rice paddy, mortar and automatic weapons fire from a bordering hedgerow raked his troops with deadly effect. With Graham stalled by the crossfire from the well-situated enemy, I called for supporting fire. When the barrage ended, Foxtrot again started forward, and advanced almost to the enemy's defensive perimeter. Halfway to the hedgerow, raking fire from two previously unseen NVA machineguns tore into Graham's Second Platoon, which was in the lead. More than half dozen men were killed or

---

wounded. The rest dropped behind the paddy dikes taking cover from the two machineguns. Some of Foxtrot's Marines were so far forward that they had been killed and wounded near the NVA spider traps.

I had been talking with Jim Graham on the radio for about three hours as well as to the other company commanders. I had a clear understanding of what was going on and where my troops were, but Jim didn't tell me he was going to retrieve his casualties that were still lying in the rice paddy. Then, on his own and without telling me, Captain Graham took a small unit of ten men from his company headquarters group to recover his wounded Marines. He was concerned that his wounded would be slaughtered by the NVA, which they would have been had the enemy been able to get to them.

In the ensuing assault, Graham forced the enemy to abandon the first machinegun. This relieved the pressure on his Second Platoon, and enabled evacuation of some of the wounded to a more secure area. Graham then attacked the second machinegun to retrieve the remainder of his dead and wounded, and shot his way into the fringes of one of the village hamlets. By this time, he had been wounded twice while personally killing fifteen enemy troops. He was now trapped himself, and radioed me for help.

Because I didn't know he had undertaken this assault, I was in no position to get an attack organized quickly to rescue him and his squad of fine Marines. We had no reserves. Everyone was committed. Alpha and Delta were fully engaged, and Foxtrot was now being led by a second lieutenant in their own firefight. We had no reserves! I told Graham we had no troops available to relieve the enemy pressure on his unit and bring him out. I asked him if he could get out on his own, but he said he would not leave any of his wounded or dead behind.

The last words Jim Graham said to me were, "We're being attacked by at least 25 enemy soldiers. Bring supporting fire down on top of us. Semper fi!"

He must have put down his radio to fight because I didn't hear from him again. When we got to the hamlet on Saturday, we found Jim Graham's body with those of his 10 men. Captain

Graham's action was very heroic, and he was awarded a posthumous Medal of Honor.

I can't tell you how upset I was over the loss of Captain Graham and his Marines because I thought we could have avoided it. If Graham had been a company commander permanently assigned to my battalion, he would have told me of his intention to assault the NVA machine gun emplacements to retrieve his wounded. I would have disapproved the idea until we could have organized a stronger effort to mount the attack. As noble as it is to retrieve your casualties, it doesn't make sense to create more and endanger the success of the operation in the process. We could have used our own protective small arms and automatic weapons fire to keep the NVA from our casualties lying in the rice paddy. The NVA weren't so intent on killing our wounded that they were willing to take heavy casualties to do so.

After Graham's action, the next senior officer in Foxtrot Company was a second lieutenant who became the acting company commander. Now we had a junior officer, unseasoned in combat, leading a heavily engaged F Company. We did not need this! This was bad break number two.

The lesson here is clear. A battalion will perform better, as a rule, when it has its own units instead of ones borrowed from another battalion. It is important for the company commander to know and have confidence in his battalion commanding officer. It is equally important for the battalion commander to know how his company commanders will think and react in a crisis.

We were now in a tough spot. We had lost the Foxtrot Company commander and a large number of his troops. Alpha and Bravo companies had also suffered heavy casualties. We needed help from another battalion to come in from the east to attack the NVA's left flank. I appraised Colonel Houghton and his S-3, Dick Alger, of the situation, and they concurred in my request for a reinforcing attack on the enemy's left flank. Colonel Houghton got the Division Commander, Major General Herman Nickerson, to release the Division reserve, Houghton's Second Battalion, less Captain Graham's Foxtrot Company.

Lieutenant Colonel Mallet C. Jackson, Jr. commanded the Second Battalion. Mal was an outstanding officer, and I liked him. Jackson, with only two under strength companies available, moved in to support me with the attack on the enemy's left flank. The helicopter assigned to transport Mal and his command group to the battle area developed mechanical problems as it was getting ready to lift off. Mal then assigned Major Dick Esau, his S-3 who was already airborne, to lead the attack. Dick came into the area after dark, landed unopposed and secured the landing zone for the rest of the Second Battalion. Once on the landing zone, and after reorganizing his troops, Esau reported to regimental headquarters by radio that he was on the ground and ready to go. Regiment ordered him to attack immediately enemy positions near a large Vietnamese archway down the road. The attack caught the enemy by surprise as they were beginning to withdraw.

This attack was successful in relieving the pressure against my battalion and inflicted heavy losses on the enemy. Dick Esau showed great professionalism and skill in this very difficult night maneuver as he brought the Second Battalion troops into unfamiliar hostile territory in the darkness of night, quickly organized them after insertion, and moved out aggressively to attack. The Second Battalion's quick entry into the battle saved the day for us.

The next morning a most unusual thing happened. There was a heavy fog over the rice paddy battlefield that morning. As it began to lift, I received a radio message from the Delta company commander, Mack McInturff, that the NVA had litter bearers out in the field collecting their dead and wounded. Mack requested permission to fire on them. I thought this might be our chance to retrieve our own dead and wounded. So, I told Mack to hold fire and send our own recovery details out to get our casualties.

"Mack, you will only open fire if the enemy starts shooting at our people. Is that clear?"

"Yes sir," he replied.

This is the way Mac McInturff remembers this part of the Union II engagement:

By the time the 3d Platoon made it back to the CP it was early morning on 3 June and still dark. Fire from the enemy had stopped, but I continued to keep the battlefield lit with artillery and "Spooky" flares.

In the light of the flares, some of my Marines observed enemy movement in the zone of contact between Foxtrot and Delta companies. Their actions and movement indicated they were searching the battlefield. My initial thought was to engage the bastards because I thought they might be looking for wounded Marines, either Jim Graham's or mine, that were still in the paddies. Lieutenant Colonel Hilgartner, my battalion commander, told me that they very well could be looking for their own killed or wounded, and that this might be a good opportunity to do the same thing. I took his guidance and had Bill Link organize a search party and go into the rice paddies to search for our wounded and dead. It was in the early morning and still dark; so, I had John Updyke suspend the battlefield illumination to prevent the enemy from firing on Link's search party.

Link's platoon brought back those Marines of 1st and 2d Platoons that they could find. This task was accomplished without taking any more casualties; one other indication that the enemy may have been looking and retrieving their guys. By daylight the enemy had "pulled chocks," as Updyke said, and departed the immediate area.

By dawn, Marines were the only ones left policing the battlefield. Just at daylight, we dug up two enemy bodies that highly resembled Chinese soldiers. After my initial report, I received orders not to mention the word 'Chinese' again.

At the break of daylight, I had the remainder of the company looking for what remained of our troops to get those that needed evacuation on incoming choppers. What I got was a chopper load of "press people" delivered to my CP. This I didn't need, and I didn't appreciate the "powers

that be" for allowing this abomination to occur. The last
thing that Delta Company needed was a bunch of "shithead
national reporters" taking away needed chopper space for
our wounded and dead in addition to questioning my troops
about the events of the previous night and early morning.
The troops were tired, hungry, and pissed.

We spent the remainder of 3 June 1967 policing the
battlefield to include the remnants of Jim Graham's Foxtrot
Company.

I agree with Mack's assessment of allowing the press into the
battlefield so early. Freedom of the press be damned; Division
should not have allowed it! Our troopers still had work to do. We
had no time to be interviewed by reporters, many of whom were
intent on asking hostile questions implying that in reality we had
been defeated, and that our command was engaged in a cover up.
Mack's commentary that they were a "bunch of shithead national
reporters" describes a press corps that had a well-earned reputation
in Vietnam. Mack and I may need more sensitivity training, but
when it comes to a firefight, I want *him* with me, and not some
rear echelon pissant who is exquisitely attuned to saying the right
things to the press and politicians.

I give the enemy commander great credit for his professionalism.
He had his troops well positioned to defend against our assault. He
was tactically very sound. Also I believe he used this casualty recovery
time both to retrieve his wounded, and to cover his withdrawal of
the main part of his troops to fight again on another day. He did
leave his KIAs on the battlefield for us to count, much to the
delight of MACV Headquarters and McNamara's "Whiz Kids" in
the Pentagon who kept such tallies in search for their "light at the
end of the tunnel." The time we spent counting NVA KIAs further
added to the enemy's withdrawal time cushion.

The NVA commander was crafty in using the casualty recovery
to evacuate his main body. He must have known that because of
our large number of casualties and the many bodies he left in the
field, that we would not pursue him until after we had recovered

all our dead and wounded and counted his KIAs. That was First Marine Division policy. Whether he knew that or not, I don't know, but the enemy's intelligence collection with undercover spies always seemed better than ours.

Colonel Houghton deserves much of the credit for the overall results of both Union I and Union II. He planned the battle strategy and tactics, and gave his troops engaged with the enemy, the artillery, the air support, and the reinforcements we needed to win. He was a superb regimental commander and all that I, or any battalion commander, could ask for.

How did we do in the Union battles? Pretty damned good! For both the Union I and Union II Operations the Fifth Marine Regiment received the Presidential Unit Citation. My battalion killed no less than 258 of the 476 NVA killed during Union II, but we suffered 55 KIA's plus 71 wounded who were medically evacuated. In the Union I and II battles, we were outnumbered at least 3 to 1 by regular North Vietnamese Army troops. They were tough fights! I am, and forever will be, proud of the way my Marines conducted themselves. Their bravery and combat skill reflect the very best that a commander can ask of his troops in battle.

I did not anticipate the change in attitude of my First Battalion Marines as a result of the Union operations. There was a new sense of confidence that they were the best. In Union I and Union II they had fought and won two major battles against the enemy's first line regiments. These were not penny-fights against Viet Cong guerrillas. These were battles with the North Vietnamese Army's best troops. The officers and men of First Battalion, Fifth Marines had performed in an exemplary manner, especially First Lieutenant David McInturff, who for his gallantry in Union II received the Silver Star medal.

My Marines became cocky bastards who wouldn't take crap from anybody, either on the battlefield or in the regimental beer hall. They were confident we could take on anything the enemy threw at us and beat the best they had. This attitude helped us immeasurably in the rest of the engagements we fought during the coming months of my command. Self-confidence, and confidence that your battalion will always win, is a force multiplier! It is a self-fulfilling belief that only the best units possess. We had it, and it remains a proud swagger we all have to this day when we gather for One-Five reunions.

The other two Fifth Marine Battalions also fought well. The Presidential Unit Citation reflects great credit upon the entire Fifth Marine Regiment. Our regiment was the best of the best. We were confident in ourselves and our ability to win. We were ready for anything, and the war was far from over.

Corporal George M. Liburdi was the type of Marine every combat unit wants. He had quick reflexes, he was an excellent marksman, and he was absolutely fearless. Liburdi loved being the point man, on small or large patrols. If his unit was involved, he took the point and led the way.

A good point man is an invaluable asset to any infantry unit. In Vietnam, the good point men were often Marines with hunting experience. The woods and jungle are noisy places, with birds singing, squirrels chattering, and a thousand other noises from nature. If it is quiet, something is wrong! It may be an ambush waiting for you. Sometimes a good point man can even smell the enemy. Liburdi was the best. He was a lifesaver. He had a nose for trouble, and could sniff it out before it struck.

But Liburdi had a dark side. When he was on liberty, or at the Da Nang recreational beach, Liburdi always got into big trouble. Booze was usually the root of his misbehavior. When Liburdi had too much to drink, he became an animal.

Liburdi would get into trouble, return from liberty in custody of the Shore Patrol or Military Police and on report. He would then come before me at office hours, and I would reduce him in rank. After getting busted, Liburdi would go on patrol again as point, kill some bad guys, receive a citation for bravery, and come before me for an award. I would promote him back to corporal, and the cycle would be ready to repeat itself. The cycle happened frequently, and I got to know Liburdi better than any other corporal in the battalion.

Liburdi's last appearance before me for disciplinary reasons came after he went to Chu Lai and trashed the Armed Forces Radio Station. I was not happy with him for that bit of mischief, and once again I reduced him in rank. I also talked with the company commander and the sergeant major about Liburdi's behavior. We decided no more trips to Chu Lai for Liburdi during the rest of his time in the battalion, no matter how well he performed in the field.

After Union II, once again the battalion gave decorations, promotions, and trips to Chu Lai to men for performing well on the operation. We had planned a special awards and rewards ceremony to recognize our battalion's best performers, and the day before the ceremony the sergeant major came to me to discuss the events for the next day.

That was when he asked me, "What are we going to do about Liburdi, Colonel? Tomorrow he's scheduled to receive a Bronze Star medal and Lieutenant McInturff, his company commander, wants him promoted back to corporal."

The sergeant major then filled me in on the great things Liburdi did during Union II. While on point during a platoon patrol, he uncovered an ambush, attacked the enemy troops, routed them, and pursued the fleeing enemy to enable his unit to continue on their mission without taking any casualties. My reaction was, WOW! If we had more Marines like Luburdi we could win this war in no time. He was a killing machine.

"Sergeant major, here's what we're going to do. I'll promote him again. Immediately after the ceremony we will send Liburdi home on R and R so his family can see what a hero their son is. Otherwise he'll be going home in a box. His good luck can't last forever."

The sergeant major's eyes opened wide, "Colonel, we can't do this," he said, "Corporals don't get sent back to the states on R and R. Officers sometimes do, but not troopers."

"Well," I said, "we are going to do this with Liburdi."

It took some doing, but I pulled strings and Liburdi went home to California with medals and stripes.

About a month later, the personnel officer came to see me and gave me the bad news. After Liburdi arrived home, he was killed in an automobile accident. I thought I had cheated his fate by sending him home to avoid what most likely awaited him in the Vietnam bush. But Liburdi's fate awaited him on the streets of his hometown in California. I felt really bad about this. Liburdi was a fine warrior. At least he had one last visit with his family.

Operation Union II ended on 5 June 1967 and for the next three months things were relatively quiet. The battalion search and destroy missions continued, and one day folded into the next. I never knew what day of the week it was until the chaplain came in for Sunday religious services.

I was bone thin after losing forty pounds, and was so tired I felt I was in another hazy world. I had commanded the battalion for seven months and my Vietnam tour wouldn't end for another four or five months. I dreaded the thought that I might be relieved and sent to the rear in a staff job. I would hate that with a passion!

One morning I was sitting on the edge of the porch leading into the Operations (S-3) hut and command center, when my S-4, Captain Art Blades, approached. Art had performed in an outstanding manner as executive officer of Charlie Company and then as C.O. of Alpha Company. I had reassigned him as S-4 when Captain Terry Cooper rotated home, and Art was doing an excellent job there. Both Blades and Cooper were fine Marines. They both became lieutenant generals. I like to think I trained them well.

As Art approached, I could tell he had something on his mind. He was not smiling, as was his usual manner.

"What's up Art?" I asked.

"Sir, I am getting ready to rotate back to the States and I am requesting a recommendation from you for my next duty assignment."

"What do you have in mind, Art?"

"Sir, I wish to enter the Marine aviation program."

"You what?"

"Sir, I wish to become a Marine aviator."

"Why?"

"Sir, I've always wanted to fly."

"Damn it, Art, you've done a superb job here. You have a bright future in the infantry. You are general officer material in Marine infantry. I want to ask you something . . . are you just tired of sleeping on the ground?" (I knew that I was!) I thought this comment might trigger that famous Art Blades smile.

"No, sir, I believe I can do more for the grunts in getting them good close air support than I can commanding them on the ground."

Now that was a good response, I thought. This officer will go far whether he's infantry or air, and the Corps will be better for it. I remembered there once was a young Marine who only wanted to be an infantry officer and had to serve a combat tour in artillery first. It was like seeing the same movie with a slightly different plot.

"O.K., Art, I'll do it. Good luck!"

With that he snapped to and gave me a big salute. Years went by before I saw Art again. When our paths crossed, he was a Lieutenant General, Marine Corps Aviation. I was, and am, as proud and happy for him as if he had been my son. And in a way he is my son, as are all of my First Battalion Marines.

After the Union operations, my Marines were in good fighting condition. They were battle-tested and proven. They knew what to do, how to do it, and when. I believed I had earned Colonel Houghton's respect, and I wanted to stay in command of the First Battalion, or in my wildest dream, command the Fifth Marines. But the road ahead was going to have some unforeseen turns and bumps.

On the 30 June, Colonel Houghton became the new Division G-2 (Intelligence), and Colonel Stanley Davis replaced him as the new regimental commander. Shortly after Colonel Davis reported aboard, he called to say he wanted to see me. I received this news with great foreboding.

Our meeting took place in an old Vietnamese chateau. I remember walking into the building and going upstairs to Colonel Davis' office. He asked me to be seated, and we began to talk. I had never met him before, but from the outset I could tell the meeting was going to be cordial, and that I would like him.

"Glad to meet you, Pete," the colonel said. "You've been doing a good job, and you've had this battalion a long time."

"Thank you, sir, but seven months hasn't been all that long."

"How do you feel about going back to division headquarters for a nice cushy staff job?"

This caused me a long moment of pause. Rumors were that several division staff pogues disliked me. I knew who they were because they were making my battalion job harder by laying on a load of chickenshit "administrivia." I had my hands full with the NVA and Viet Cong. I didn't have time for asinine gamesmanship with staff idiots who were trying to let me know they were boss. I clearly had a problem with some members of the division headquarters staff. They didn't like me and I had no use for them. If I were to go back to a division staff job, it would only be a matter of time before I decked one of them after Happy Hour at the O-Club. I really didn't need that on my record.

"Well, sir, I'd probably get into trouble at headquarters. I've had disagreements with some of the division staff. They don't like me, and the feeling is more than mutual. I think dying in combat would be preferable to putting up with a lot of chickenshit nonsense and backbiting. Colonel, forgive me for being so candid, but the truth's the truth, and I hope you won't hold it against me for speaking frankly."

"I can handle the unvarnished truth," Colonel Davis replied. "If I couldn't handle it, I wouldn't have asked your opinion. So, you're telling me that you would rather keep your battalion until your end of tour in Vietnam?"

"Yes, sir, I would. If this meets with your approval. I would, however, like a little break. Frankly I'm a bit tired right now."

"How about a few days at Chu Lai?" he said.

"Well, sir, my family is in Hawaii. I'd rather go there, if that is appropriate and possible."

"You know that division policy is not to give an officer R and R until he completes his combat command assignment," he said. "However, I too want you to stay on as battalion commander. I'll see what I can do. If you get R and R in Hawaii, it will be the only one ever given prior to completion of a combat command assignment that I know of."

"Thank you, sir. I would really appreciate getting that R and R, and I do want to stay with the First Battalion."

Frank White's tour as executive officer was about over and his replacement, Major Ernest Cheatham, had reported in. I told Colonel Davis that these two could run the battalion very well while I was gone, and Ernie Cheatham would benefit by working with White. I had complete confidence in both of these officers and knew they would not disappoint me.

Diana, David and Pete

A short time later I received word that the R & R request was approved, and that I would retain command of the battalion when I returned. A group of us flew to Honolulu and were bused to Fort De Russey where my family was anxiously waiting. I was so excited about seeing them that I wasn't sure I would be able to control my emotions. I didn't want anyone to see a Marine with tears in his eyes; so, I donned sunglasses. My daughter Diana told me later that was the only time she ever saw me wear "shades".

The ten days in Hawaii were wonderful. We had a complimentary suite in one of the famous old hotels on Waikiki Beach with the ocean only a few steps from our room. I had a wonderful time playing with the three girls and my baby boy in the ocean. All had grown while I was gone, and each of the girls was prettier than ever. My new son, David, was a joy to me, and the salt water felt wonderful on my tired body. The visit was far too short.

I slept most of the way on the plane trip back to Da Nang. When I arrived a helicopter returned me to Hill 51. Corporal Billy Long, my driver, greeted me on my return.

"Welcome back Colonel. We're all glad you are back. We sure have missed you. We have a patrol out now and it's lost. We don't know where it is."

"What?" I shouted and ran for the operations bunker. Both White and Cheatham greeted me when I walked in and confirmed what Billy told me. They had just received the word on the patrol and were getting a platoon saddled up to go find it. A couple of hours later we found the patrol and brought it in. My little welcome back crisis ended on a good note.

The operations during those summer months were ADAIR, CALHOUN, and COCHISE. I quickly returned to the grind of daily operations, and each combat mission blended into the next. I do, however, remember one operation in particular.

We had moved out of the combat base early in the day, and been walking a long time. There was no enemy contact; however, during the day, we moved into an area where we knew enemy forces were operating. Soon enough, we discovered several caves of the kind the Viet Cong and NVA troops used for shelter. We brought up a German Shepherd dog to sniff out the caves, and found one to be "hot"—bad guys were inside. Rather than sending in a Marine to deal with them, I decided to seal the entrance. We didn't know how many were in the cave, but the dog revealed the presence of at least one enemy soldier hiding inside. So while the engineers were coming forward to plant demolitions to seal the entrance, I sat down on a stump near a large tree.

I had no sooner been seated when a Marine said in a low, firm voice. "Colonel, don't move and don't even turn your head. Sir, freeze right where you are. You are sitting next to a booby trap that is primed to explode."

The Marine then called to the engineers who were nearby

working on the cave entrance. Thankfully, the engineers showed up quickly and diffused the booby trap, which was a hidden satchel of explosives that would have blown me all the way back to Honolulu, or at least into Cambodia. I confess that I had some very uneasy moments while the engineers were defusing the booby trap. I kept wondering if the parting view of my family at Fort De Russey before going back to the plane was to be the last time I would ever see them. I closed my eyes and tried to remember what they looked like. If I had to go, I wanted my last vision to be of my family. The engineers did their job quickly. Thank God they knew what they were dealing with and how to disarm it. That was my second close call with a booby trap! Those Marines saved my life.

Now we had a river to cross. It was turning dark and beginning to rain. At first the crossing was easy, but the current soon became more swift and treacherous. We lost a machine gun, and several more pieces of equipment followed it down river. About the time my sergeant major told me that all hands were across, the rain came and it poured torrents. The sky was so black we could barely see one another.

With this torrential downpour, we couldn't go anywhere. For me, control of my battalion troops became of paramount importance. I passed the word for the troopers to bunch up like a herd of cattle and hold hands. I wanted every man to close into a circle as tight as possible.

When I gave this command, my ever so tactful sergeant major said, "Colonel, this is the craziest thing I've ever seen you do. One round from the enemy and they'll get us all."

I always welcomed frank opinions from my sergeant major, but I growled right back, "No, they're all under cover too, and trying not to get soaked."

Then the rain stopped as suddenly as it began. We had made so many night movements before that the troops knew exactly what to do. They uncoiled from the circle and quietly began to move out in single file. I took a position near the point to ensure that we stayed on the trail. Then the moon came out. All was deathly quiet along our route as a shimmering silver-blue cast from the moonlight bathed the trail and surrounding trees in a surreal glow. It looked like a dream.

The lead company commander came to me and quietly said, "Sir, I believe we are near our objective."

The entire battalion knew the plan. Our objective was a remote village that the enemy was using as a base. We would attack at dawn from the east so that the sun would be in the enemy's eyes. Two companies would attack abreast. The reserve would follow in the center of the formation on my command.

It was about four in the morning. The company commanders and officers were positioning their troops and getting them ready for the fight set to begin at thirty minutes before sunrise. I decided to take a break while all this was going on. The grass was wet, but I put my helmet on the ground and lay down with my head resting on it.

The next thing I heard was the sergeant major whispering in my ear, "Colonel, if you don't wake up you'll miss the fight."

As I sat up the attack began. It went like clockwork. With the sunrise at our backs, the enemy had trouble seeing us, and we took them completely by surprise. They woke up to the sound of our small arms and automatic weapons fire, and stepped out of their hooches into a hail of death. We totally destroyed the enemy, and my Marines had no casualties. It was like picking low hanging fruit.

I recalled the time in the Korean exercise when I successfully employed a similar tactic to surprise and capture a U.S. Army company. I may have ruined the planned tactical exercise and incurred my battalion commander's wrath, but I learned a lesson in Korea that I put to good use in Vietnam. I was in a very fine mood.

We received orders to occupy the village for the night, so we spent the day organizing a defensive perimeter. The H & S company commander selected a grass-roofed hut in the village for the command post. The hut had a dirt floor, and in the rural Vietnamese custom, chickens, pigs, and a mother duck with ducklings shared the hut with the people who had lived there.

The usual assortment of forward observers and communications personnel accompanied my command group on this mission. In addition, we had a naval gunfire support coordinator with us, a fine looking young Navy lieutenant. He reminded me of Staff Sergeant Mallard who worked for me years before in Quantico. I thought Mallard and this young officer could have been brothers they looked so much alike.

When night came, we tried to get some sleep in between standing watches and keeping alert when we weren't on watch. We knew we were in hostile territory, and bad guys were out there waiting for an opportunity to do us harm. There was always someone awake to make sure we didn't get an unpleasant surprise. When I woke up the next morning, I noted that our gunfire officer was still soundly asleep on his back with his arms folded across his waist. The mother duck, with her ducklings tightly nestled beneath her, sat in the center of his chest. It was a most peaceful sight.

Everybody in the command post group was awake by this time, except our naval officer. As he awoke, mother duck with her brood moved quietly off his chest and the whole place was filled with laughter. In the Marine Corps, almost anything can get you a nickname. If someone asked, "Where's Lieutenant Duck?" there was no question about who they were looking for. The moniker stuck as long as he was with us.

In a way, the operation was typical of those we conducted that summer. Most of our movements were at night. The troops ate only two meals a day. Our rations had three meals, but we could move an extra day without resupply if we only ate two. Resupply was usually by helicopter, and that brought a major disadvantage that we were anxious to avoid. When the choppers came to our positions the enemy knew exactly where we were. The longer we could keep the choppers away, the safer my men were. Better safety was an easy tradeoff for the inconvenience of missing a meal every day.

•

Military regulations stipulate that sleeping on watch is a serious crime. In fact, if a soldier were to fall asleep while on watch in combat, he could be court-martialed and shot. In Vietnam we were always tired, but I know of no Marine who was caught, court martialed, or executed for falling asleep while on watch. With the schedule we had to keep, sleep was a luxury. I rarely got more than three or four hours of sleep a night in the Que Son Valley, and my Marines were lucky if they got that much with their combat patrols and Hill 51 work schedules.

Since we were all tired, and for our safety while in a defensive posture, I directed that *all* officers and senior noncommissioned officers would walk the lines each night. This would keep the troops alert, and protect us from unpleasant surprises. The battalion X.O. and I walked the lines until 10 p.m., majors and captains between 10 p.m. and 2 a.m., lieutenants from 2 a.m. to 6 a.m. The X.O. and I alternated nights. I usually had the sergeant major and Vince Capodanno, our Navy Catholic chaplain, with me. I'm sure the captains also took their first sergeants with them. It was good to have company while making the rounds, and Vince Capodanno always had warm words of encouragement for the troopers. Vince had a wonderful way about him, and the troops all loved him. They looked forward to Vince's nightly visits from which they seemed to get a feeling that God was in His heaven and all was right with the world.

Our defensive position had a landline telephone network that we laid on the ground to encircle the entire Hill 51 perimeter. Each foxhole had a telephone connected to the landline, so they could pass important information along. Walking the lines was good for troop morale, and also kept the men awake and alert. Until 10 p.m. they could expect to see Major Cheatham or me. When we appeared in one fighting position, the word would be passed to alert the next Marine that we were on the way. I wanted this information passed on. I didn't want some nervous trooper to shoot me.

One night I was walking the lines and came to a Marine stationed in a small cave with a machine gun aimed over the battlefield. When I appeared I usually greeted the Marine and asked him how he was doing. The usual answer was, "I'm fine, sir."

When I approached the machine gun position, I gave the usual greeting. The Marine answered saying, "I'm okay, sir, but this cave sure is a lousy position." I asked him why he thought that. He replied that when the enemy attacked, bullets could come into the cave and ricochet around the walls.

"It's a death trap," he said.

The Marine had a point, but he was overlooking something. So, I asked him what he would be doing when he saw the enemy coming across the rice paddy.

"Oh, I'd be shooting them, sir."

"That's right and you'll be killing them, and they'll be real busy trying to get out of your line of fire. In fact they will be so busy I doubt if any of their rounds will find their way in here at all."

That seemed to settle him down. I was certain this was one Marine who wouldn't give anyone coming across that rice paddy in front of him the time or opportunity to fire any rounds into his cave.

When we reached the next fighting position, I noticed that Chaplain Capodanno wasn't with us. "Sergeant Major, where is the chaplain?" I asked.

"He's still talking with that machine gunner in the cave. I think the Padre is giving him a bible or something."

"Let's wait for him to catch up. He shouldn't be running around here in the dark all by himself. I don't want some nervous trooper shooting him by mistake."

Walking the lines was dangerous stuff, and for the chaplain alone it could have been fatal; so, we waited for him to catch up. When Father Vince accompanied us in walking the lines, it always took longer to make the rounds because he stopped to chat with each Marine, and to give each his blessing and often a gift. I have no idea where Father Vince got all those gifts he passed out, but I do know his visits to the fighting positions cheered the troops beyond anything I can describe. The Padre was a monumental morale booster!

I had so little sleep while we occupied Hill 51 that I can only remember one place I had a cot. It was summer time and extremely hot during the day. The coolest place I could find at night was in a small banana grove near the operations "hooch," which was an old Vietnamese house that was covered with tenting because the tile roofing had been blown off. I had a telephone extension from our base landline next to my cot so that I was always immediately available to all my troopers on watch. Communications with headquarters and other higher authorities was via radio.

One morning about 2 am, I had just stretched out on my cot, positioned the mosquito netting so no bugs could bother me, and was almost asleep when the phone's little bell rang.

I picked up the phone and said the usual, "Cottage Six."

What I heard was not one of my Marines. This call was from the White House in Washington, D.C. I was in "Indian Country," and we damn sure had no landline to Washington.

The voice said, "This is Mr. XYZ, Chief of Staff for the President. What are you trying to do Colonel, start World War III?"

At that, I was now wide awake and really ticked off at being so rudely awakened. I replied testily, "I don't know who you are, sir, but I am out here fully occupied fighting the enemy. I follow the orders I've been given. If you have a problem with what I'm doing, you need to speak with my regimental commander or division commander." Then I slammed the phone down on the receiver. I may have also said, ". . . and the horse you rode in on!" If I didn't, I wish I had.

I then called the regimental commander and told him about the White House phone call. I have no idea whether Colonel Davis later received a call complaining about me, and I never found out what that self-important White House staffer was concerned about. That was my one and only call from Washington to my digs in Indian Country, but it really opened my eyes to the communications capability that we had. The Pentagon and political bureaucrats could micromanage this war down to the foxhole level with this capability. Can you imagine my Marine in his cave firing at enemy troops coming across the rice paddy being interrupted by a phone call from some pissant Washington bureaucrat asking him if he's trying to start World War III?

That little vignette of White House bureaucratic command and control still raises my ire. Lives are at risk in combat, and some politico who has never heard a shot fired in anger has no business on the battlefield, in person or by phone.

The summer of 1967 was hot, like it is every summer in Vietnam. During the day we would endure triple digit temperatures even in the shade, as much as 120 degrees at times.

In early July, two new Navy medics reported to the battalion for duty. One was a corpsman and the other was the new battalion doctor. At the initial briefing I noted that the corpsman was very overweight. My first inclination was to send him back to the rear. He wouldn't make it because he was not in shape, and I told him so. However, he protested and told me he would keep up. I told him, that he had better not fall behind, because we weren't going to carry him anywhere.

"We'll leave you where you drop to be captured or killed by the enemy," I said.

Then one day while we were on a battalion operation, strung out on an open trail, I received word that our overweight corpsman had collapsed on the side of the road. I walked back to the rear with the company commander to check on the collapsed medic.

I said in a loud voice, "Captain we are not going to wait for that fat S.O.B. Leave him here to die." Then I gave the order for the battalion to move out.

After we had gone around a bend in the road, a short distance and out of sight, I instructed the company commander to drop off a fire team to cover this slob. "Have the fire team catch up with us when he gets up. They *will not* carry him. He must catch up on his own."

A short time later I received word that the corpsman and fire team had rejoined the column.

A month or so later I was sitting in the C.P. in a shady place when a fine looking Marine appeared. The young man saluted and requested permission to speak with me.

"Sir, do you remember me?" he asked. Well, to be honest, I did not. Then he said, "I'm that fat corpsman you said wouldn't make it. I just wanted you to know I'm still here."

"Congratulations," I said, "and you look a whole lot better. You must have lost about fifty pounds." He smiled and departed.

This next incident occurred a few days after the two medics had joined us. The X.O. told me that the new battalion surgeon wanted to speak with me. "He's pretty angry," the X.O. said. At the time I was sitting on the front steps of the porch to the operations hut.

The doctor marched up and said, "Colonel, I'm placing you on report to the regiment for disobeying orders."

"What orders?" I asked.

"You are disobeying the division order that requires Marines in this battalion to wear flak jackets."

"Well, Doc," I answered, "we do wear our flak jackets, at night in defensive positions, when it's cooler. It's too hot during the day, and we have a lot fewer cases of heat exhaustion doing it this way."

"Orders are orders, Colonel, I'm still going to put you on report."

My hackles began to rise. "Well, Doc, you can put me on report, but since you haven't done so yet, and before you do, I'm going to give you a direct order. If you violate this order, you will be court-martialed. I order you to wear a flak jacket day and night for the next thirty days. That includes when you sleep. You will not take it off at any time, except to bathe. Is that clear? You will do this for thirty days, and then come back to see me. I am entering this order in your file!" (I never did, but he didn't know that.)

I had a lot on my mind and forgot all about this affair. Time must have flown, because one day the doctor showed up again. "Colonel," he said, "my thirty days are up. I have carried out your order to the letter. You are right, sir, that flak jacket is too hot for the men to wear during the day. I request that my complaint be withdrawn."

"I'm glad you now see the light, Doc. There's a reason for everything we do out here, and it's to try and keep these Marines alive while still accomplishing our mission. If you see something you don't like or understand in the future, you are welcome to come talk with me about it. By the way, I think you've lost a little weight. You look a lot better. You can remove that flak jacket now. You may want to put it on again after dark when it cools down."

That lesson was also applicable to the SLF battalion. They came ashore wearing flack jackets, and suffered heat casualties in much greater numbers than did Marines stationed ashore. The heavy SLF heat casualties were caused by a combination of not being conditioned to the Vietnamese heat and weather and wearing flack jackets. Watching the SLF fire and maneuver, was like watching slow motion. They appeared to be hardly moving when they wore flack jackets. The SLF quickly learned that unless there was a threat of mines or booby traps, flack jackets were detrimental to daylight operations.

The summer operations had an effect on the enemy beyond the damage we inflicted on him during the Union operations. We appeared to be firmly in control of the valley, and had introduced the Que Son District to the beginnings of electoral democracy. In fact, elections were soon to be held for the first time ever.

We had hurt the NVA and Viet Cong badly during the Union operations and the follow-on search and destroy operations during the summer. They had retreated to their sanctuaries in North Vietnam and across the border into Laos and Cambodia to bring their organizations back up to strength with replacements for their casualties, and to undergo training to get themselves combat ready again. The elections in Que Son most likely prompted the NVA to move back into the Que Son Valley before they were fully ready. I say this because regular NVA units appeared to have integrated VC units into their organizations. We found a large number of VC guerrilla KIAs among the uniformed NVA dead after the coming battles near Vinh Huy and Chau Lam.

Operation Swift began on 4 September and lasted for eleven days through 15 September when we helolifted the last unit of the

First Battalion, Fifth Marines out of the battle zone to return to our battalion combat base on Hill 51. The most intense action happened the first day, with scattered engagements following until the enemy withdrew from the area.

During the engagement we identified the First NVA Regiment, consisting of the 40th, 60th, and 90th Battalions with an estimated strength of 600 men per battalion. The enemy augmented the 1,800 man core units of the First NVA Regiment, with elements of the Third and Twenty-First NVA Regiments plus VC guerrilla units. Total enemy strength was about 2,500 troops.[18]

September 4: Day 1

Because of the elections, we received word to step up our patrolling activity to provide increased security for polling places. This meant patrolling in strength; so, I sent Delta Company on a mission to screen a polling place in the village of Dong Son. At 4:30 a.m. on 4 September, the enemy attacked Delta Company. The company commander, Captain Robert F. Morgan, who had assumed command of Delta Company in July, reported enemy troops on at least two sides.

Devastating NVA automatic weapons, mortar, and grenade fire wounded several of D Company's Marines and the forward air observer. Lance Corporal Thomas B. Driscoll immediately assumed all the duties of forward observer for air and artillery supporting fire. At about 5:30 a.m., Driscoll held a strobe light over his head to guide medevac helos in to recover D Company's wounded and to direct aircraft to the target. The enemy also saw the strobe light and targeted it with increasing accuracy to their fire, which became more intense. Driscoll exposed himself to heavy enemy sniper fire to guide the medevac helicopters into the LZ to evacuate his wounded comrades.

Enemy troops infiltrated the western part of the defensive perimeter throwing hand grenades into D Company's position.

---

[18]   Combat After Action Report; Headquarters First Battalion, Fifth Marines, First Marine Division, 16 September 1967.

Delta returned fire, and Driscoll called in artillery support and an armed Huey to break the enemy assault. Driscoll adjusted 105mm artillery fire with superb accuracy to assist Delta in destroying the infiltrators, and then attacking the enemy position in the village to the west. When D Company swept into Dong Son village, they received intense automatic weapons fire that fatally wounded Bob Morgan, D Company's commanding officer.

At this point, Second Lieutenant Carlton W. Fulford, Jr. assumed command of the company, and immediately radioed me for help. Fulford, a platoon commander, was the only officer left in the company who had not been killed or seriously wounded. He did a magnificent job in stepping into company command, organizing the survivors, and repulsing enemy attacks until reinforcements could be brought in to help bring D Company safely back to the First Battalion defensive perimeter.

After Swift, we promoted Fulford to First Lieutenant. In October, Regiment reassigned him as Commanding Officer F Company, Second Battalion, Fifth Marines, where he remained until his return from Vietnam in June 1968. For his Vietnam service, Fulford received the Silver Star, two Legions of Merit with Combat "V", the Bronze Star with Combat "V", and two Purple Hearts. Carl went on to a very distinguished Marine Corps career and became a four star general. He showed his stuff to us all that day in Swift when he took over D Company and brought his troops safely home.

In response to Fulford's call for help, I ordered Bravo Company under command of a fine warrior, Captain Tom Reese, to join up with Delta Company. I knew Bravo and Delta would still be outnumbered, but all my troops were otherwise committed. This was developing into a hell of a fight!

In a 1994 article by Eric Hammel that appeared in *Vietnam Magazine*, he wrote: "In typical reactive mode, the local battalion commander (*that was me*) attempted to relieve Delta Company with another company, a force too small to take on a larger NVA force."

That comment is just plain bullshit! If Hammel had better judgment, he would have called me to check his facts before publishing his article. Alpha Company was sidelined by an encounter with a rabid puppy. Now that's a story! Charley Company had been loaned to another battalion, and was on Nui Lac Son where they stayed until they were relieved by Delta after the fight at Dong Son so Delta could regroup. Bravo Company was all I had to commit to the rescue of Delta Company. I was out of rifle companies.

Let me come back to Alpha Company for a moment. I had well-publicized standing orders to all my troops that they were never, but NEVER, to adopt Vietnamese dogs or puppies for mascots. I love dogs as much as the next Marine, but many dogs in The Republic of Vietnam had rabies, which is not always easily detected in its early stages. Alpha Company violated my standing order and adopted a puppy that turned out to be rabid. The entire company remained at Hill 51 undergoing rabies shots, sidelining them during Swift. You have no idea how angry I was, and still am, about this. My only consolation was in knowing that the rabies shots, which go into the stomach, hurt like hell. I made the company commander get the shots along with his troops, and the battalion surgeon cooperated.

I was certain that this was going to be the major battle of my command, and I requested help from Colonel Davis, our new regimental commander. Colonel Davis responded by giving me operational control of companies K and M from the Third Battalion, Fifth Marines. These I then committed to the fight. I hope Eric Hammel reads this, and gets his facts on Operation Swift squared away before he writes any more Marine Corps history.

We dispatched medevac helicopters to extract D Company's wounded, but the enemy fired smoke grenades to mislead the incoming helos. When they neared the enemy position, the NVA opened fire and shot down two of our medevac helos. Delta was taking heavy automatic and semiautomatic weapons fire from an estimated NVA company in the vicinity of Dong Son that was backed up by the full enemy force of about 2,500 men throughout the area.[19]

---

19   Ibid.

At 8:20 a.m. my Bravo and Delta companies linked up on the west side of Dong Son and were in a heavy firefight. At about 9:00 a.m., an armed Huey dropped 400 pounds of tear gas on enemy positions. The NVA always thought our CS gas was poison; so, they broke off the engagement and fled the area to the north across the Song Ly Ly.[20] Our Bravo and Delta Company Marines pursued and attacked the fleeing enemy.

Later in the morning, about 10:00 a.m., we helolifted Captain Heinz into the battle area to take command of Delta Company for the fallen Bob Morgan. Heinz did an excellent job stepping into command a new company in the midst of the chaos of battle. He and Carl Fulford deserve great credit for keeping Delta Company an effective fighting force until I withdrew them from the area under orders from the regimental commander. We sent Delta to regroup at Nui Lac Son after the heavy casualties they suffered.

The NVA slipped back into the area around the village complex of Chau Lam and Vinh Huy. About noon, Bravo Company again received heavy automatic and semi-automatic small arms fire from well dug in and camouflaged enemy troops concealed in one of the three hamlets that comprised the village of Vinh Huy. Bravo Company returned the fire and called in an air strike. After the air strike, Tom Reese led B Company in an assault on the NVA position in the village and drove them out, killing 9 confirmed and 35 probable enemy troops, while taking 2 prisoners. This assault and the air strike's tear gas drop caused the enemy to abandon his position and flee once more to the north across the Song Ly Ly. Captain Reese kept the retreating NVA under small arms and machine gun fire. During this engagement, Captain Reese was severely wounded.

Also at noon, the Third Battalion, Fifth Marines K and M Companies linked up with my First Battalion command group at the landing zone, and we moved out to join the fight that was to the west of us. Captain William R. Tenny commanded K Company

---

[20]   The Song Ly Ly is a large river in Que Son province. In Vietnamese, "Song" means river.

and First Lieutenant John D. (JD) Murray commanded M Company. I had never operated with these officers before, but I knew they both were fine Marines for whom I had the utmost respect.

There was a trail leading to the east side of the villages of Chau Lam. I had the companies in column with Kilo leading and Mike Company trailing. I placed my command group and myself with part of Mack McInturff's H&S Company in the middle behind K and in front of M. I had recently reassigned Mack as H&S Company commander. With K and M plus my command group and Mack's H&S troops, we had about 350 troops on the east side of the enemy's position. Companies D and B were positioned about 1,500 meters away on the west side of the NVA and just south of the Song Ly Ly. See the Operation Swift battle map in appendix B.[21] We had the enemy position bracketed between my four companies.

When my command group and I were helolifted out of Hill 51, the only troops my executive officer, Major Ernie Cheatham, had to defend the hill were the cooks, supply troops, motor transport people, a few sick or lame Marines, and Alpha Company, which was undergoing rabies treatment. The mortars and perimeter defense troops of McInturff's H&S Company were with me moving into the fight. Ernie Cheatham could be backed up with Delta Battery field artillery and a few tanks, but it would be a thin line of defense against a determined NVA assault had they elected to attack our base on Hill 51. Fortunately, the enemy didn't attack while it was so thinly defended.

As my K and M Companies with Mack's H&S units moved out in a column toward the battle area, the company commanders put scouts out on each side of the column. With the sun filtering through the overhead canopy of dense foliage we moved out making no more noise than the muted sounds of troops making their way cautiously along a bush trail. It was very quiet, almost eerie with the sun breaking through the leaves to bathe our column in alternating sunlight and shadows.

---

21   Telfer et.al., op. cit., p112. See Appendix B for battle map and explanation of map symbols.

Now I recognized the area! We had been here before on a sweep and clear operation several months before. I remembered that Chau Lam had defensive trenches surrounding the entire village complex. I was bringing the village and its defensive works back into my mind's eye when one of the scouts on the right flank came running in, directly towards me.

"Sir, there's an AK-47 teetering back and forth on that large rock over there," he said pointing to the rock.

This was of major importance! I halted the column, walked over to the rock, and sure enough, there was an AK-47 still rocking back and forth. We must have surprised one of their out-guards. This was major good luck! I surmised the enemy was waiting for us, about 500 yards ahead in an ambush formation, but would they be on the left or right side? I had to make the correct decision to deal with this. It was truly a life or death call. The AK-47 was on the right side of the trail; so, the out-guard must have been in front of the NVA position. I thought the enemy would be waiting for us in a backward "L" setup on the right side of the trail to ambush us as we were proceeding along the trail in a column. I thought they most likely positioned themselves with one side of the "L" in the trenches perpendicular to the trail we were on and the other leg in trenches parallel to the trail. This positioned the enemy so they could engage our column with one leg of the "L," then envelop us from the rear after we made contact. Thank God that I had been here before, and remembered the terrain and the Chau Lam defensive layout.

The K and M company commanders, and Mack McInturff, were already by my side waiting for orders. I gave them my battle plan, "I want bayonets fixed NOW! K Company will be in a V formation and guide on the trail. M Company will move up on K's right side off the trail and form a line of skirmishers. This will let our wall hit their wall. The CP group and Mack's troops will follow behind K."

We had no reserve, all my troops were committed, and I was certain we were outnumbered. As I later learned, we were indeed outnumbered by about 1,200 NVA troops to our 350 Marines . . . almost four to one! This time I was blessed with being able to talk directly with Bill Tenny and JD Murray, the company commanders from the Third Battalion. Both completely understood the planned deployment of our own troops and the probable positions of the enemy.

Just as we were beginning to go in, Ernie Cheatham appeared. "I've brought everyone I could on Hill 51 with me, Colonel."

"Good," I said. "We need all the troops we can muster. If you brought any of Alpha Company's troops, I'll send them in to bite the enemy and give 'em rabies. Follow me."

I didn't know, nor did any of my company commanders know, that Chaplain Vincent Capodanno was with us too. Father Vince had been reassigned from my First Battalion to the Fifth Marines staff and then to the Third Battalion some time prior to Swift. In retrospect, we believe that when he heard about the coming big battle, Father Vince decided to join one of the M Company platoons without clearing his action with his regimental commander, his battalion commander, or with me, the battalion commander in control of tactical operations. Just before lift-off, Father Vince jumped aboard a helicopter carrying M Company's Third Platoon to the fight, and moved right into the front lines with them. I would never have authorized this. I didn't feel our chaplain belonged in the front lines during a battle, but Father Vince thought otherwise. He wanted to be where his grunts were, to give comfort to the wounded and last rights to the dying.

I turned to my company commanders and said, "When I give the order, attack on the double. Yell like hell as you go in. I want those bastards to think we have more troops than we do."

Just as I finished giving these orders, Billy Long said, "Colonel, Major Alger wants to talk with you," and handed me his radio handset.

"Pete," Dick said, "we've just gotten word there's a large force waiting for you in the Chau Lam-Vinh Huy complex."

I answered, "No shit! Well, we're almost there, and we're attacking now. This will be one hell of a fight. Get another battalion mounted up to assist ASAP. See you."

"CHARGE!" I shouted.

With a roar, the attack began! We had to get into those enemy trenches and take them quickly. The battle began with fierce fighting at close quarters. My assessment was correct. The enemy was in an "L" shaped ambush position on the right side of the trail, and we had one-upped them.

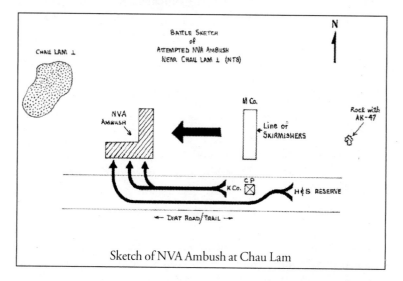

Sketch of NVA Ambush at Chau Lam

K Company hit the NVA right flank and slugged their way into the trenches parallel to the trail, with my command group right behind. I found an abandoned enemy trench and jumped into it with Billy Long right beside me. McInturff's H&S group continued the envelopment of the enemy's right flank and pounded into the trenches next to K Company. We received heavy automatic small arms and mortar fire, which we returned with a heavy volume of our own. The after action report cites that we expended 35,000 rounds of small arms fire, 300 M-79, 35 60mm mortar high explosive rounds and 20 rounds of 105mm high Covering his movement with 60mm mortar counter battery fire, Captain Tenny maneuvered his K Company to close with the enemy in fierce hand-to-hand fighting. explosive shells.[22] That seems high in retrospect. I don't think we traveled carrying that much ammo, but I cite those statistics to give you a measure of the intensity of the fight.

While K Company was hotly engaged with the enemy, JD Murray's Mike Company was also in a heavy fight with well

---

22 Swift After Action Report, op. cit., pg11.

entrenched and camouflaged NVA troops. His First Platoon came under intense semi-automatic weapons fire from an estimated NVA company. Murray maneuvered M Company's Second Platoon into a position to support the First Platoon, and the Second Platoon immediately came under intense automatic and semi-automatic small arms fire from another estimated NVA company.

At this stage in any battle, there is massive confusion. This is the time the company commanders and platoon leaders become the principal players in the battle's outcome. The battalion commander is no longer in total control of the fighting. At this point, Marines do what they have been trained to do.

Sergeant Lawrence D. Peters of M Company's Second Platoon maneuvered his squad in an assault on an entrenched and camouflaged enemy position on a knoll that was hitting M Company with intense fire. He completely disregarded his safety and stood in the open, pointing out the NVA positions. Enemy rounds hit all around him until he was painfully wounded in the leg. Disregarding his wound Peters moved forward and continued to lead his men. As the enemy fire increased in accuracy and volume, his squad lost momentum and was temporarily pinned down. Exposing himself once again to devastating enemy fire Sergeant Peters consolidated his position to render more effective fire, and was wounded again in the face and neck from an exploding mortar round. When the enemy attempted to infiltrate the position of the adjacent First Platoon, Peters stood erect in full view of the enemy, firing burst after burst and forcing them to disclose their camouflaged positions. Peters continued firing until he was critically wounded by a gunshot wound in his chest. Although unable to walk or stand, Peters continued to direct his squad in spite of two additional wounds until he lost consciousness and died. Inspired by his valor and fighting spirit, the squad regained fire superiority and successfully carried the assault to the enemy.

In another nearby M Company fight, Sergeant Howard Manfra skillfully deployed his team to give them effective fields of fire into camouflaged enemy emplacements. Then exposing himself to intense hostile fire, he stood erect and located two NVA mortar emplacements that were inflicting numerous M Company casualties. With a 3.5 inch rocket launcher, Manfra calmly fired one rocket, which destroyed a NVA mortar position killing four enemy soldiers. In the process, he received a severe leg wound. Despite the wound, Sergeant Manfra stood again and fired on a second target, which he destroyed. He was wounded again, but continued his efforts to silence other hostile mortars by directing his team's fire as he lay critically wounded in a dangerously exposed position. While attempting to seek cover, Manfra was struck by enemy fire that rendered him unconscious.

Sergeant Clyde Craig Sullivan also exhibited the kind of leadership and bravery that we've come to expect from our grunt Marines. Sullivan's platoon serving as point element for M Company absorbed the brunt of a fierce attack by massed NVA troops using small arms, automatic weapons, and mortar fire. The platoon commander was one of the immediate casualties of the enemy assault, and summoned Sullivan to come up and assume command of the platoon. While on his way to his new position, Sullivan came under heavy fire that forced him to seek cover. While waiting for an opportunity to move, he heard the cry of one of his squad leaders who had been wounded. Under cover of an M-79 grenade launcher, he retrieved his wounded companion, and moved him to a safe position behind a large rock where he skillfully applied battle dressing to the disabled man's wounds. In the meantime enemy troops had moved behind Sullivan's entrapped unit, and had commenced to deliver a heavy volume of fire. Sullivan ordered his men to move to a bomb crater about 30 meters away. During this movement he was wounded in the forehead by an enemy mortar fragment. As the intensity of the enemy attack increased Sullivan radioed for assistance, but other nearby units were also heavily engaged and couldn't come to Sullivan's aid. Realizing the need to move the critically injured to safety, he organized a team to evacuate them, but the enemy fire was so heavy that they could only gather them in the crater. When one ceased to breathe, Sullivan gave mouth-to-mouth resuscitation until the man revived. Upon receiving direction to leave the area in preparation for an air strike,

Sullivan radioed that he was pinned down in the bomb crater only 75 yards from the enemy positions. He courageously recommended the air strike commence. Subsequently the strike silenced the enemy fire allowing Sullivan to lead his men back to the M company positions.

Father Vince heard radio reports that M Company's Second Platoon was in danger of being overrun by a massed NVA assault force. With total disregard for his own safety, he ran through an open area raked with fire to join the Second Platoon. In spite of the intense enemy small arms, automatic weapons, and mortar fire, he moved about the battlefield administering last rites to the dying, giving medical aid to the wounded, and dragging some wounded Marines to safety behind a hill. When an exploding mortar round inflicted multiple wounds to his arms and legs, and severed a portion of his right hand, he refused all medical aid, and directed the corpsmen to render their aid to others. Seeing a wounded corpsman in the direct line of fire of an enemy machinegun positioned approximately 15 yards away from the fallen corpsman, Father Vince ran to the wounded man and was struck down by a burst from the machinegun.

This is an account of Vince Capodanno from an M Company Marine who was there.[23]

> Sometime late afternoon we heard scattered fire. We had stopped close to a small hill. Sergeant Pete came running up and told us that First Platoon had been hit hard, and we were going to help them. We ran some, walked some, and approached the top of the hill, and then the carnage started. All I can remember was Sergeant Pete screaming, "Get that gun! Get that gun!" Then I took a hit in the left arm that spun me to the ground. Another shot shattered my rifle. I was screaming along with other members of my squad. We were being shot at every move we made. The machinegun

---

[23]   Excerpt from a web site for Mike 3/5 Vietnam Vets

was close, 15 to 25 yards away in a thicket part way down the far slope of a small hill. This is very hard for me. I can remember seeing North Vietnamese troops moving and coming toward me. There were Marines lying all around me, and I was calling for help, while with every beat of my fast pumping heart, my life's blood was spurting on the ground. I could hear someone holler, "Corpsman," but every time I moved that gun would shoot at me and the other Marines. At a distance I could see Doc Leal moving from Marine to Marine, and he was looking at me. I knew I was going to die. I was not able to defend myself, and the NVA were coming after me. That was my fear.

Through all the noise and hearing myself scream, someone touched me. To slow the blood loss, I had rolled myself on my left side to put pressure on my left arm and elbow, and someone touched me. It was Father Vince. As I looked into his eyes, all things got silent. I couldn't hear a sound. There was no screaming, nothing but the sound of his soft voice, and the look of compassion in his eyes. "Stay calm Marine. Someone will be here to help. God is with us all this day!" I could see Sergeant Peters lying on the ground, blood coming from his mouth. Corpsman Leal was moving in my direction, but I was not scared any longer. I was at peace. Father Vince was bareheaded, blood on his face, and neck. His right hand was mangled with a bloody compress hastily attached. He cupped the back of my head in an attempt to raise me off my arm, when all of a sudden I heard a scream, "My leg! My leg!" and I was back in the war.

I glanced over at Corpsman Leal. He was sitting on the ground about 25 feet from me screaming. Father Vince blessed me with his good hand, leaped up and darted to Corpsman Leal. I had come to my senses and was ready to fight again. The words, "Get that gun! Get that gun!" were still ringing in my head. I made an attempt to move when that gun opened up once more, not at me, but at Father Vince and Corpsman Leal and ended their lives. A long burst killed my savior and my friend. Father Vince was gone. That image haunts me, remains foremost in my mind today. I got mad at God and mad at the enemy. I will not go into what happened later between that gun and me.

This was the fourth time I met Father Vince, and it was the same as the first. His steadfast determination, calmness, and dedication to his "mission" will always be in the minds of those who came in contact with him. We still feel his presence. At the time of his death the entire First Marine Division was in shock. "The Padre is dead," spread from trooper to trooper.

Sometime during the dark hours, I was found and dragged back to a large shell hole. I had survived. I began then, during the night, trying to push that memory of Father Vince out of my mind, but it was not to go. Father Vincent Robert Capodanno is still with me. He is still doing his work. He is not finished with us yet.

Those words are, in their own way, a beautiful and powerful tribute to a truly remarkable and wonderful man. Father Capodanno ministered to all our troopers, be they Catholic or not. He was beloved by all, and his death brought great sorrow throughout the battalion and the entire Fifth Marine Regiment. All the troopers called him Father Vince. Regardless of your faith, you couldn't help having a good feeling around him because he radiated an essence of spirituality and strength. When you were in his presence, you had a feeling of tranquility and security that was almost palpable. It was not easy to feel at ease with a sense of peace in Vietnam, but that's what Father Vince gave us all. He was quite remarkable. Father Daniel Mode describes Capodanno's heroic actions in detail in his book, *Grunt Padre*. It is a great story about a magnificent man who most of us thought of as a saint. When we lost him, the entire First Marine Division mourned his death.

After assessing the situation with M Company's First and Second Platoons, Lieutenant Murray deployed his Third Platoon forward. Murray exposed himself to enemy fire in order to observe and control the fire and movement of all M Company elements. When the commanders and key noncommissioned officers of his lead platoons became casualties, Murray quickly reorganized his company to establish strong defensive positions. He then skillfully called in close air support, and accurate mortar and artillery fire to repulse NVA attacks on his positions. Four air strikes and an aerial tear gas attack over the company battle area forced the NVA to withdraw. Murray then launched an aggressive attack that took the NVA positions. After recovering all his casualties, he arranged for their evacuation and consolidated his company into a night defensive perimeter.

The fiercely contested engagement continued until nightfall when the battalion consolidated positions to form a defensive perimeter to medevac casualties and conduct night activities. At the end of the first day, our combined casualties were 54 Marines KIA, 104 WIA. The enemy body count was 139 confirmed KIA and 250 probable KIA. We also captured 19 of the enemy, 22 individual weapons, and two crew served weapons.[24] The battle was a fierce close-quarters encounter. It was a slugfest with bayonets and rifle butts. I lost track of time.

During Swift, the regimental command post remained at the Fifth Marines combat base at Tam Ky. Colonel Davis, the regimental commander, was in overall control of the battle, and was in constant communications with me as his on-scene commander. In response to my recommendation for an additional company, Colonel Davis ordered the Third Battalion's Item Company to join me and operate under my control. Item Company arrived in my area at about 9 p.m. that night, and immediately took position in our defensive perimeter.

Delta Company was the first of my units to be engaged by the enemy that long ago morning of 4 September. It had only been two days, but it seemed like two years. In the prolonged heavy fighting, Delta Company suffered 14 KIA, including the loss of the company commander, and 15 WIA. This reduced Company

---

[24]   Ibid, pg12.

D by almost 25 percent of its normal strength. Delta was so beat up that Colonel Davis later directed me to helolift Delta to the Nui Lac Son outpost so the new company commander, Captain Heinz, could reorganize and regroup his command. This I did on the third day of the battle.

Even the worst of times can have their element of bizarre humor. So did Day One of Operation Swift. Several days before this operation, the battalion corpsman had lanced a large cyst on my right buttocks. The medics had been very attentive in coming to see me every four or five hours to change the dressing. In the heat of battle, a medic appeared to take care of this routine chore. I was standing there with my trousers down while the corpsman changed the dressing when Dislodge Six came up on the radio. During Swift, the regimental command post was located at the Fifth Marines combat base at Tam Ky. Billy handed me the radio handset.

"Cottage Six, this is Dislodge Six," Colonel Davis said. "We just received word that you are wounded. How serious is it?"

"What?" I replied. "I haven't been wounded. The corpsman is just changing the dressing for a huge cyst I had on my butt that was lanced."

"Huge cyst on your butt, aye," Davis replied. "Carry on Pete."

Then I turned to the group, "Now, who called regiment without telling me?" No one replied, but I saw Billy Long looking very intently at the ground. "You all know my policy. When we need to talk with regiment, I'll do the talking. You will not send back any message unless I tell you to. Is that clear?" Everyone nodded.

And to think that I almost got a Purple Heart for a cyst on my butt!

September 5: Day 2

On the second day of the battle, Lieutenant Colonel Webster's Third Battalion, Fifth Marines command group was helolifted into a position to the west of me near Companies B and D. Colonel Davis at that time directed Webster to assume operational control over both B and D companies. We still had the enemy bracketed between Webster's and my positions; however, they were far from trapped. We were hitting them on two flanks, from the east and west, but they could still retreat across the Song Ly Ly.

Throughout the day, companies Kilo, Mike and Item searched the battle area with no enemy contact. The NVA seemed once again to have withdrawn to the north across the Song Ly Ly. We found abandoned enemy weapons, ammunition, equipment, and 7 freshly dug graves. Three of the graves contained bodies dressed in black and green clothing as opposed to the uniforms regular NVA troops wore. This indicated that Viet Cong units had participated in the battle in support of NVA units

September 6: Day 3

On 6 September, I turned operational control of Companies K and M over to the Third Battalion, Fifth Marines, and regained operational command of my battalion's Companies B and D. Colonel Davis also gave me control of Company D, First Battalion, First Marines, and I retained control of Item Company, Third Battalion.

At 10:30 a.m. we commenced a sweep of the area. All was quiet until 11:30 when snipers fired ten to twenty rounds on Company D, First Marines. About the same time, Company D, Fifth Marines took sniper fire that wounded two of our troopers. We returned fire and searched the area, but found nothing. Shortly thereafter we did find four Vietnamese males between 30 and 40 years old hiding in a bunker. All wore black clothing. They surrendered and came out with their hands raised above their heads.

A short time later, we found three Vietnamese hiding in another bunker. When they refused to come out, we threw a hand grenade into the bunker killing two NVA and one VC. We recovered weapons and documents and forwarded them to Regimental Headquarters for intelligence evaluation.

The rest of the day continued like this, sweeping the battle area and capturing small contingents of the enemy. Then at 3:15 p.m. things began to get interesting again. Companies B and D started to receive sniper fire, which became more intense as Bravo Company moved towards the source of the fire. Company Delta maneuvered to attack the enemy's left flank, and it became obvious that they had come across at least a battalion size enemy unit. The engagement continued through the rest of the afternoon.

At nightfall we consolidated our forces in a defensive perimeter. The enemy began hitting us with intense mortar and small arms fire, and NVA troops attempted to infiltrate our positions. At one point 5 to 15 enemy troops were within 10 meters of the perimeter before we detected and killed them. Once again, Lance Corporal Driscoll distinguished himself. He played a decisive part in defeating this enemy probe by boldly exposing himself to withering small arms fire and making a one-man assault on the enemy, hurling grenades and breaking up the enemy attack.

After returning to Delta Company's position, Driscoll saw two Marines who were wounded and lying in an open area approximately 100 yards from him. With the NVA still in the vicinity, he courageously moved forward and retrieved one man, and then returned for the second man after bringing his first wounded comrade to safety. Lance Corporal Tom Driscoll displayed a loyalty to his fellow Marines and a gallant fighting spirit during those two early days of Swift that earned him a Navy Cross.

Sergeant Rodney Davis of the Second Platoon, Bravo Company also demonstrated Marine heroism in the fight that day. Elements of the Second Platoon were pinned down in a trench by a large force of NVA troops. Sergeant Davis directed the fire of his men while repelling the NVA attack by throwing hand grenades at the onrushing enemy. When an enemy grenade landed in the trench, Sergeant Davis threw himself on the grenade absorbing the full force of the blast. Through his selfless sacrifice he inspired his men to repulse the enemy attack and hold their vital position. Sergeant Rodney Davis received the Medal of Honor posthumously.

After the initial heavy exchange, the enemy continued sniper and mortar fire then gradually ceased his probing action. We called in medevac helos to evacuate our wounded. The enemy fired on them as they came in, but otherwise all was quiet. Both B and D Companies rejoined the battalion and provided perimeter defense throughout the night. When B Company entered the perimeter they brought with them their severely wounded company commander, Captain Tom Reese. Tom had been wounded by small arms fire in a village. Lieutenant Drollinger then took command and brought B Company back to our perimeter. Later, we medevaced Tom out, and he survived.

At the end of the day, we had lost 35 Marines KIA and 92 WIA. We found 61 enemy KIA and another 106 probable KIA.

September 7: Day 4

At first light on 7 September, both the Third and First Battalions searched the battlefield to look for items of intelligence value among the enemy dead. We found a map that contained the defensive positions of a battalion of the First VC Regiment.[25] The map pinpointed company, command post, mortar, and ammo storage positions. As a result, Colonel Davis ordered my battalion to attack these sites. With the help of supporting arms, we assaulted the positions to find that the enemy had already withdrawn.

At noon my friend, Lieutenant Colonel William K. Rockey, took command of the Third Battalion Fifth Marines. I was happy to see him again, and we had a great reunion.

Operation Swift Wraps Up

The remainder of Swift, from 7 September through 15 September was an area sweep with no major enemy contact. My First Battalion took several dozen Viet Cong prisoners and killed another ten during individual encounters that were not part of any organized NVA resistance. Essentially, it was all over, and we had won.

On 8 September, Alpha Company, First Battalion relieved Item Company, Third Battalion and completed Operation Swift. Because of the rabid puppy, 28 Alpha Company Marines had to undergo rabies antidote shots and remain in quarantine, which didn't expire until 8 September. The rabid puppy incident caused Alpha, much to their disappointment, to miss much of one of the major engagements of the Vietnam war.

At 10:30p.m. On 13 September, we began helolifting units of the First Battalion, Fifth Marines out of the area and back to our

25   Telfer et.al., op. cit., pp 115-117.

combat base on Hill 51. By 2:00 p.m. on 15 September all our First Battalion, Fifth Marines were back on Hill 51, and Operation Swift was officially terminated at 4:00 p.m.

Although again outnumbered, we fought and beat two regiments of the Second NVA Division. Sadly, we lost 54 of our brave Marines and 104 were wounded in action. We lost Chaplain Capodanno who was awarded the Medal of Honor, as were two more of my Marines, Sergeant Rodney Davis and Sergeant Lawrence Peters. During the time I was battalion commander we had fought in every action in the First Marine Division sector, and had suffered many casualties. There are two panels on the Vietnam Memorial Wall in Washington, D.C. that attest to our sacrifice.

For each Marine lost, though, the enemy paid dearly. We had taken four of theirs for every Marine in my battalion they killed. My heart is still filled with sadness after all these years for the families of those heroes. I have to this day, a very hard time visiting that memorial wall. Every Marine who served in my First Battalion, Fifth Marines was, and is, a hero to me. While others may write about our battles, it is important to me that I record my recollections to let it be known that this battalion commander loved those men like brothers. I deeply appreciate what they did, not only for me, but also for the battalion, the regiment, the Marine Corps, and most of all for our country. GOD BLESS THEM ALL!

In Operation Swift, we had none of the mishaps we had in Union I. Our battle dispositions were exactly as they should have been to deal with the enemy. Fortunately, my B and D Companies were on the west side of the NVA after the first day's engagement. Colonel Davis and Dick Alger positioned me with K and M Companies attacking from the NVA's eastern flank. We were hitting them on opposite sides of their positions. We had the enemy in what Mack McInturff calls a "shit sandwich." All company commanders performed with distinction and according to battle plan, especially Captain Tenny and First Lieutenant Murray with their fine Marines. JD Murray was awarded the Navy Cross for extraordinary heroism.

Operation Swift was by far the toughest battle the Fifth Marines fought during my time with the regiment. We were outnumbered, as always, but in Swift the fighting was with bayonets and rifle butts. Swift was tough, close-in, hand-to-hand fighting with no quarter asked or given. We prevailed because of the tenacity and fighting spirit of our Marines, so evident during the first days of the operation. It has always been a mystery to me why the Fifth Marines did not receive a Presidential Unit Citation for Swift. We received that award for Unions I and II, and although the Presidential Unit Citation was well earned for the Union Operations, the regiment was equally deserving of this award or a Navy Commendation for Swift.

My time with the First Battalion ended on 20 September 1967. The ten and one half months had flown by. The battalion gave me a wonderful send off with a formal change of command ceremony, as Lieutenant Colonel Oliver Vandenberg, an old basic school classmate, assumed command of the battalion. Ernie Cheatham presented me with a gold watch with the inscription: "To the Dragon, from First Battalion, Fifth Marines."

That watch is still keeping time, and is more precious to me than any medal I ever received. The "Dragon" may have been what the officers called me, but it was not until years later while attending a First Marine Division reunion that I learned that the troopers called me, "Highpockets." It could have been worse, but it fits and I carry the title with pride.

Before flying home, I paid a visit to Lieutenant General Don Robertson at the Da Nang First Division command post to say good-bye. General Robertson said he was sorry to lose me, paid me some nice compliments, and wished me well. In a way, I was sad to be leaving. I wouldn't miss the heat, being wet, the lack of sleep, the bugs, the snakes, the enemy, but I sure would miss my troops and the comradeship we shared. That is tough to leave behind. The First Battalion had fought hard and well in every engagement with the enemy. We had **never** been beaten. It was an experience I will never forget.

My grandson, John Basset, once asked me, "Granddad, were you ever afraid you would lose in battle?"

"Never," I replied. "Marines don't lose in battle."

The day came to fly home. My new orders were to report for duty with the Plans and Programs Branch, G-3 (operations) at

Headquarters Marine Corps in Washington D.C. after thirty days leave. I was on a Pan Am passenger plane jammed with troops going home. As the plane started rolling down the runway the enemy began mortaring the airfield. In spite of the good friends I was leaving behind, I was glad to be going home.

For all of us, Vietnam is a place of tangled emotions and mixed memories. Like most Marines, I have recollections that range from the unpleasant to the downright traumatic. The bugs, rain, chronic fatigue, and sleeping on the ground are nobody's idea of fun. Those are "no-account" compared to the pain of losing good friends and fellow warriors as the inevitable part of combat. The futility of defeating the enemy, and not being allowed to pursue him in retreat for total victory hurt the spirit of our troops. When we had him on the run, we wanted to chase him all the way to North Vietnam, kicking hell out of him every inch of the way. I never knew why we were ordered to cease pursuit, and to concentrate on counting enemy dead and weapons captured. It didn't make sense, and it pissed me off!

In spite of the painful memories, each of us has his own warm memories of our individual experiences in Nam. The good thing we all extract from the bad is the feeling of fellowship and *esprit de corps* that comes from the hardship and travail of combat. This was eloquently stated in a recent letter to me from Corporal Philip Johnson, which I would like to share with you. Phil Johnson was a good Marine, and is now a successful investment banker in Boston. In his letter he captures the essence of the shared hardship and comradeship of troops in battle. He also projects the appreciation troops have for commanders who genuinely care for their well being, and who lead by example. Marine troopers are a smart and cagey bunch. They are quick to spot the pretenders. To young Marine leaders yet to come: Be honest, be caring, and lead from the front.

> Dear Colonel Hilgartner,
> We have not talked since September 10, 1967 when I suddenly left you on a small hill in Viet Nam. At that time, I was Corporal Philip Johnson, a 20-year-old bodyguard assigned to guard the battalion commander who just happened to need a very deep foxhole most evenings. I am

now a 56-year-old investment banker from Boston, but some of my proudest memories emanate from the months we spent together leading First Battalion, Fifth Marines.

During the past 36 years you have never been far from my thoughts and conversations. My months in Viet Nam, and certainly my commitment to the Corps, have always been easy for me to discuss. My conversations are most often with men who did not serve, or were too young for the war. I am always proud to tell people about my time serving in the Marines and especially about the efforts that were made by the Marines in Viet Nam. I know now, from reading your letter to the recent graduating class at USNA, that you had a tremendous amount of battle experience in Korea.[26] I should have known then that you could not have learned all of your battle skills at the USNA, but I did realize that you were a very good commander. I did not always understand the tactics and I was too immature to ask you all the questions I should have during our long hours together. I have even matured to the point of realizing the possibility that you may not even remember me. I was one of so many yet you were the focal point of leadership in my Marine Corp career. Well, maybe there are one or two DIs that I still remember, but not quite as fondly.

I would love to know a little bit about your life after September 1967. I was able to get your address through a friend who also graduated from the Academy. I called to tell him that you had written a letter to the graduates of 2003. Thanks to some premonition, I had checked the USNA web site and was fortunate enough to see the letter. I read it and it brought back great memories and made me very proud to have served with you. Once, a few years ago, I found a book in the bookstore at the Smithsonian that described Marine

---

[26]   This was the address I gave to the 16th Company midshipmen that appears in section 4.1. The Naval Academy posted it on the World Wide Web, where Phil Johnson found it.

operations in Viet Nam, You were mentioned several times and the book discussed operations like Prairie, Union, Swift and others that we fought during my time serving with you.

I would just like you to know that at least one Marine never forgot the impact and Influence you made on my life. I am sorry that we were not able to say goodbye or talk again after 1967. Perhaps it was best that we have had time to reflect on everything that happened in Nam. I now have a 23 year old son who has just graduated from college, and I have even more respect for those who gave their lives with us during the war and what their father's sacrificed to have them serve. I wanted my son to try to go to USNA, but he never quite understood my reasoning. I am not sure that I fault him, but I wish he could experience the *espirit de corps* without the suffering of battle. Perhaps you can't have one without the other. Well Sir, I really just wanted to make contact and to tell you that you were admired and appreciated. You were a very good leader and taught me how to lead by example while caring for those around you in a very meaningful way. I trust you will have a very long life, and will always be confident that I thought you would have made a great Commandant. Thank you for every memory.

Respectfully yours and Semper Fidelis,
Philip Johnson

I deeply appreciate Phil Johnson's sentiment. His praise means more to me than letters from the president of the United States, or a bag-full of medals. His comment about having his son experience the *espirit de corps* without the suffering of battle is probably a feeling shared by many parents. But it is impossible. That true feeling, *that real spirit,* comes from the suffering of battle. Parade ground soldiers and rear echelon "pinkies" may think they have "the spirit," but it isn't the same. Battle bonds men into brothers, for from the carnage and suffering of battle comes the kind of nobility that proclaims, "There is no greater love than that shown by a man who will offer his life to save another."

In a recent letter Brigadier General Jerry McKay recalls the following events that occurred shortly after he joined the battalion in 1967 as a captain:

Pete . . .

My recollections of the First Battalion, Fifth Marines are memories of following Lieutenant Colonel Pete Hilgartner over some very large hills and through some deep rice paddies. There are naturally numerous memories, but two instances have remained with me. One night as the battalion was preparing to go into its night defensive position, the battalion command post was totally bunched up. You didn't say anything. You just continued walking over the proposed command post site with the headquarters element in tow. Eventually, you had covered the site to a degree that we were finally spread out to your satisfaction. This may seem trivial, but this was your way of leading and teaching.

A second instance, among many, was a night march back to the battalion base camp on Hill 54. We had been in fairly heavy contact throughout the day and were supposed to be airlifted out. Because of the volume of fire, the helos were unable to get into us. We had to walk home, and unfortunately the way home was through a large number of rice paddies that didn't always have dikes to walk on. As we walked through the night, supported the entire way by flare drops, Lieutenant Colonel Hilgartner was always visible to us as we moved along. Naturally this was not difficult, not only was he very visible because of his height, but because he was constantly moving up and down the lines providing great encouragement to the Marines in his command.

There are many memories of Vietnam and the battalion, some unpleasant, but mostly I remember a superb battalion with strong leadership and sense of mission. It was my honor to be counted as a member of the First Battalion, Fifth Marines and under Lieutenant Colonel Hilgartner's command.

I can't tell you how much I treasure Jerry McKay's praise. He was, and is, a fine warrior, a superb Marine, and a great friend. Jerry's letter has two messages that I would like to pass on to the next generation of Marine leaders. First, lead from the front. That is a leitmotif that you will hear again and again throughout your service career. Don't become jaded or dismissive because you have heard it before. Pay attention each time you hear it and refresh yourself with it, because leading from the front is fundamental to combat leadership. Be where the grunts can see you.

Jerry's second point is: A good leader is a teacher, and the best teaching is with patience and showing rather than telling, or shouting. Leaders teach by training and demonstration that requires repetition. Training repetition may seem tedious to the troops, but it is that tedium that makes combat skills instinctive and habitual; what your troops do without thinking. In combat, you can depend on imperfectly learned skills to be the first to desert you when you need them most. Troops that keep their heads and remember their combat skills are the ones with the best chance of coming home whole.

Final Day, 20 September 1967

The Dragon and
his new gold watch

Change of Command

Gen. Chapman says Thanks

7.0 HEADQUARTERS U.S. MARINE CORPS

After leaving Da Nang, the plane ride went smoothly. We were packed in like sardines, but no one seemed to care. We were going home!

I had heard about the war protests in the U. S., but I was busy fighting. The extent of these did not register with me; so, after returning home, I was shocked to learn that I was no honorable Vietnam veteran. Many of my fellow citizens thought I was a bum!

I've always believed in our Constitution and those freedoms enumerated in the Constitution's Bill of Rights, which include freedom of speech. Those protesters were free to express their opinions, and I, along with all our military in Vietnam, had placed our lives in harm's way to help preserve their right to say their piece. However, that freedom of speech did not give them the right to insult, and in some cases physically abuse, those of us who answered our nation's call to military service in Vietnam. There was nothing noble or patriotic in their noisy, petulant demonstrations that demeaned those of us who fought in Vietnam. Their treatment of combat veterans was shameful. The behavior of people like Jane Fonda, Peter Arnett, and their ilk among that sorry group was a national disgrace, and the rancor they left with Vietnam veterans still exists.

When I reported for duty in the Plans and Programs branch of the G-3 Operations Division, I was pleased to learn my immediate boss would be Colonel Calhoun Killeen. I had known Cal at the Naval Academy and he had been my artillery battery commander in Korea. He was a very fine officer and later retired as a major general. Above Cal was Brigadier General Gordon Gayle, a brilliant officer with an outstanding combat record in the Corps. General Gayle had lived across the street from my family and me in 1955 to 1957 during my supply and basic school assignments at the Marine Corps base, Quantico, Virginia.

My new job involved the deployment and redeployment of forces to and from the Pacific, with emphasis on Vietnam. This was similar to the job I had on the CINCPACFLT staff in Hawaii. Back in those days we didn't have the computer capability of today. The record of unit deployments and the troop strength of those units were tabulated by hand. Keeping those records was a tough and important job. In doing it by hand, though, there were times I felt like Bob Crachit with his green eyeshade and quill pen, but Cal Killeen was no Ebenezer Scrooge.

When the Commandant of the Marine Corps (CMC) wanted deployment information he called for Killeen and Hilgartner. I remember one instance when the commandant, General Chapman, asked for a deployment briefing. Colonel Killeen said he wanted me to brief the commandant to get face time with the boss. The two of us would represent the G-3 Operations Division at this briefing, which would be in CMC's office.

General Chapman had recently awarded me two medals, a Silver Star and a Legion of Merit with Combat V, for my service in Vietnam. My family attended the ceremony in his office; so, I knew he would remember me. I was determined to make a good showing at the briefing.

Getting ready for such an event was a real ordeal. I wrote and rewrote (with Colonel Killeen's supervision,) the presentation many times. At about 0400 in the morning, Cal felt we had finally gotten it right. Then he told me to go home and get suited up for the briefing to be held about 0900 that morning. That meant a drive down to Triangle, Va. where we lived and a drive back in the awful morning rush hour traffic coming from the Woodbridge and Quantico area.

I calculated that I should be back by 0800, allowing a fair sized cushion in case of traffic problems. The drive each way was about an hour and a half. That left me approximately one hour to clean up put on a fresh uniform, and grab a quick breakfast before heading back to my office.

I called my wife and explained the situation and asked her to put out my khaki gabardine uniform, khaki shirt and tie, and please to have something ready for me to eat. When I arrived home it was about 0530. I rushed into the house, showered and put on the clothes she had laid out for me. Breakfast was cold cereal, doughnuts, and coffee. I jumped in the car after eating and headed back to D.C.

It was no later than 0800, maybe a little earlier when I arrived back in the office. Colonel Killeen called me in to inquire if I was all set to go. When I entered his office, what I heard was not what I expected.

"Pete, you are out of uniform, look at yourself!" I was shocked. I looked myself over and could see nothing wrong.

Then he said, "Look at your trousers—they are wash khaki's—not gabardine. CMC is going to have you for breakfast."

I was in deep *kimche*. We had worked very hard getting everything ready and our whole effort was going to be ruined because I put on the wrong pair of trousers. What could be done? There weren't any Marine officers in the headquarters that wore trousers my size.

Then a green light went on. I said, "Colonel, may I have your permission to go down to CMC's office and look around at the briefing setup?" I thought maybe I could hide behind a podium or desk. He concurred with my request.

I raced down to office of the Commandant's aide and requested that he allow me to make a recon of CMC's office, and arrange things for the briefing. We went into the office. A spindly lectern was in the room flanked by a flipchart stand. A potted palm tree stood in a corner just to the right of the entrance to CMC's office.

General Chapman would be sitting in a large chair facing the lectern. I moved the lectern into position, and arranged the location of the flip chart so it would partially screen my body as I entered. I then asked the aide if I could place the potted palm in front of the lectern, to improve the esthetics of the presentation. The aide looked a little puzzled, but approved my request. So I moved the palm in front of the lectern so that as I stood behind the lectern there were enough leaves on the palm to break up the outline between the bottom of my wash khaki trousers and the contrast they would make with the gabardine coat. It was creative camouflage at its best.

I then returned to the office and told Colonel Killeen what I'd done. He added one more thing. I would walk into the general's office directly behind him. He would be sitting on the General Chapman's right side. Cal would make some light chitchat as I was organizing the materials on the lectern to keep the general's attention focused on him instead of me until I began.

When all was ready, I stood at attention and the general gave me the word to commence the briefing. I have no detailed recollection of the briefing, but it went very smoothly. After my presentation, Colonel Killeen fielded General Chapman's questions, and I used the question period to make a low profile exit.

I was in my office when Colonel Killeen returned. He entered with a smile on his face and said, "Pete, we did it! CMC seemed very pleased with the presentation, and he made no comment about your uniform. That palm tree was a very effective screen. What made you think of that?"

"Just a little thing I learned in the infantry called camouflage!"

He laughed and said, "Good job, Pete, now go on home and take the rest of the day off. You might also look for those gabardine trousers." Colonel Cal Killeen, an artilleryman, later retired from the Marine Corps with the rank of Major General.

I tell you this story to draw a contrast between things that are important in Washington D.C. and those that grab the attention of troops in combat. A day in Korea and Vietnam involved problems of life and death. Mistakes in combat don't result in a service record black mark; they result in an MIA or KIA statistic. A day on a headquarters staff brings problems of over-inflated importance that can be "career enders." Most problems a headquarters staff deals with are trifles and pale to insignificance when compared with combat. It doesn't make sense that surviving a tour in the Pentagon is fraught with more dangers than duty tours in Korea and Vietnam. Maybe that's why we called the Pentagon "The Five Sided Crazy House." Any sane man would ask, "Why must it be this way?" Any other sane man would answer, "It doesn't have to be!" Someday, a leader with vision will change it.

Colonel Tom Stuart was one of my very closest friends. Both of us had to struggle to get through the Naval Academy. When we graduated and received our numerical listing in rank, Tom was one number behind me followed by his brother, Jerry. We used to joke about my being one number senior to Tom. Whenever I reminded Tom of my seniority, he would say, "Careful, Pete, don't turn your back on me."

Tom and Jerry were "Marine Juniors." They were the sons of Lieutenant General James Austin Stuart, USMC, USNA Class of 1924, the same class as my stepfather, Boney Close. General Stuart was one of the Corps' most distinguished generals in the Pacific campaigns during World War II. Tom and Jerry were very close, not only as brothers, but also as Naval Academy classmates and fellow Marine officers. Jerry was killed in action in Korea, and Tom was detached from his battalion to escort Jerry's body home for burial in Arlington National Cemetery with full military honors. That was a sadness Tom never got over.

Tom later served with distinction in Vietnam in command of the Third Reconnaissance Battalion. He established reconnaissance tactics and command and control procedures for long-range reconnaissance patrols that became Marine Corps doctrine. Tom's "Stingray Patrols" would go out into the bush for extended periods, find the bad guys, then set up straight lines of communications to get the division's firepower and other supporting arms to hit the enemy hard. With direct communications to supporting arms, Tom took the initiative from the enemy by inflicting surprise heavy punishment on their troops. He took away the enemy's safe sanctuaries. They never knew when they were going to be hit hard with big guns and air strikes.

Colonel Jack Grace USMC, a USNA classmate, who also commanded a reconnaissance battalion in Vietnam says, "Recce guys are all a little bit weird. If you weren't before you went out on an extended mission in the Vietnam bush, you were when you came back." Jack said that Tom's innovative communications direct to supporting arms that bypassed much of the headquarters staff review and approval allowed Marine reconnaissance teams to be fully effective. Our Marine "recce guys" may have been a little weird, but they knew how to bring the war home to the enemy when he thought he was safe in his sanctuary.

Before leaving the subject of "recce weird," let me relate the story of Tom's Naval Academy roommate who paid him a visit in the Vietnam bush. Sam Jones, Tom's Academy roommate, was the executive officer of a cruiser in the Seventh Fleet. After a meeting in Da Nang with members of the First Marine Division Headquarters, Sam mentioned that his Academy roommate was in country, and inquired if it might be possible for him to pay Tom a visit. Headquarters immediately arranged for Sam to be helolifted into the jungle where Tom's unit was taking a breather after some very "hairy" operations. Unfortunately for Sam, Headquarters didn't pick him up for four days, and Sam didn't relax until he got back aboard his cruiser. Later, he kept classmates regaled with tales of his four sphincter puckering days in the Vietnam jungle with Tom Stuart and his band of psychopaths. Sam said he had never been so scared in his life, and that he didn't know who was scarier, the VC or Tom and his Marines. Recce Marines and the Vietnam jungle, lots of thrills!

Happily for both of us, Tom Stuart's tour at headquarters Marine Corps and mine coincided. About once a month, Tom, a few other Naval Academy classmates, assorted Marine Corps friends, and I would meet for lunch at the Army-Navy Country Club. Sometimes it would just be the two of us. At these "twosome" luncheons we talked about many things.

Tom shared my sadness and concern for Paul, my youngest son and fifth child, who had been born with Down's Syndrome. Tragically, there is no cure for this, but Paul is an exceptional young man who has dealt with his handicap in an admirable way. He earned a regular high school diploma, and is enjoying his job at McDonald's. Recently, Paul was named "Employee of the Month," and now trains other handicapped employees in their duties. We are all very proud of his accomplishments.

Paul's affliction was a serious blow to my wife, Frances, who was truly the perfect mother. Her dedication to his needs, seeking out other mothers with similar problems, and learning about infant stimulation, is a major reason for Paul's achieving the success he has in dealing with his handicap.

Sometimes Tom and I discussed our futures in the Marine Corps. We had good service careers, but saw our poor Naval Academy academic records as a hindrance to further advancement. I loved the Marine Corps and "war" was my best subject, certainly better than electrical engineering, but we both agreed that the possibility of commanding troops in combat again was remote. With the end of the Vietnam War, the Cold War was once again on a slow simmer, almost like peacetime. Going to one of the top war colleges (Army, Navy, Air Force, National, or Industrial) seemed to be a prerequisite for promotion to general officer grade. Competition for the limited number of places at these institutions was tough, and a board at Headquarters, Marine Corps similar to a promotion board, selected attendees. Tom and I both felt that with our lackluster academic records we had little chance with the Headquarters war college selection board; so, we decided to try another route to advanced professional education.

Tom wanted to try for the George Washington University program in finance, and I wanted to try for the Naval Postgraduate School in Monterey, California. The Navy PG School offered a one-year Master of Business Administration degree with the option to major in a business field of interest. Economics had always interested me, and I tended to do well in courses that interested me; so, I figured Business Administration with a major in Economics would suite me just fine. Happily, both of us were admitted to the school of our choice. The George Washington

University admitted Tom, and in late May 1970, I checked in to the U S Naval Postgraduate School in Monterey, California.

Before leaving for Monterey, I had a family matter to settle. My eldest daughter, Linda, was now ready for college. This is her account of how we selected a college for her to attend.

My father had definite ideas about where I should and should not go to college. He wouldn't tell me what those ideas were until I told him where I wanted to go, and then I bumped smack into "No's." I mentioned schools in California, he said, "No," and X'd off the state of California on the spot. Then I mentioned Brown, in Rhode Island, and he X'd off Rhode Island. (Like the game of battleship, I had two negative hits in my first two choices.)

"Then we settled on some women's colleges, Smith, Mount Holyoke, and Connecticut College for Women. At the recommendation of my college counselor, we added one co-ed college, Dickinson, in Carlisle, Pa.

That summer of 1969, Dad and I went on a trip to visit these schools, starting with Smith College. I liked the admissions officer right away. She had great energy and passion for the school, and agreed with Dad on the value of women's institutions. Dad liked her as well. But I had lingering question in my mind, due to knowing that buses of anti-war demonstrators came down from New England to Washington, D.C. regularly. I asked her, 'Would it be a problem for me on campus, being the daughter of a Marine?'

At this, the interviewer's face fell, lost all its enthusiasm, and she looked briefly at the floor. Collecting herself, she gave me an honest answer, 'Yes, it could be difficult for you at times.' I thanked her, and ended the interview. I informed her that I would not be applying to Smith College after all. I was disappointed at the way it turned out, after such a good initial impression, but never regretted the decision.

After visiting all the colleges on our list, I applied for

and was accepted as an 'early decision' applicant at
Dickinson. What a stroke of good luck! There, I met my
future husband, David Bassert, who was an R.O.T.C. cadet.
Our senior year, my father considered David 'a nice guy for
someone in the Army.' Semper Fi!"

After getting Linda squared away for college, it was my turn to
get to work on my post-graduate education. We packed our bags
and headed for California and one of the most pleasant times of
my life. My one-year tour at the Naval Postgraduate School was a
wonderful and peaceful time in my life. I did what good students
do. I studied hard and tried to do well on my exams and academic
projects.

I was the senior officer in our student section. We devised a
study plan for helping each other. For example, in preparation for
an exam we held review sessions where the best student in each
subject would conduct the review. Major Jon Easley, USMC, was
a very smart student in the computer course. Jon helped us all,
especially me. I will always be grateful to him for his patient
explanations of computer arcana.

In June 1971, the Naval Post Graduate course ended. I graduated
with a master's degree in business management, with emphasis in
economics. I made the best grades I ever made in school, which leads
me to believe that taking courses I selected because I was interested in
them made a big difference in my academic success. The added
maturity over my undergraduate days at the Naval Academy was a
further boost to my new-found scholarship. I must confess that my
Naval Academy experience with electrical engineering never sent my
heart into heavy palpitations. That must be why "Juice" was such a
struggle for me when I was a midshipman.

After graduation from the Post Graduate School, I requested
another tour in Vietnam. I thought my previous experience as a
battalion commander might bring me another combat command,
possibly a regiment. This was a long shot, but it didn't hurt to
hope. Unfortunately, I was in for a big surprise.

8.0 SECOND TOUR IN VIETNAM

We departed Monterey and made the long drive back to Falls Church, Virginia. We were lucky and found a nice two-story house for rent near Lake Barcroft in Falls Church. I devoted the balance of my thirty-day leave to moving in and helping my family get settled. Our Collie had just died; so, one evening we purchased a little black and tan mongrel puppy to ease the loss of our family dog. David named him Mike. He was a lovable little mutt, but very naughty. No one seemed to mind chasing after him when he ran away. The kids got lots of exercise doing the chasing. To the pup, it was all a game. But all good things come to an end, and way too soon the time of my departure for Vietnam arrived.

I arrived in Saigon on 1 August 1971. Instead of a combat command, I was assigned to the Agency for International Development (AID) in Saigon. I was to be the chief of the civic action division. This was a new AID Saigon organization, and I was not relieving anyone.

This assignment was a payback tour for the Naval Postgraduate School. Payback tours usually happen after an officer goes to a school at government expense. I had no problem accepting this; however, I was appalled at what I saw going on in this AID Saigon outfit. It looked to me to be a place for a lot of civilian dead wood. They did little more than plan where they were going to eat lunch, and what they were going to do that evening. Most of them had mistresses.

While with AID, I made one trip into the "boondocks" to check on a civic action division pig farming program. That was my most important assignment. From commanding a battalion of Marines to pig farming, what a comedown! And I needed a masters degree from the Navy PG School to do this?

Fortunately, I knew a Marine Brigadier General in the G-3 section at Headquarters MACV; so, I went to see him. After I gave him the scoop on what was going on at AID, he agreed to get me transferred to MACV to work for him in G-3. After two months at AID, I was transferred to the Surface Operations Division, J-3 as executive director of the Combat Information Center.

While this assignment was an improvement, I had to scramble to find enough to keep me busy. The Army Colonel I worked for tried to make a meaningful job for me, but there really wasn't enough work for both of us. The Army colonel tolerated the situation because his boss was the Marine Brigadier who had rescued me from AID. Word also came through that I had been selected for promotion to full Colonel. My Army Colonel boss needed me like a hole in the head, but he kept a smile on his face and made the best of it.

I tried to keep busy by volunteering for duty as the all night watch officer in the J-3 command center. The MACV Headquarters was overloaded with Army and other service types getting their Vietnam "combat ticket" punched so they could go home and finish out their careers. My disillusionment with high-level staff duty began after seeing the useless waste of manpower. As an operational battalion commander I had a hundred times more responsibility and things to do than I had at MACV Headquarters. My biggest and most pleasant daily activity was playing tennis at noontime on the COMUSMACV tennis court.

One incident occurred during my tour where I made a difference. A Marine lieutenant colonel, named Gerald Turley, had performed an arduous and heroic deed that was totally unappreciated by MACV Headquarters. This was the same Gerry Turley whom I tried to take with me when I took command of the First Battalion, Fifth Marines. Turley gives a full account of this incident in his wonderful book, *The Easter Offensive*. I will summarize the events and try to fill in some of the blanks in his story from my perspective.

In Easter of 1972, the North Vietnamese invaded South Vietnam's Quang Tri Province as the first step in invading all of

South Vietnam. This was their second offensive. The first was in 1968, which was repulsed in the now famous battle for Hue City. In the Easter Offensive, the North Vietnamese launched a full-scale invasion of Quang Tri, and came across the DMZ with tanks and heavy artillery. South Vietnamese troops did the fighting with the support of a small cadre of U.S. Army and Marine field advisors. Lieutenant Colonel Gerry Turley and Major Jon Easley (my Monterey classmate) were two of these Marines.

Lieutenant Colonel Turley was thrust into an unprecedented and controversial leadership position when a U.S. Army general ordered him to take charge of all military personnel and combat operations in the northernmost area of I Corps (called Eye Corps). An Army general's bypassing more senior Army officers to select a Marine lieutenant colonel to command combat operations was unbelievable! It was, however, a drastic response to a serious situation, and Turley, with help from Major Jon Easley, stepped up to the job of halting the North Vietnamese attack. Gerry responded aggressively with counter attacks and delaying actions including destruction of the Dong Ha Bridge to foil an NVA tank attack.

Back in Saigon, at MACV Headquarters, senior Army staff officers were raising hell over Gerry's assumption of overall tactical command in Quang Tri. They began undermining Turley's credibility by raising serious objections to his tactics and command maturity. Essentially, they did not want a Marine officer, and a relatively junior one at that, taking command of all military operations in Quang Tri Province, and they were determined to stop it with bureaucratic sabotage.

They further objected to Turley making his reports through Navy channels rather than going through MACV Headquarters. MACV was also outraged that Turley requested, without MACV staffing and approval, an amphibious landing by U.S. Marines to provide tactical support to the beleaguered South Vietnamese troops in Quang Tri. In tactical operations, called "Operation Deckhouse," Marines aboard Seventh Fleet ships were often temporarily deployed in combat ashore to reinforce U.S. and ARVN troops heavily engaged with the enemy. These Seventh Fleet

Marines were the same as the Special Landing Force Marines that had been deployed in support of the Fifth Marines during Union I. So, Turley's request for Marine intervention in Quang Tri as another Deckhouse operation was not an out of the ordinary tactical move. It made good sense. It wasn't Turley's request of Operation Deckhouse support from the Navy and Marines that upset the Army command. It was the fact that Turley didn't go through normal MACV command channels.

MACV ordered Turley to be relieved from his emergency assignment in I Corps, and to report to Headquarters in Saigon. They wanted his head! They were going to rip his buttons off and drum him out of the regiment! They were going to drive a stake thorough his heart!

My Marine brigadier told me that when Turley arrived I was to interview him and then bring Gerry to his office. I was to sort out the facts and give the general a clear picture of the situation.

I had known Turley since 1959 when we were company commanders in Okinawa. When it came to the Marine Corps and war fighting, Turley was all business and a serious professional. When it was *monkey business,* well . . . he and I had lots of fun together, especially at the Air Force Officers Club in Kadina, Okinawa. But Turley was not in trouble for high-spirited nonsense. He was in serious trouble for carrying out his general's orders, doing his best to stop the North Vietnamese offensive, and getting "cross-threaded" with the MACV bureaucracy.

When Gerry entered my office, I hardly recognized him. He had come straight from the field. He was unshaven, and in a torn, filthy uniform. Gerry looked a mess! He immediately began to brief me on the I Corps circumstances. I had never heard a tale such as this. I asked him a number of questions and let him know that General Abrams, who was Commander U.S. Military Assistance Command Vietnam (COMUSMACV), was personally embarrassed by his actions in circumventing the MACV chain of command to request a Deckhouse Operation.

As the conversation progressed, I began to realize that Gerry was telling the truth about the deteriorating military situation in

Quang Tri. He was doing the right thing tactically, the Deckhouse request was not impulsive and poorly conceived, and he needed to be back with his troops, not giving briefings, and being "wire-brushed" by headquarters staff. He may have been insensitive to headquarters protocol and the MACV chain of command, but Gerry's job was to beat the enemy, and that he was doing. General Abrams wanted Gerry replaced by a more senior Army colonel and removed from Quang Tri.

Gerry did not deserve to have his helmet "dinged" and to do penance at MACV Headquarters. I had to find something else for him, and fast. Gerry said he had the "trots," a normal ailment in Vietnam, and excused himself to go to the head. While he was out of my office, I called my friend and Naval Academy classmate, Captain F. Trent Shaver USN. Trent was the Navy engineering duty only (EDO) officer with duties on both the Commander Naval Forces Vietnam (COMNAVFORV) headquarters staff and COMUSMACV headquarters staff. I felt Trent understood the political intricacies in the relations between the two staffs, and that Trent could get Gerry strong support at COMNAVFOR. Trent was the consummate professional and the right person to help in this situation. During Turley's absence from my office, I moved quickly. My boss, the brigadier, had concurred with getting Gerry out of MACV Headquarters. When Gerry returned to my office, I filled him in on my actions. I told him to get over to NAVFORV Headquarters immediately, which he did.

In Turley's book *The Easter Offensive* he describes his meeting with Admiral Salzer and how the Admiral, after listening to his account, took him back to MACV Headquarters and went to bat for him. MACV would not back down. Gerry was replaced by a more senior Army colonel and removed from Quang Tri Province.

MACV Headquarters won that skirmish, but Lieutenant Colonel Turley did return to Quang Tri later. He served with the Vietnamese Marines, and was decorated for his actions in Quang Tri Province. He retired from the Marine Corps with the rank of Colonel, and subsequently became a Deputy Assistant Secretary of Defense. He always has been, and still is, a good friend. I felt then, and still do, that Gerry was badly used by General Abrams. His picture may not be on General Abrams' piano, but Gerry came through this mean-spirited mess with the respect of his fellow grunts. I played a small part in this whole sorry affair, but my contribution was to help save Gerry from the purgatory of finishing his Vietnam tour on the MACV Headquarters staff. That would have been worse than death for a grunt!

My second tour in Vietnam ended in July 1972. This time I had orders bringing me back to Washington for more staff duty. Events that occurred during my trip home and afterwards were instrumental in my making one of the most painful decisions I ever had to make.

9.0 FINAL MARINE CORPS TOUR

My orders detaching me from MACV Headquarters in Saigon directed me to report for duty in the Office of the Chief of Naval Operations as Assistant Branch Head Program Appraisal and Information Branch (OP-09) as a relief for Colonel H. J. Redfield USMC. This was a choice assignment and I was elated.

When I arrived in Washington, I went down to Headquarters Marine Corps to let them know I was back. I learned my orders had been modified. I was now to report to the Commandant of the Marine Corps (CMC) headquarters for duty. From being assigned the top job available that summer, I went to the bottom of the list because all other colonel slots had been filled. I tried to find out what had happened, and learned that the Assistant Commandant of the Marine Corps, General Anderson, a Marine aviation general, had my orders changed so that the OP-09 job could be filled with an aviation colonel. This upset me greatly! That switch was a political change. It had nothing to do with me except that I was an infantry officer and General Anderson wanted an aviator, one of his own, in the job. I now had to find another assignment, hopefully one that would enhance my career.

My former regimental commander in Vietnam, Colonel Fred Haynes, was now a Major General commanding the Second Marine Division in Camp Lejeune. I called General Haynes and told him what had happened. General Haynes said he would try to get me assigned to the Second Marine Division. Initially I would be an excess colonel, by one. However, within a couple of months, a vacancy would open up and he would give me a regiment. General Haynes said he would call Headquarters Marine Corps, (HQMC) and make the appropriate request.

Headquarters Marine Corps was already over staffed with colonels; so, there was no sense in sending me to HQMC if I had an assignment elsewhere. I was very optimistic that HQMC would approve the request, but that was not to happen. The "Colonel Detailer" was a Naval Academy classmate. He told me he would recommend disapproval of General Haynes' request, and to my amazement the G-1, brigadier general backed my classmate. Headquarters rejected General Haynes' request for my assignment to the Second Division.

One of the first things we learned at the Naval Academy was never "bilge" a classmate. And in my four years at the Academy and the 24 years I spent in the Marine Corps, this was the first time a classmate had been disloyal or failed to support me when I needed help. If he had a good reason for recommending disapproval of General Haynes' request for me, he never made the effort to tell me, and if the reason had been sound, I would have accepted it with good grace. The episode reeked, and I do mean "reeked," of pettiness.

My new orders, thanks to my classmate, sent me to the HQMC Division of Reserve as an excess colonel. With the war in Vietnam ending, our forces were coming home. The Marine Corps had more colonels than they needed. From being much in demand when the shooting was going on, I was now one of the excess.

I reported to the Division of Reserve as an assistant branch head to another colonel who did not need me. Our office was in a room so small that our two desks were butted together facing each other. Papers were placed in my in-coming box. After reading them, I would put them in the branch head's box. Can you get a mental picture of this? It was not good for either of us. I knew I could not do this for the next two years.

Things were not going well on the home front either. My wife's health had deteriorated substantially. The kids, especially Diana and Dale, were covering for her. They fixed the meals and did the housework. They were great! I blamed myself for my wife's severe depression and the sad condition of my family. I had gone to war too many times, and now my family needed my full attention.

I was one unhappy Marine. There was, though, one bright spot in my life. We had just acquired a Brittany spaniel pup. We named him Pat. He was the one bright, happy thing around our house. Pat and I would go for walks, and I would tell him my problems. Was God sending me a message? If so, what was it? Pat may not have spoken to me, but he got the message to me. I had a duty to my family now. They needed me, and I was not "in excess" with them.

I had one of the best combat records in my seniority group. My staff record was good. I had received two Navy commendation medals: one for my staff work while in Hawaii and the second for my job in the G-3 at Headquarters Marine Corps. I loved the Marine Corps. It had been a very rewarding career to this point, but now it was drudgery. I was not proud of what I was doing.

I was certain of one thing, I was at my best in combat, and I would never again lead troops in battle. Peace was here, and it looked to be a long-term proposition. If I did make general officer, which seemed highly unlikely now, I would just be a "paper pushing" general with no combat troops to lead. I was forty-five years old. Now was the time to find out if I might be successful in the business world. That could be an acceptable alternative to staying in the peacetime Marine Corps.

I couldn't soldier forever. It's a young man's game, and one doesn't acquire financial wealth in military service. In a second career I wanted to gain the wealth to provide amply for my family; so, I decided to pursue a second career in the world of finance. Finance is about making money, and it seemed that was the field to be in if I wanted to acquire wealth.

As a Marine Corps retiree I would have a monthly check, which would provide me with financial security until I could get started in a new career. My talks with my Brittany pup, Pat, and self-analysis led me to believe I should try to become a stockbroker. I had learned about business and finance at the Naval Postgraduate School. The accounting course I took would help me read financial statements, and the economics courses would help me understand investment trends. I had also invested in the stock market with good results. Pat seemed to be giving me good advice.

So, I went to Washington, D.C. and walked into the main office of Ferris and Company, a small brokerage firm. I met with the branch manager, a lady named Carol Rollins, who told me what I had to do to get hired. I had to take an aptitude exam and be interviewed by the executive vice president. I took the exam and a few days later received a phone call from Carol. She told me I had done very well on the aptitude test, and invited me to come in for an interview with the executive vice president.

After the interview, the executive vice president told me to come back after a few days while he "thought about it."

My reply was very direct. "Sir, I came down here for your interview. If you want me, I'm prepared to go back right now and submit my request for retirement from the Marine Corps. I'll just sit out here in the lobby until you make up your mind."

In less than an hour, Ferris and Company offered me a job. I became the highest paid trainee in the brokerage house. The hiring terms were to pay me a salary for a period of time, after which I would be on a full commission as a stockbroker. This was assuming I passed the other required exams to become registered as an investment broker. I went back that day and submitted my request for retirement.

When my request for retirement reached the desk of Lieutenant General Foster Lahue, he called and asked to see me. He wanted to ask why I was leaving the Corps. Not many colonels seeking to retire, are personally interviewed by the Chief of Staff of the Marine Corps, but I was. He asked why I was retiring, and I told him why with no holds barred, no soft soap, no fuzzing up the message. General Lahue was upset with me, but he understood and accepted my decision gracefully. He even offered to give me a retirement parade ceremony at the Marine Barracks at 8th and I Streets in Washington, D.C., which I thanked him for and politely declined. General Lahue asked me to reconsider my decision to retire, but it was too late. I had made up my mind, and had no intention of turning back.

When the news of my retirement became public, I was totally surprised and immensely pleased to hear from friends both in and out of the Marine Corps. Their thoughts and letters touched me deeply, and their sentiments made my decision to leave even more painful. I am proud of the Certificate of Appreciation from the President of the United States, but I treasure most of all those letters from my troops.

One thing was left for me to do before I could be officially transferred to the retired rolls of the Marine Corps. I had to take a physical exam. After reporting to the medical facility, a doctor examined me from head to toe. When he finished, he told me to get weighed and measured.

The person doing that small task was, if I may use this expression, a "grizzled old Navy nurse." Somehow that sounds better than "hoary" Navy nurse, which means the same thing. This lady had been around the Navy for a long time. She ordered me to get on the scales. I did so, assuming the customary stance I had used for many years.

Whereupon, she growled, "Colonel, you can stand up straight now. You are not coming into the Marine Corps, you are going *out!*"

On 31 March, my thirty days of terminal leave from the Marine Corps began. On 1 April 1973, I went to work at Ferris and Company, and began a rewarding career as an investment broker. This may have been April Fool's Day, but it was a great move for me, and one that was to last a little more than twenty-five years. I have never regretted my decision to change careers. However, I was then and always will be in my heart—a United States Marine!

10.0 LIFE AFTER THE CORPS

Transition from one way of life to another is never easy, but going from the military to the civilian world is truly culture shock. At least it was for me. The adjustment is a monumental effort that takes concentration, desire, will-power, and all the diplomatic skill you can muster to make your new colleagues accept you into their order of things. In my new world, I was not in command. I was starting all over again at the bottom. It was like being a "third lieutenant," just out of the Naval Academy all over again.

The broker-training program at Ferris and Company was loosely structured. It consisted of a heavy dose of rules laid down by the National Association of Security Dealers, (NASD), some by the New York Stock Exchange and some by Ferris and Company. Trainees were also expected to perform "scut-work" chores such as stuffing envelopes for mailings. In short, the training programs lasted until the trainee passed the various required examinations to become a registered and licensed broker.

Right off the bat, I incurred the enmity of one of the established brokers in the firm. He had been with Ferris for many years and did not like the fact that the company was paying me a salary while I was receiving retirement pay from the Marine Corps. He made his feelings very clear stating, "I worked my way into the business the hard way. I started out selling vacuum cleaners door to door." Mr. "Hoover" even carried his hostility to the point of trying to get me fired. Fortunately, his complaints fell on deaf ears.

As soon as I had passed the exams I was directed to begin building a book of clients. The firm wanted me to go to Quantico and prospect the Marines there. I refused to do this. I knew that Marines do not have extensive financial assets and even less in the way of an investment mindset. They were warriors and lived month-to-month on their meager paychecks.

Instead, I began talking with various brokers and inquiring where their main client bases were located. I plotted this information on an area map, and learned that none of them had a meaningful base in the Warrenton, Virginia area.

The brokerage business is mostly a sales oriented business. There are three main ways for brokers to obtain clients: by cold calling on the telephone; through mailings; and by face-to-face solicitations. Established brokers primarily relied on referrals to build their book, which they supplemented by conducting investment seminars. These seminars reflected the concept that an educated client is the best client. They filled a big gap in financial education for the general public. There was no such thing as a TV business channel or computer on-line stock market reports in those days.

I abhorred the idea of making cold calls, and decided I would never do that. I didn't mind face-to-face solicitations or mailings, and I felt very comfortable with the idea of holding classes and seminars. I decided to start my program in the Warrenton area, and drove down there for that purpose. I spent three days sitting in an old-fashioned drug store located across from the county courthouse. I must have consumed a gallon of coffee during those three days. I sat at the store counter and chatted with people who came into the drugstore. I also visited the local library and arranged to conduct a series of investment seminars one night a week for three weeks in a row.

The Warrenton area has a large number of affluent people, and the results from my first seminar were very encouraging. Many of the attendees were the same people I had met in the drug store. When the seminar series ended, about eighty percent of the class opened accounts with Ferris and Company as my clients. Investment TV programs were non-existent then, and similar radio programs were just beginning; so, I continued my Warrenton investment seminars every three months. After I became established in the Warrenton area, I continued these highly successful seminars semiannually for a number of years.

Since my efforts in Warrenton were so successful, I expanded the seminars to Loudon, Prince William, and Fairfax counties. Later, I branched out into Maryland. To supplement my seminars, I started an investment newsletter, and arranged to give a radio investment commentary daily after the stock market closed. At the end of my first year in the business, I had created a client book of sufficient size that I asked to be put on full commission status. It worked, and I never looked back.

As a result of my efforts in Warrenton, I received a telephone call from the president of the old Virginia investment firm of Scott and Stringfellow. He offered me the job of branch manager in their Warrenton office if I would leave Ferris and join them. I thanked him, but declined his offer.

I continued to build my business, and worked hard at it. I usually worked ten-hour weekdays and half a day on Saturday and Sunday. If I didn't drive to D.C. on Sunday, I worked at home. Sunday was the day I made my plan for the next two weeks. This was a demanding schedule. During my first ten years in the business, I never took a vacation. I knew this was not easy for my family. The years of separation in the Marine Corps had taken their toll, and I had left the Corps with the idea that I would have more time for my family. I had, though, set goals for myself, and I had to take care of my family financially. I had to work hard to succeed. There was no other way.

After about two years in the firm, I was appointed vice president of investments. This classified me as a senior broker and I remember that Mr. Hoover came over to my desk and congratulated me. We got along okay from then on. His title was merely senior broker and that was as far as he ever got.

George Ferris, Jr. was the president of Ferris and Company. He usually held meetings every Tuesday morning with the brokers in his Washington, DC office. In the beginning of my tenure with the company as a trainee, the meetings were interesting, but as I learned more about the business they became increasingly boring.

During one such meeting, I glanced over at a nearby small coffee table. There was a copy of *Financial World* lying face up. On the cover it had a photo of a bovine animal with a modest set of horns. In big letters right above the picture were the words, "Is It For Real?" The article inside was presumably about whether the current market was then a bull or bear market.

I looked at the cover and said to myself, those idiots don't know the difference between a bull and a cow. Why should I believe they know the difference between a bull and a bear? I proceeded to jot down the following letter to the editor, "You all should be ashamed of yourselves for misleading the public. This is a cow and not a bull and a pregnant one at that—and that's **no bull!**"

About ten days later I answered the phone on my desk and a voice said, "I just received your letter. Are you sure that this is a picture of a pregnant cow?" He then identified himself as Alfred Kenyon, editor-in-chief of *Financial World*.

I answered, "Yes sir, I'm positive. My father had a ranch in Texas, and I know the difference between a bull and pregnant cow. One difference is the shape of the head. A bull's head is broader, much more 'V' shaped. A pregnant animal has distended sides and looks pregnant."

He asked if he could have this observation checked out. I told him to go ahead, because I knew I was correct.

After another week went by, I received a second call from Mr. Kenyon. This time he told me that he had consulted some ten different sources, cattlemen and veterinarians alike and they all verified my comment, 100 percent.

Then he said, "I've just called Merrill Lynch, and if you look out your window you'll see a mushroom cloud in the sky. Donald Regan, the chairman of Merrill, has just gone ballistic and fired their ad agency. They're also going to change their logo."

So whenever you see the Merrill Lynch bull displayed, you can be assured that there is no mistake about that bovine animal. It now is in fact a bull. That was my most enduring contribution to Wall Street. *Financial World* published my letter in their July 1, 1978 issue with appropriate commentary. As Paul Harvey says, "And now you know the rest of the story."

By design, Ferris and Company remained a small operation

with only a one-person stock research department. My business continued to grow to a point where their research could not adequately support my business. It became time to move elsewhere.

At home, my marriage continued to deteriorate because of my wife's mental illness. Our Episcopal Church parish tried to intercede with well-intentioned parishioners and our clergyman. The parishioners, who wanted to patch things up, were out of their depth. They were good people, but they were interfering in something that none of them understood, or were capable of handling. The clergyman was equally unhelpful. He came at me with an attitude, and became very vitriolic. He declared that I was the cause of my marital problems. I had run off to war too many times . . . as if I had run off to Las Vegas too often and spent the family milk money.

The clergyman suggested that I consult my wife's psychiatrist to help me understand her severe depression. That was a reasonable suggestion, and I agreed to do so. I met with him hoping that he might offer the guidance I needed to save my marriage and family. It was another totally unproductive exercise. In the end, my wife and I separated and were divorced a year later.

After the divorce, I moved to a small one-bedroom cottage near Herndon, Virginia. To make life more difficult in those crowded conditions, my female Brittany Spaniel had just produced a litter of pups. One day, in response to my newspaper ad concerning the pups I had for sale, a gentleman appeared and wanted to purchase one of the puppies for his son. During our conversation, I asked him what his profession was. He told me he was the branch manager of the local Legg Mason office at Tyson's corner, Virginia. His name was David Farrington.

Legg Mason was a regional brokerage firm with an excellent reputation. They had corporate headquarters in Baltimore, and were much larger than Ferris with a strong stock research department. I already knew these things, and on several occasions had considered transferring to Legg Mason. A few days after the sale of the puppy, I called David Farrington, and he arranged a luncheon meeting for me with the Legg Mason executive vice president, James Brinkley. Our discussion lasted about an hour and Brinkley offered me a position with Legg Mason as vice president-investments and appointment as assistant branch manager. This gave me a personal secretary and more leverage to solve problems. As assistant branch manager I would have direct access to department managers in the Baltimore headquarters to help resolve problems and answer questions, which would benefit my clients. The move was to be effective on the first working day in January 1980.

Jim Brinkley immediately impressed me, and my admiration for him grew steadily over the years we worked together. He knew the financial management business, was a superb leader, and always encouraged and supported me to the fullest. I learned a great deal from him about how to succeed as a broker.

We were having a cold snowy winter, and a water pipe in my home broke a day or two before Christmas. I had to attend to the situation immediately. The house had been flooded; so, I had a perfect reason to ask for time off during Christmas week. I hired a plumber to repair the pipe, and my son, David, helped me clean up the mess the water made. Even with all this frenzy, I found time to finish the necessary paperwork to move to Legg Mason. On the last working day of December 1979, I told Mr. Ferris that I was leaving. As abrupt as it may seem, this was the way broker transfers took place in those days, and we parted good friends.

After reporting to the Legg Mason Tyson's Corner office, I began notifying my clients of my new firm. About ninety-five percent of them moved their accounts with me to Legg Mason. Jim Brinkley was impressed that so many clients had followed me, and told me so. The move to Legg Mason was one of the best decisions I ever made. Chip Mason, the chairman and founder, is a truly outstanding leader of his firm and a respected member of the securities community. In Jim Brinkley, David Farrington, and Bill Jones, the regional manager, Chip had surrounded himself with superior people to make a solid brokerage team. The brokers I met in the Tyson's Corner office were also a fine group. Jack Glenn, who had been with the office longest, gave me a warm welcome and helped me to adjust quickly to the Legg Mason routine. Richard Cripps, Nadine Van Orsdel, Laurie Kent, Andy Flowers, Steven Skousgaard, and others who joined us in the months to come added to the congeniality of the office. All were professionals of the highest caliber. This firm is as fine a civilian organization as the Marine Corps is a military organization. Turnover in Legg Mason was practically nil, and the company has grown to a billion dollar international investment firm. My life had changed for the better.

11.0 SARA

I had opened a small account with a young man named Greg Fernlund. He was a recent graduate from Wake Forest, and wanted to start a program to grow his wealth for later years. A proper goal, I thought.

He called one day and asked me, if I would speak to his mother about opening an account. I agreed to do this, and one day in early April 1982 an attractive lady came to see me at my office. She was Greg's mother.

A broker must make every effort to know his customer when opening a new account. This is a Securities and Exchange Commission rule, and a good one. I had a standard procedure in opening new accounts that included a detailed one-on-one interview. Mrs. Fernlund entered my office shortly after 11:00 A.M. The interviews usually lasted about thirty minutes, followed by some paperwork that took a few minutes. I asked her a number of questions, concerning her investment objectives, and for married women I usually asked something about their marriage because I needed to know what role, if any, the husband would play.

"Mrs. Fernlund, what role will your husband have in your investment decisions?" I asked.

With that she burst into tears. "My husband and I are getting divorced."

I decided to get her out of the office, before everyone thought I had insulted this poor lady. So I said, "Mrs. Fernlund, let me take you to lunch. We can leave right now. There's a place a few doors down the street where they have a very nice lunch. I am sorry I upset you, but I am required to ask these kinds of questions"

We went to lunch and it was very pleasant. I learned she was working as a realtor. Just before I said good-bye she asked me if I ever gave investment seminars, and if I did would I give one at her office? I thanked her and said I would be pleased to make such a presentation.

After lunch, we parted, and I went back to my office. The investment seminar that Mrs. Fernlund had mentioned passed from my mind. Several months later, in early June, I received a call from her.

She said, "This is Sara Fernlund," and after passing conversational pleasantries she said, "I'm calling to see when you can hold an investment seminar at our Great Falls Long and Foster office."

We agreed on a Tuesday morning. At 9:30 A.M on the appointed day, I appeared at her office. I was expecting about fifteen or twenty people, but the place was jam-packed. As I stood in the room and surveyed the crowd, Sara stood and made the introduction. Wow! She's really quite stunning, I thought.

The presentation went very well. I apologized for not bringing enough handout literature, and said that I would go back to my office to bring more that afternoon. I sensed I was going to receive some business from this group. At that point, Sara said she was holding a property sale open house, and I could return with the material and leave it with her.

"Besides," she added, "we'll be serving sandwiches so you can get something to eat for your trouble."

I agreed to return and drop off my material with her. When I later returned, I opened the door and stood there with my arms full of handouts. Then I saw Sara come gracefully downstairs to the hallway. My eyes flat-out crossed!

After leaving the handout material Sara and I went into the kitchen where she had a table loaded with good things to eat. Even though we had never dated, nor had I ever made such overtures, as a matter of ethical principle, I had to tell her I was interested in her for more than platonic business reasons. So when we were alone, I told her, "Sara, I'm a whole lot more interested in you than just being your stockbroker. I can't combine business with pleasure; that wouldn't be right, and certainly it would not be fair to you. I will find you another good stockbroker, if you will consent to go out with me. I have tickets to a concert at Wolftrap. Will you go with me to the concert?" She accepted and offered to bring a picnic supper. The Wolftrap evening was a success.

In early December 1982, I asked Sara to marry me, and she accepted. It was a happy night, for both of us. When we began discussing the events leading to my proposal and her acceptance, she told me that it was the invitation to go to the Wolftrap concert that did the trick. Sara said, "I had always wanted to go to a concert at Wolftrap and have a picnic on the lawn there. When you extended the invitation I was thrilled."

During Christmas 1982, I went with Sara to meet her parents, Hugh and Mille McNown, in Indiana. They were wonderful, unpretentious people whom I liked immediately. Hugh, nicknamed "Ace," had been a master sergeant in the Army Air Corps during World War II. He left the service after the war and devoted his life to helping handicapped youngsters. Mille and Ace were a warm, Midwestern family that made me feel right at home.

I asked Ace if he would give me permission to marry his daughter, which he did. In April 1983, I married Sara in Centreville, Virginia in a tiny church with a history going back to the Civil War when it was used as a hospital. My mother was with me at the church, and when the time came for the ceremony there was **no** Sara. She arrived a few minutes later with both of her sons, Greg and Scott. To get through the evening rush hour congestion, Scott had printed, with Sara's lipstick, "Bride Late for Wedding" on the car window and they shot down the shoulder of the road.

Not all my children were able to attend, but my daughter Dale and my sons, Paul and David, were there. David was my best man. Sara has been a blessing, a great supporter and my best friend for over twenty years now. I thank God and Greg every day for sending her to me!

One of the most enjoyable days at Legg Mason I can remember was the day the firm scheduled a trip to New York City to visit the New York Stock Exchange. Neither Sara nor I had ever been to the Exchange. My stepbrother, Bill Close, was a floor broker on the "floor" of the Exchange. He is a wonderful person much like his father. He and my brother, Tex, had been roommates at Princeton. Both were members of the Navy ROTC there, and each had been commissioned a Navy ensign upon graduation.

When we arrived on the floor of the Exchange, we surprised Billy. He recovered quickly and gave us a tour I'll never forget. Now we exchange visits as often as possible. His lovely wife, Stephanie, and Sara look so much alike they are often mistaken as sisters.

Over the years my business at Legg Mason flourished. We had acquired some international clients, and my "book" grew to over 1000 clients. I credit much of my success to my wonderful long time assistants. The first was Lou Ann Brown. After she retired, Dianna Rodgers took Lou Ann's place. My clients loved both of these ladies and so did I. They were outstanding, and my success was in no small measure attributable to them.

In order to keep up, I had to grow in capability. As luck would have it, Dick Martin appeared on the scene and became my partner. Dick was a West Point graduate, number two in his graduating class. He was a wonderful man with ethical principles of the highest order. In fact, it was with his encouragement and support that I was able to help Legg Mason establish an ethics course for our broker trainees. Dick and I began to specialize more and more in the pension arena. One of the larger law firms in Washington became our client, as did one of the most prestigious girls' schools on the East Coast.

Permanently living in the Northern Virginia Village of Great Falls, I had time for other activities. I became actively involved in establishing the Northern Virginia Brittany Club. I also joined the Rotary Club of McLean, remaining a member until 1995 until my retirement from the business world. I then became active in the State of Virginia Hunter Education Program. Both the Brittany Club and Rotary Club honored me by asking me to serve as president. I have remained a member of the Brittany Club to this day.

In the spring of 1997, while jogging one Sunday, Dick Martin succumbed to a massive heart attack. I came out of partial retirement to handle the client load. Six months later, I was carried to Fairfax Hospital in an ambulance. The diagnosis was heart disease. On 30

June 1998, I retired from Legg Mason officially, having served with them for over eighteen wonderful years, for a total of 26 years in the brokerage business.

God has blessed me in so many ways. He has given me twelve wonderful grandchildren, with Joshua Louis being born to David and Kay on 1 October 2003. Now He has given me the years to pursue my life-long passion for the wonders of the great outdoors, and for hunting and fishing. My story would not be complete without a few hunting and fishing tales. Much of what I learned through hunting helped me tremendously in Vietnam. Hunting gave me a sense of how to live in the forest and jungle. It taught me to understand forest sounds, and to know that when I heard total quiet, things were not normal. Hunting gave me a sense of how to be stealthy and track my quarry. It taught me patience to wait for the right moment to take my shot. I suppose that in many ways, hunting "Charley" wasn't all that much different from hunting deer . . . except hunting "Charley" was dangerous. I don't mean to imply that war is an enjoyable game. It isn't! My point is that hunting skills and combat skills have much in common. Perhaps that is why so many Marines enjoy hunting.

Sara, Pete and friends

12.0 HUNTING TALES

I love hunting and fishing. I love the out-of-doors and all the wonders in the forest and streams that God created. Hunting is my passion. I live for my family and hunting. Part of that love is my hunting dogs. Currently, I have five dogs, four Brittanys and one Lab. The Brittanys, Minx, Maggie, Penny and Rufus, are for hunting upland game birds, like grouse, pheasant, quail and woodcock. Ruby, my young Lab, is for retrieving geese, ducks, and other waterfowl.

For me, hunting is not really a sport the way tennis and golf are sports. It is an important part of my life, a link to the way things were in simpler times in our land. Whatever I hunt and bring home, we eat. Sara can create magnificent feasts with venison or game birds.

Woodsmanship, ethics, gun safety, proper gun handling and patience are all part of the hunting game. A good hunter must also know the game laws. They are his rules of engagement. Hunting is a privilege and a learning experience. Gun owning is a right that requires common sense and responsibility. Every time I go hunting I learn something. No two hunting days are exactly alike. Each hunt is different from the last.

The traditions of hunting point in one direction: generosity, fair play, and respect for the hunted and the environment in which game lives. Wildlife is a resource that will thrive if it is properly managed. Deer, for example, are now overly abundant in places where they did not exist a hundred years ago in this country.

Hunting is a great adventure. I've been able to enjoy it for more than sixty years. I do not consider myself a great hunter, but I am experienced enough to teach others about the right way to be a hunting sportsman. That is why I became certified as a Virginia State Hunter Education Instructor. As a teacher, I am still learning new things each year. That is one of the enjoyable aspects of being a hunting instructor.

Buckshot Sparks was my first hunting and trapping teacher. Buckshot took me on my first deer hunt. We rode horses one very early morning to a high ledge jutting out from one of the hills on his ranch. We brought a third horse in tow as the packhorse. My job was to hold the rope tied to the packhorse's halter.

When we arrived at a spot near the ledge, but out of sight of it, we dismounted and secured the horses. We then walked to the ledge. I remember I had on a warm jacket, but I had no long johns on under my blue jeans. No self-respecting cowboy would ever wear long johns . . . so I thought. There was a light wind blowing from the north into our faces. After we sat down on the rocky ledge, Buckshot told me to sit real still, otherwise I might spook the deer. Well, it was pretty chilly that southwest Texas morning up in those hills. I wanted to sit still, but my legs didn't. After telling me to sit still several times, I could sense my hero was getting a bit annoyed with me. Fortunately, a nice buck showed up, and Buckshot dropped him with one shot. I learned a good lesson that day: Smart cowboys wear longjohns when it's cold!

I did almost no hunting for many years after I left the Sparks ranch. When I was stationed at Quantico in 1955 to 1957, I began hunting again. These hunts were infrequent and by myself. I was a novice hunter, and my game take was meager. In spite of my small take, I loved being out in the woods. There was so much to see, and when I sat still for a time, the woods seemed to come alive with all sorts of wildlife and sounds. When the woods sensed me, or some other creature that didn't belong, it sensed danger and became eerily quiet.

The best thing that happened during this time was that I became friends with another basic school instructor and hunter, Major Dean McDowell, USMC. That friendship lasted for forty-two years, until Dean passed away in 2001

Dean was already an experienced hunter and woodsman when

our friendship began. Many of the things I learned from Dean, I used in Vietnam. I believe I was a better field commander because of Dean, and more men survived in my battalion as a result.

Dean and I began our big hunts together when we were stationed in Hawaii on the CINCPACFLT staff from 1963 to 1966. Molokai Island was our favorite place to hunt, but we did make a memorable trip to Hawaii, the biggest island of the Hawaiian Islands chain. In fact, our first big hunt was on the "Big Island." This was a feral sheep hunt in the area of Pahakaloa, the Marine training area base camp. It was a two-day hunt with a day set aside to arrive and another to return home, four days in all. On 22 May 1964, we flew over to the Big Island, and spent the night in one of the camp huts there. The next morning, we were up early, ate and saddled up with packs and rifles. On hunts like this, for safety reasons we designated a "first shooter" by a coin toss.

I was the first shooter the first day and Dean had the honor the next day. We were both in good shape. The hike up the mountain above the tree line took about two hours. We sat down for a short break, and as luck would have it, some sheep headed right for our spot. I took a nice young ram with horns about fifteen inches in length that turned down and into a half curve upwards. I earned the horns, but we would each be taking home some mutton. Good hunting friends always share the meat regardless of who bagged the game.

The next morning was a repeat hike up the mountain, well above the tree line and onto lava rock that began to do a job on our Marine Corps boots. We climbed up about as high as we could go in three hours and stopped on a long narrow ridge with a steep gully on each side. The ridge sloped down in a westerly direction.

Dean had binoculars. I did not. He spotted the herd at the very top of the mountain. "There are two nice rams in the herd, Pete, a black one and a white one."

"Which one do you want?" I asked.

"The black one," he answered.

As soon as he said this a huge black cloud appeared over the herd, causing a stampede downhill. We hastily got ready. Dean was on my right side covering that gully. I set up in the prone position to cover the left gully. The white ram was coming down on Dean's side, the black one was coming down on my side. This meant we were going to make crossing shots. They came roaring down, closer and closer. I was sighting in on the white, waiting for Dean to shoot. He did and the white went down. I didn't have time to kibitz. I swung my rifle to the left and fired, just before the black would have gone out of sight. He went down. Both rams were beauties.

I stood up and called, "Dean, I thought you were going for the black."

"I was," he said, "until I saw that the white's horns were bigger."

When we laid them out, side-by-side, both rams' horns made a full curl and a half. Dean's ram's horns were about an inch longer. How he could have noticed that small difference, I'll never know.

After two great days of hunting, we had a heavy load packing out the heads and meat from these two animals. By the time we reached the bottom of the mountain, our boots were shredded by the lava rock. Our boots were finished, kaput, beyond repair, totally gone! That was the bad news. The good news was: we would be eating mutton for a long time. Good news? . . . Well, yes, if you like mutton stew.

Molokai is an island of high mountains and lush lowlands. On the eastern side of the island the mountains have sheer walls that drop down to the sea. There is a small peninsula that juts out from those high walls, but more about this later.

October 1964 was one of the first hunts Dean and I made to Molokai. This was an overnighter and campout hunt in the mountains for feral goats. This was going to be an exciting adventure. Our plan was to backpack in, crawl through an old Hawaiian tunnel leading into a valley, and then camp overnight. Our goat hunt would take place very early the next morning.

When we arrived at the tunnel, Dean (being *the* Lieutenant Colonel and senior to me) elected to go through first. Since I was taller (and a newly appointed junior major), I would follow. I was also a little heavier. If I got stuck, he would pull me through with a rope. The tunnel crawl went well. We got our knees and dungarees a little wet, but that was about it. We walked for some distance, selected a good spot near a stream with a waterfall, and pitched our shelter halves making a two-man pup tent. We then heated up our rations, ate and turned in. During the night, it began to rain. It was still drizzling when we woke up just before daylight.

"Morning, Dean," I said, "Why don't you stay in your sleeping bag for a few more minutes. I'll get my clothes on, and wait for you outside the tent."

"No," he said, "that's not the way we'll do it. The senior officer will get dressed inside the tent and the junior officer will dress outside the tent."

"Are you serious?" I asked.

"Yes, I am," he answered.

So I crawled out and dressed in the rain . . . very quickly I might add. Even on goat-hunts *Rank Hath Its Privileges*.

We ate cold rations and moved out. We had very good success that day. Dean bagged a handsome black and red billy and I dropped a beautiful black with one shot from my 30-06 Winchester.

Three months later we made another hunt to Molokai. We had each drawn deer tags so we could go after bigger game than goats. Brigadier General Marion Carl also had deer tags, and Dean invited him to go with us. General Carl was a war hero and combat aviation ace. We considered it an honor to have him with us on our deer hunt.

When we arrived by jeep in the area we were to hunt, we dismounted, and got our packs and rifles ready for the hunt. General Carl had a new rifle and long-range scope. He seemed very proud and pleased with this firearm and began showing it to us. The first thing he did was to take the scope off the rifle and pass it around for us to look at, which we did examining the scope admiringly. I was thinking to myself—General, you should have waited until the hunt was over to show us these items. We passed the equipment back to the general. He remounted the scope on his rifle, and we were off. The general had a specific area he wanted to try; so, Dean and I went to a different place.

The morning passed and no one had any luck. I decided to eat my lunch, and sat on a stone wall atop a hill. While munching on a sandwich, I scanned the area. Down to my right front was a gully with a dried up streambed at the bottom and a copse of trees on one bank. This looks like a good spot for deer, I thought. I picked up my rifle and began scanning the area through the riflescope.

Suddenly a doe came out of the thicket, climbed up the right side of the bank, and ran off. She was about 400 yards away. We were hunting only bucks; so, I didn't shoot. A second doe came out and ran the same route as the first. For the fun of it, I swung my rifle keeping the scope on her as she moved. A third doe then came out. I did the same thing swinging my rifle on her as she moved. Then all of a sudden a nice six-point axis deer buck came out of the thicket, and I swung my rifle squeezing the trigger as I did so. BOOM! The rifle fired and I saw the buck stagger, roll down the hill and run back into the thicket. Dean had been working the same draw only he was several hundred yards further to my right. I heard him shoot. Soon he came out carrying a small Axis buck on his shoulders. It was a spike buck.

I congratulated him on his kill. He said, "I heard you shoot, did you score?"

"Yes," I said and told him what had happened.

"That's too long a shot, Pete. You probably missed or crippled him."

"Let's go down there and look, I know I hit him."

Dean preceded me down the hill and immediately moved into the thicket. I continued looking around closer to the spot I saw the deer fall. Then I heard Dean call, "Pete, I found him. It's a beautiful six-pointer. Congratulations, that was one helluva shot!"

When we arrived back at the jeep location with our deer, General Carl was still out hunting. We heard him shoot, a little while later he came in, empty-handed. He had missed a nice buck.

We offered our condolences and drove back to the place we had started from. Dean and I were in the same jeep. The General was in the other one.

As we rode along, Dean said out of the side of his mouth, "If General Carl had not removed that scope he might have gotten a deer too. When you remove a scope, the rifle needs to be 'zeroed-in' all over again."

I just smiled and thought the general was lucky he was in aviation and not the infantry. Mistakes like that can be fatal for a grunt.

Pheasant hunting on Molokai without dogs was not very difficult. Several times daily the Hawaiian Airline "island hopper" would make the rounds from Honolulu to the other Hawaiian Islands making brief stops at Molokai airport. A hunter could board a "hopper" early in the morning, debark at Molokai, walk across the airstrip, and begin hunting immediately.

One day I decided to make a solo pheasant hunt. After landing in Molokai I debarked and hunted for a few hours. It wasn't a big day for me. I shot only one pheasant. It wasn't much, but at least I would be "bringing home the bacon," which always makes a hunter happy.

On this particular day, when I boarded the plane to go home, I thought I was going to be the only passenger. Then two more people boarded, a man and a pretty woman. I had taken a seat near the front, and they took seats seven or eight rows behind me. They seemed to be very happy and very interested in each other. I had looked at the man when he boarded only casually, but he seemed familiar. When I heard them talking I knew I had heard his voice before.

Finally, I decided to turn around and take a better look. There he was, my movie hero, John Wayne! I was delighted, but decided the last thing in the world he wanted was for some fan to interrupt his conversation with his lady friend. So I did nothing to disturb them, and disembarked in Honolulu with the warm glow from my close encounter with "The Duke."

My family was having severe car problems in Hawaii with our Volkswagen camper; so, I decided to trade it in as part of the deal on a Jeep station wagon. During the process, the car salesman and I struck up a friendship.

For some time, I had been thinking about hunting goats in the eastern cliffs of Molokai Island. It would require a boat to make the trip to Molokai and landing in a remote, uninhabited part of the island. It would be a tricky expedition, but no problem. Marines are amphibious, aren't they? This would be an amphibious goat hunt.

My car salesman, who was nicknamed "Boomer," mentioned that he had an outboard motor boat. He said I could use his boat if I took him with me on the hunt. Boomer had never been goat hunting, and said he would love to have a try at it. So, I hatched a plan for an amphibious assault on the remote eastern side of Molokai using Boomer's outboard motorboat as our assault craft. I, of course, would be in command, and the hunting guide.

Being young and immortal, neither of us considered the hazards of this adventure. The body of water separating the island of Oahu from Molokai is called the Kaiwi Channel. The distance we had to travel was about five or six miles of water that sometimes gets damned rough. We planned to cross the Kaiwi Channel in Boomer's Chris Craft boat, which was built for sporting around on lakes, not on the waters we were going to navigate. We didn't know this at the time, but the Kaiwi Channel is one of the most shark infested and dangerous bodies of water in the Hawaiian Islands. Our plan was to cross this channel, motor around to a landing area that opened up into a large canyon, beach the boat, camp out overnight, and hunt the next day. We would return to Honolulu on the day after the hunt.

The big day came. We loaded our gear, rifles, and provisions aboard the Chris Craft, and took off. I rode in the bow cockpit with Boomer at the helm. When we got out into the channel, the unexpected began to happen. We encountered HUGE waves!

Boomer kept the boat headed into them as water crashed over the bow. We were being tossed around like a cork. Boomer got sick and began to throw up. I wasn't feeling so good either.

As we cleared a large wave and slid down its backside, we had another unexpected piece of excitement. Our motor died! There we sat, fortunately the wind was at our back from the north. This left us drifting towards a small peninsula, called Kalapapa, that jutted eastward from Molokai. In the early days, lepers and criminals were exiled to Kalapapa. Today, it is still a state supported leper colony where badly disfigured lepers can live out their days in isolation from society—a society that still doesn't want to look at them. For thousands of years, leprosy was the scourge of mankind, but fortunately, today the disease is rare and well controlled by modern medicine.

We continued drifting for about an hour when we spotted a small boat with some fishermen in it. They saw us, and one shouted, "You need help, brudda?"

"Yes!" we replied.

They motored over to us and tossed us a line. "We tow you in," one of them said.

Then I noticed this man had no fingers on either hand. Another man in the boat had no nose. Lepers were rescuing us! They towed us into the small harbor, and told us they would fix our motor. They also suggested that we take a look around since we said we had never been to Kalapapa before.

They tied our boat to the dock as several more lepers joined the group. A leper in the boat tossed a crescent wrench to one of the men on the dock, who had no fingers either, and the tool fell into the water. The man who dropped the wrench dove into the water, and after what seemed like at least five minutes, he surfaced with the tool. He had to go down fairly deep, find the wrench in the darkness, and grab it with hands that had no fingers. I don't know how he did this.

As the men started to fix our motor, Boomer and I took a walk around the leper village. It was beautiful. The cottages that housed the lepers were all painted white. Everything was clean and neat.

They had planted flowers and small vegetable gardens to give the entire area a sense of stability and hominess. There were also signs telling tourists where they could go and not go, which served as a reminder that this was no ordinary neighborhood.

After an hour or so, one of the men called to us and said the boat was fixed. We thanked them profusely and offered to pay them. They politely refused payment saying that they had a good time fixing the motor. Besides, they had no use for money. The State of Hawaii took care of all their needs.

It was now early afternoon and we still had a fair distance to go before we reached the canyon. After a long ride, we had almost reached the canyon when it began to rain, and the sea became rougher. Boomer and I discussed the situation. We were on the windward side of Molokai and didn't know how violent the storm might get. The boat had no cabin. We had no raingear. The situation had become tense again, but we decided to keep on going until we reached the harbor on the lee or westward side of Molokai, where the sea would be calmer. Also, I had hunted goats from that side before and knew where we could find them in that area.

It was well after dark when we finally motored into the harbor. It was very calm, and the rain had stopped as we tied up to the dock. Two tired and very lucky adventurers ate their supper, and then went to sleep on the boat under the stars.

The next morning we got started early and by midday had taken two nice billy goats. I saved the horns from mine and mounted them on a beautiful piece of monkey pod.

The trip back to Oahu was not exactly uneventful either. We now had to ride those huge waves down and get away from them before they broke over the stern of our little boat. Boomer also had to make sure we didn't capsize in the rough seas. He did a good job and brought us safely back to Oahu, but as we entered the Honolulu harbor, we had one last bit of unexpected excitement. Our engine broke down again. Once more we were lucky. An ocean going motor launch came by and towed us in. It was a humiliating way to return, but return we did from a great, once in a lifetime adventure.

When I tell my Naval Academy classmates about "The Great Amphibious Goat Hunt," they shake their heads in amazement and say we were lucky to come through that caper alive. They know what happens to idiots who venture forth into the open ocean in a small craft built for lake sports. In fact, they recommended that I entitle this narrative "The Ship of Fools" rather than the "Amphibious Goat Hunt."

There are three parts to a hunt: the preparation and planning, the hunt itself, and post hunt stories and discussions. When one goes hunting with good friends, there is a heightened sense of excitement and joy that is an integral part of the experience. The night before a hunt, or fishing trip with friends, I can hardly sleep I'm so fired up. I hope I never lose that sense of excitement.

I always enjoy hunting with good friends who have excellent hunting skills, sound ethics, and demonstrate a spirit of sharing. We share the cost of the trip, food and some of the game we harvest. Dean McDowell and Tom Casmay are two great hunting friends, with whom I share many wonderful memories. Dean passed away, but Tom is still around to add spice to my hunting adventures.

Tom and I have hunted pheasants and deer on the McDowell farm many times. Tom is a fine rifle shot, and always brings home a deer—or even two—when we're hunting for venison. However, for eight years we trudged through the mountains of western Virginia and West Virginia bird hunting, and in those eight years Tom never got a grouse. That is, until a couple of seasons back. Let me tell you about how we ended Tom's run of bad luck with grouse.

When George Washington was at Yorktown, he wasn't sure he could defeat the British. He did know about a beautiful little valley ten miles west of Front Royal that was surrounded by mountains. On the east, west and north sides of those mountains were the two branches of the Shenandoah River. Washington thought the valley would be a good place to retreat to in the event he had to fall back from his encounter with the British at Yorktown.

Like all good generals, Washington planned for all possible outcomes, good and bad. In his engagement with the British at Yorktown, he knew Cornwallis to be a formidable foe. It was far from certain that he would defeat the British at Yorktown; so, Washington planned a line of retreat in the event that it became inevitable. Washington ordered Captain Morgan, an engineer under his command, to build a fort and a road from the south fork of the Shenandoah over the eastern range of mountains and into the valley, which Washington named Fort Valley. Morgan and his men built the fort and road, but fortunately Washington never had to use it.

In our wanderings around the Fort Valley Mountains looking for game, Tom and I discovered Captain Morgan's road. It is now a trail for hikers marked with an appropriate sign. On this particular day, two of my Brittanys, Penny and Minx, were searching the mountain laurel and brush piles. My other two "Britts," Rufus and Maggie, were in the truck. We had used them that morning, but had raised no grouse. Tom and I had hunted from sunrise to about ten minutes after five. We were pressing the limits of legal hunting hours, which were from a half hour before sunrise to a half hour after sunset. Sunset was at five-thirty that day, giving us another twenty minutes of legal hunting time. At about ten minutes after five the dogs began getting "birdy" and up flew a beautiful cock grouse. Tom fired one shot and his grouse drought ended.

There were high-fives all over the place. I don't know who was happier, Tom or I. That was the only grouse we flushed that day, and he harvested it with a great shot. Tom had that first grouse mounted and it now adorns a wall in his office . . . a testament to a goal finally achieved after nine years of effort.

Bart Edelen is another friend I often hunt with. I don't know a better wing shot than Bart, especially in goose hunting. Bart, a retired airline pilot, is a former fighter pilot who is used to hitting the target, whether in the air or on the ground. His father taught him to hunt waterfowl on the Potomac River when he was a kid in the early 1950s. I met Bart in 1990 when he joined the same real estate firm where Sara worked.

Goose hunting is a sociable endeavor that offers as much fun in the socializing as in the hunting. For the past four years, Bart and I have been privileged to hunt geese on a beautiful estate in northern Virginia with a ten-acre pond. A fine gentleman named John Bond manages the estate for the owners. Interestingly, John served in Delta Company, First Battalion, Fifth Marines in Vietnam. He joined the battalion shortly after my tour ended. John has three purple hearts, and is a real war hero to me. Both John and his wife are wonderful people.

In the year 2000 when we hunted there, the pond was iced over. We couldn't tell how thick the ice was, and we weren't certain it would hold us walking on it. Neither could we tell what the ice might do to the canoe if it were sufficiently thick to damage the hull enough to sink it. This was a dicey situation. If a goose fell on the ice, we would have to retrieve it in my canoe. It would be very risky. If the ice broke and was thick enough to damage the canoe's hull we could sink. I wasn't happy with our chances of the ice breaking and our ending up in ice-cold water, especially without life vests.

On this day we set up our decoys on shore. That way, the geese we shot would most likely drop on land. Two geese flew in. We both shot. Bart's goose dropped at the shore's edge. Mine didn't cooperate. He kept flying until he was over the ice before dropping forty feet off shore.

Now we had a problem. We couldn't leave that dead goose out there. The owners wouldn't like that. We decided to get it with the canoe. Since it was my bird, I went out in the canoe to retrieve it. We pushed the canoe out onto the ice as far as we dared. Then I gingerly flopped in head first, thinking any minute I'd crash through the ice. Bart then carefully slid onto the ice so he could push me out farther using his legs and feet. We had a line attached to the canoe so he could pull me back in, if the canoe broke through the ice. I had found a rake on the shore that I brought with me to snag the goose and drag it into the canoe.

The maneuver worked and after retrieving the goose, Bart

hauled me in. We were both relieved. I vowed never to try that dumb stunt again in a wintertime hunt. After that adventure I decided it would be smarter to own a retriever dog that could go out and get the birds for us. A couple months later Sara and I were the proud owners of an eight-week-old Fox red English Labrador Retriever puppy.

It was great fun training her. I used the Richard Wolter's books and video to do it. Ruby is now three years old. Her lifetime record to date is twenty-nine goose retrieves from the water or ice at our estate pond. She has sixteen duck retrieves that Roscoe Tippett and I harvested on Eastern shore duck hunts. Not a bad record for a young dog. She is a real sweetheart as well.

I really enjoy bass fishing, and I don't know a better bass fisherman than Bart Edelen. When we go bass fishing together, Bart catches the first fish, the most fish and the last fish. I am lucky if I catch one at all. I guess the reason I find fishing with Bart so enjoyable is that he keeps me laughing. He can tell more tall yarns and sea-stories than anyone I ever met outside the Marine Corps.

I have another fishing buddy, "Miss Sara," my wife. When she fishes it's with a determination unknown to the rest of mankind. She is not always successful, but when she is, it's in a big way.

We went fishing in Alaska for king salmon several years ago. I was fortunate and landed, with the guide's help, a nice one. Sara hooked a big one, brought it to the surface by the boat twice, but the guide failed to net it. She was crushed!

On another occasion we went on a charter fishing trip with some friends for Chesapeake Bay stripers. Sara hooked a monster. Would she let anyone help her? **No way!** This little thing, my wife, probably didn't weigh a whole lot more than that fish, but she fought it and fought it and brought it to the edge of the boat. A big deck hand netted it and brought the prize aboard. Sara had caught a citation striper, and later received a certificate attesting to that fact from the state of Maryland. The certificate is now framed with photo, and hangs proudly on our wall.

Three happy hunters with their quota.

Twice during a hunting season several years ago, snow caused one of my hunting partners, Jim Monroe, and me to cancel West Virginia grouse hunts. We were both eager to get in one last hunt, and West Virginia's season was ending soon. Jim was particularly anxious because he hadn't bagged a grouse yet that year.

On the February morning of our third and last scheduled hunt, I woke up and saw snow falling. Jim arrived promptly at 5:30 a.m. and we loaded his gear and my Brittany, Minx, into the truck. Because of the bad weather, we had only the most reluctant of blessings from our wives. However, our desire to hunt overcame our good sense. We had no idea that before day's end, we would come close to losing our lives. In retrospect, we should have stayed home by the fire and re-read Bob West's *Safe Hunting Tips* in the Dec/Jan 1995 issue of *Gun and Dog*.

The drive to the West Virginia mountain hunting area took about three and a half hours because of the snow. The road up the mountain was a narrow gravel road with a six to nine degree slope. There were three sharp left turns on the way up, all at relatively level spots. A steel gate with heavy steel posts was located at the middle turn. Going up the mountain road, we would be bounded on the right by a drainage ditch (which was rocky and about a foot deep) next to the mountainside. On the left there was a sheer drop of 300 to 500 feet. Trees grew along the left side side, and soon, as we drove higher we could see the treetops.

As we started our ascent we noticed tire tracks. This seemed to be a good sign. At least one other hunter had preceded us this morning. Because of the Dodge Ram's heavy weight, we initially had little difficulty moving up the mountain road. I had the truck in the lowest gear and in four-wheel drive. When we reached the second landing, both of us noticed two things: First, we had some slippage, signaling a possible traction problem; and second, at the gate the tire tracks from the earlier vehicle had disappeared.

"They're just gone," Jim said. Maybe the snow had covered them up—but it was as if that vehicle had just vanished into thin air!

Now we realized we might be in trouble. There was no way we could turn around, and the gate was open. We decided to continue to the parking area located at the top of the mountain. We could turn around there. As we moved higher, we noticed that the Ram's four wheels were having increasing difficulty maintaining good traction.

On passing through the final open gate into the parking area, I suggested we stop and check the road's surface. When we dismounted from the truck, both of us slipped and fell. Jim exclaimed, "Holy cow, Pete, there's six inches of ice under the snow!" We knew then we were definitely in trouble.

"Okay," I said. "We're parking here." We could have called for help on the car phone, but we didn't. We even discussed hiking down the mountain for tire chains, but the hike back up would have been difficult and long. Besides, we had made this trip to hunt. We'd deal with driving down the mountain later.

As we moved out, the wind picked up and the snow continued to fall. I was glad the wind was at our backs. At high noon we reached the "grouse area." The road turned past a feed plot, and as Jim and I turned to walk down it, we noticed the snow had stopped falling.

At this point, Minx began getting birdy. Jim was looking to the right. I was looking left. Suddenly, there was an explosive sound like a whole covey of quail and Jim shouted, "Grouse!"

Minx had been trying to climb the bank on the right side, and flushed the grouse. We thought we could find the bird again farther down the hill in a large patch of laurel. As we climbed up the bank, we heard a second grouse flush off to our right. Neither of us saw it, so again we took no shots.

As we moved downhill into the laurel, Minx began acting birdy again. Jim and I spread out properly to deal with the grouse if it got up. Then the bird exploded into the air. I raised my gun to fire, but nothing happened. The safety was frozen in the no-fire position.

Jim fired twice but missed. "Do you think we can locate him again?" he asked. I said we could try, but we needed to be back at the truck while we still had daylight.

At 2:00 P.M. we reached the road. We hadn't raised the grouse again, but we both felt good about having the three flushes. You don't score on every hunt, I reminded myself, especially when you forget to occasionally click the safety to keep it from getting frozen.

We went back to the truck along the same route we had come. At 3:20 P.M., we were in our seats and buckled up buckled up. I looked at Jim, and he looked back and smiled. "I'm ready," he said, "but let me suggest this, Pete, since the road is *sheer* ice, if we start sliding, head for the drainage ditch next to the mountain. Also, tap your brakes so you don't lock 'em up. The rocks in the ditch will help slow us down."

Good advice, I thought. I said, "Okay . . . let's go." I cranked up the engine, released the brake, and put the truck in the lowest gear, ready to creep **SLOWLY** back down the hill.

At that moment Jim said in the calmest voice I've ever heard, "Pete, I think I'd take it a little slower, the truck isn't supposed to be a luge."

I noticed he hadn't turned to talk to me; his face was glued toward the front. As I looked up, I realized for the first time we were already moving downhill.

"Jim, I hate to tell you, but I haven't touched the gas yet!" I said.

"No problem, just gently tap the brakes," he replied.

I did as I was told. It didn't seem to make any difference. We continued to pick up speed.

"Get in the ditch, Pete!" Jim ordered.

Like me, he's a former Marine. I knew the situation was getting serious even though you couldn't tell it by his voice. I turned the wheels slightly to the left and the Ram responded. So far so good . . . Tapping the brakes now helped, but we were still moving at a good clip. We passed through the first open gate and I was able to slow the truck down almost to a stop. The second incline was steeper.

Jim said, "Good job so far. Use the same tactic again."

"I'm not sure we can," I said. "There are two big boulders in the drainage ditch and a large pothole in between."

"Well, do the best you can, but Lisa is going to be really mad if we don't make it," Jim said.

"I don't think Sara will be too happy, either," I said through clenched teeth.

As we worked our way down, the truck began picking up speed again. This incline was much steeper and we were soon almost flying . . . into the ditch . . . boulders rushing up at us. We fishtailed out to the right. Then we were back in the ditch again, hurtling toward the middle post. I struggled with the steering wheel and somehow we missed the post by inches. Now, with nothing to stop our momentum, we were out of the ditch and again racing down the slope, totally out of control. Suddenly we were back in the ditch again. We both felt a tremendous bounce that slammed us down in our seats and sent us headlong toward the cliff's edge and a sheer drop of 500 feet into a rocky bottom below.

"Pete, we're heading for the cliff!" Jim shouted.

I would have congratulated Jim on his grasp of the obvious, but I'd long since lost my voice. All I could do was imagine the three of us going over that cliff, probably outdistancing the Wright brothers' flight. With incredible effort and a quiet prayer, I finally got the wheels turned hard left, hoping they'd grab hold of something. They did! Praise God, we were back on the road, and the brakes were slowing us down. We slid to a stop on the third level. **Hallelujah**!

Sweat was pouring off my brow. I couldn't look at Jim. He took a deep breath and said, "That was a quite a ride—one more leg to do. How do you feel about this one?"

"Well, let's hope we won't have to deal with any more ice and we'll get some traction if we can keep from going too fast," I said.

The last leg began. We again started slipping, and I decided now was the time to get into those tire tracks maybe we'd get some traction and stop fishtailing. It worked. The fishtailing stopped. The tracks were deep enough to hold us to the center of the road. We came to the first house on the left, and the brakes started grabbing. Our speed slowed and we came to a gradual stop at the bottom.

I said, "Jim, I don't know what to do first—get out and kiss the ground, or drink some coffee."

He said, "Both, then share this bottle of beer with me."

That was an enjoyable hunt and one helluva ride. Just think— we've developed a new Olympic sport . . . *Ram sledding in a huge luge!*"

We both let out a whoop as two very lucky hunters headed home to Virginia—*very slowly.*

I am not one of those hunters who hunt strictly for trophies. I guess you might classify me as more of a meat hunter. I try to be, above all, safe and ethical in the way I hunt. As much as I enjoy hunting with friends, my most memorable hunts have been when I've gone out alone, or with only my dogs.

My first grouse hunt took place in Fort Valley not far from where Sara and I now have our property. This first grouse hunt was in the early seventies, shortly after I retired from the Marine Corps. I had two Brittanys then, Pat and Misty.

I had heard about Fort Valley, but had never been there. That morning I loaded the dogs into the truck along with my bird hunting gear, and took off for my hunt. I drove down the Fort Valley road, which bisects the valley floor marveling all the while at the beauty of the place. After about ten miles, I turned right and went up the Woodstock Tower Road. After a mile or so I saw a cornfield on my left at the base of a rather high cone shaped hill. Then I saw a beautiful stream that I later learned is called Peter's Mill Run. I came to a state camping ground, parked the car, forded the stream, and began to climb the hill.

The dogs were out in front having a dog's good time and sniffing everything. When we reached the top of the hill, I sat down on a stump admiring the scenery. Pat and Misty took off downhill toward the cornfield. Suddenly, a magnificent bird came flying over the crest of the hill about ten feet above the ground. It was brown with a large tail spread out like a fan. The tip of the tail was flecked in a white band with a black band about ½ inch wide inside the white band. It was a grouse. The first I'd ever seen.

In bird hunting, the dogs find the bird's hiding place and point to the bird's location. The hunter then walks to where the dogs were pointing, flushes the bird, and shoots it when it takes wing. This bird hunt was proceeding a bit differently. My dogs had not pointed the bird, and I watched the grouse as it flew over my head and landed about 20 yards away.

I wanted to do things the way they are supposed to be done because I was still training my dogs; so, I called the dogs and waited until they came to me. I planned to get them over to where the bird came down so they could find it and point it. With everything by the book, I would then shoot the grouse. My heart was pounding so loudly I could hear it.

No such thing happened. The dogs came up, scented the area where the bird came down, but never could find it. I saw my first grouse, and could have bagged it if I hadn't wanted to involve the dogs. The dogs searched for quite some time, but never found my grouse. That was a great disappointment for me, but you can't win every time. And the sooner you learn that in hunting, the more reasonable will be your expectations.

My most memorable solo pheasant hunt was the day I shot a

My champion Leroy points out a pheasant,

pheasant cock with a twenty-three inch long tail at Dean McDowell's Merrimac Farm. Not only was this a beautiful bird, but my champion dog, Leroy, found and pointed it for me. I have hunted many pheasants, but never one as majestic as the one on our fireplace mantle with that twenty-three inch tail.

In Virginia, and most other states, turkeys are classified as big game along with deer, bear, elk, and other large animals. There is one big difference, however: Turkey hunting is more of a solo endeavor. Turkeys have wonderful eyesight and the slightest false move by a hunter will spook them. With two hunters in the same area, the chances are greater of being seen by the turkeys. When I hunt turkeys with a friend, we split up into different areas.

I once had unexpected results on a turkey hunt that gave me a trophy that was "one for the books." It was in the fall, and I was near Dean McDowell's farm. I had loaded my over and under shotgun with turkey shot, which is quite different from buckshot or slugs used for hunting larger animals, such as deer or bear. I had walked into a little clearing and stopped to look around. To my surprise, the field was loaded with turkeys, perhaps as many as a dozen, but they were too far away to get a good shot. I froze, not even daring to blink, but there was no way I could move without spooking them. I tried to move closer for a shot, but sure enough I spooked them.

I thought I might find them across the narrow stream that would put me on Dean McDowell's Merrimac Farm property. Dean had just retired from the Marine Corps and taken a job at a university in Connecticut. He asked me to keep an eye on his property while he was in Connecticut, and had given me permission to hunt there. After I crossed the stream I hooked to the right, walking slowly through the woods looking for those turkeys. The wind was blowing briskly towards me. As I moved out of the woods there was a section of brambles and multiflora rose that I had to clear before I could enter a small glade. Just as I did, I saw a buck lying nearby in the sun. He saw me and quickly began to rise. He was only about ten feet away and had no chance. I took him with one shot. As he lay there, I marveled at what had just happened. I had taken a twelve-point buck, a once in a lifetime trophy, with turkey shot.

Of my four most memorable solo hunts, the most significant was the spring gobbler hunt on a friend's place near Hillsboro, VA. That was on 2 April 2000. I arrived well before daylight, and began walking down a dirt road running across the property. The idea in spring turkey hunting is to locate the gobbler, and make hen sounds so that the gobbler will come to the hen sounds. Normally, the gobbler wants the hen to come to him; he does not want to go to the hen. Chauvinism extends even to the kingdom of birds. The hunter must make hen turkey sounds enticingly enough to trick the gobbler into going to the hen instead of waiting for her to come to him. Can you imagine arousing a turkey gobbler to a state of high passion?

I had located a turkey several hundred yards downhill from me by using an owl call. Turkey gobblers don't like owls and crows. They gobble to run them off. I gave an owl hoot and received an answering gobble. I quickly moved down the road to a clearing. A nice tree dominated the hilltop up the road where I could sit facing the sun. I put three turkey decoys below me on the road and sat down at the base of the tree. My strategy was to do a little hen clucking, then quietly watch and wait. I made my best hen noises and sat quietly with my shotgun cradled in my lap admiring the sunrise.

There was a large, half-moon shaped rock sticking up out of the ground directly down hill from me and on the far edge of the dirt road. Suddenly, a head popped out from the right side of the rock. It was a gobbler. Then the head disappeared behind the rock just as quickly as it had appeared. I shouldered my shotgun in the firing position. The head popped out from the left side. I saw more of the body this time. Then he ducked behind the rock again.

Pete Bags a Trophy

I said to myself, "Turkey, if you come out from behind that rock and take two steps towards my decoys, you're going home with me."

That's exactly what happened. He came out, took two steps, and I pulled the trigger. I stood up to see if I needed to shoot again. I didn't. I walked down to see him close up, and there lay a magnificent bird. This was a monster. He had a 10 ½ inch beard and weighed 22 pounds. He was gorgeous too. He was a spectacular combination of gold, brown, black, red white and blue. My taxidermist told me it was the second largest bird ever brought into his shop. I had waited nine years for this. I was euphoric and floated on clouds for weeks afterwards.

My hunting partner, Tom Casmay, came over and took pictures. Later, he posted a sign in front of his wine store telling the world about my prize. That was embarrassing, but understandable since a true hunting partner takes pride in the success of his hunting buddy.

I've always had a dream, that in my senior years I could go hunting with members of my family. At an early age, Linda, Diana, Dale, and David all shared my love for hunting. I took each of the girls out to experience the adventure of deer hunting before they became teenagers. Of the three girls, Dale seemed to like hunting more than the others did, but it was not until recent years that I found out how much. She's always ready to accompany me on a hunt for birds or deer, no matter how bad the weather.

David began hunting at an early age, and when he was older did some guiding for Dean McDowell at his preserve. David began following me through the fields at McDowell's Hunting Preserve before he could see over the top of the grass. He took to hunting like most kids take to baseball. As a teenager, he worked for "Colonel Mac" as a guide on McDowell's Hunting Preserve. I remember driving down to McDowell's one afternoon to check on David's progress. Dean told me where I could find him, and I drove to the edge of a field where I could observe David's actions.

From a short distance, and concealed, I was pleased to see my Brittany dog holding a staunch point and David telling the hunters, "Sam, the dog is on point. You stand over there. Tom you stand over here. Both of you get ready to shoot. I'm going to move in front of the dog and flush the bird." He handled the situation like a pro guide.

Now married, and a father, David lives in Colorado, and is a superb elk and antelope hunter. A few years ago David took me on an antelope hunt in Wyoming. He had planned this hunt in anticipation of my visit, and made arrangements with a rancher for us to camp on the ranch. Early into the hunt, David began having problems with his rifle. He had missed several antelope at relatively short ranges, and was clearly frustrated.

"Dad, I went to the rifle range and zeroed in my sights. I can't understand what's causing me to miss those easy shots."

I examined his rifle, and we both suspected there was a malfunction of his weapon. That disappointment added to David's frustration. He wanted everything to go perfectly, with each of us bagging several antelope. David wanted to show me that he was a great shot, and he wanted me to have a wonderful time.

"Dad, can I borrow your rifle on the next opportunity?" I was hunting with a Model 70 Winchester that had never let me down. "Sure," I said, "but you've never fired this gun. Let's go down the road where it's isolated, and let you take a few practice shots. Let's see if the gun works for you."

As we drove down a remote, back road on the ranch, David spotted an antelope in the distance. "Dad, I'm going to try and take this one," he said as he stopped the truck, got out and ran over to the berm on the side of the road. I remember thinking that it was a long shot to take that animal, and it was even harder with a rifle he had never fired.

Then, "Boom!" To my surprise the animal went down. It was a beautiful shot! When we measured the distance, David had dropped his antelope at a distance of 350 yards. What a fantastic piece of marksmanship, and I was one proud father!

Sara and I call our property in Fort Valley, Virginia "Arrowhead," because the borders of the property form an arrowhead shape. It is only twelve acres, but the acreage is ideally situated in a place that is a magnet for wildlife. Deer, bear, grouse and turkey abound in the areas adjoining us, and are frequently on our property. It is a wonderful place to hunt. Sara and her boys, Greg and Scott, have gone goose hunting with me, and my nephews, Bruce, Peter, and Henry have hunted deer, pheasant, and geese with me.

Last year one of my grandsons, Jonathan Cirillo, bagged his first squirrel. Another grandson, Andrew Boyd, missed taking a deer when two does passed under his tree stand, and he had to let them go because does were not in legal hunting season. To my delight, both boys' fathers also hunt. David Boyd and Jim Cirillo are fine shots and good company. I love it when these "dads" and my "grandsons" go hunting with me. It just doesn't get any better than that.

One of the best hunting stories at Arrowhead is about my nephew Henry, whom we call Huck. It was the last day of deer season in Shenandoah County, and both bucks and does were legal. About noon Sara said, "Pete, why don't you and Huck head on down to Arrowhead and hunt deer this afternoon?"

That was all we needed to change clothes, get our guns and gear, jump into my Yukon, and head down to Arrowhead. The drive takes just under two hours. We arrived there at about 3 P.M.

On the way down we talked hunting and Huck began asking me some very good questions. He asked how far away should the deer be when he fired his shotgun? I told him the proper distance to give the best chance for a kill. He asked if he should shoot when the deer was running? The answer was, no, don't shoot if the deer is running. Wait until it is grazing or walking, because this means less chance of just wounding the animal.

I posted Huck in the center position, in a blind called the "outhouse tent." After showing him his safe zone of fire, I proceeded down to the right side of the property and climbed up into a sixteen-foot tree stand we call "tree stand number two." Dry Run Creek runs through my property at the point of the arrowhead with ponds on either edge. I built tree stand number two to cover this area with a clear line of fire. I had been in the tree stand almost two hours when I thought I heard some rustling off to my right. I got ready, because it probably was a deer. Then I heard— **"boom"**! About five minutes later Huck called and said he had shot a deer.

I climbed down and went to join Huck. He told me he had hit the deer behind his left shoulder. It had fallen down hard and then got up and limped off. We started to trail the deer, and although it was almost dark the blood stains made the tracking easy. We were looking at the ground so intently that we walked within fifteen feet of the deer, which was lying down. When we got that close the deer jumped up and headed for the creek.

I felt our best bet was not to trail the deer any further because it was getting dark. I was sure the deer was mortally wounded, and that if we waited we had a good chance of finding it and bringing it home. So, we went back to the cabin. I made hot chocolate, and we sat and talked for a while.

After an hour and a half, the hunting season was officially over. We couldn't take our guns with us; so, armed with flashlights we set out to find the deer. After about thirty or forty minutes we found it lying dead in the creek.

By majority vote, remember RHIP, I elected Huck to pull the deer back to higher ground. We had a cart to load the animal onto, so we could wheel it back to the cabin. Huck kept his cool during all this, and made me very proud of him. Then I asked him how many deer he had taken before.

"Uncle Pete," he said, "this is my first one ever!"

As I look through my hunting photo albums, I see pictures of many more friends who have hunted and fished with me. There are fishing friends like Mel and Nina Vogel. There is a photo of my friend from the McLean, Virginia Rotary Club, Ed Holman, who invited Tom Casmay, my nephew Bruce, and me to hunt geese at his Lake Anna place. I see photos of Dayton Robinson who went on Molokai goat hunts with me. Another old hunting buddy, Bill Kean, is there. I hunted geese with Bill on the Eastern Shore and dove at his farm in South Carolina. Jim Robison and I had a great and memorable wild boar hunt on the big island of Hawaii. We killed a 250-pound boar with Sara's .410 single shot shotgun after the herd of wild pigs had treed the guide, Jim, and me.

I have photos of Warren and Pat Kitterman's farm in King George, Virginia, where my son, David, shot his first deer. Kitt Kitterman was my Naval Academy classmate and fellow Marine. Kitt and I went to war together in Korea and Vietnam. Sara's son, Scott, harvested his first hunting trophy, a squirrel on the Kitterman farm. These are wonderful, warm, and supremely happy memories. There's a picture of Bernie Bernhardt, who was in the Northern Virginia Brittany Club with me. Bernie showed my son, David, how to fly fish. I had a memorable goose hunt with Bernie when I shot my first Canada goose.

With Dave Stingl and my next-door neighbor, Bill Borland, I had happy pheasant hunts at the McDowell Hunting Preserve. Waterfowl hunting and pheasant hunting with Roscoe Tippett was great fun. My friendship with Roscoe began the day he came to my home and bought a Brittany pup from me. With Roscoe I harvested my first wood duck. Together Roscoe and I joined forces with our two young retrievers, his Chessie and my lab, Ruby. On two occasions we downed, and the dogs retrieved, a bounty of

Mallard ducks. Roscoe and I bagged some Reece's Pheasants, magnificent birds, much larger than the Ringneck Pheasant.

Some of these people have gone on to a better place and I pray they are keeping a spot open for me in "The Happy Hunting Grounds" when my time comes. When I get there, if I can bivouac with my Marines, and hunt with my family, my friends, and my dogs, ol' Highpockets will be in tall cotton.

When I look back on my life, I see a long and common thread of adventure, friendships, and caring throughout all that I have done. My life has been a wonderful mixture of privilege, challenge, and blessing. The road was at times bumpy. I had my share of disappointments and heartaches, but no one travels the road of life without a few tears. God has been good to me, and my guardian angels have watched over me. Would I do it all over again without changing a thing? In a heart beat!

APPENDIX A

Marine Corps Rank Structure

OFFICER
General
Lieutenant General
Major General
Brigadier General
Colonel
Lieutenant Colonel
Major
Captain
First Lieutenant
Second Lieutenant

Warrant Officer
(4 levels)

ENLISTED
Sergeant Major
Master Gunnery Sergeant
First Sergeant
Master Sergeant
Gunnery Sergeant
Staff Sergeant
Sergeant
Corporal
Lance Corporal
Private First Class
Private

APPENDIX B

Battle Map Symbols

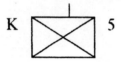 First Battalion, Fifth Marines.

 K Company, Fifth Marines

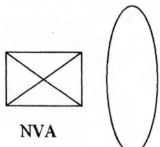 North Vietnamese Troop Dispositions

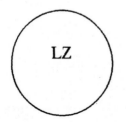 Landing Zone for Helicopters

APPENDIX C

Organizational Structure,

U.S. Pacific Forces

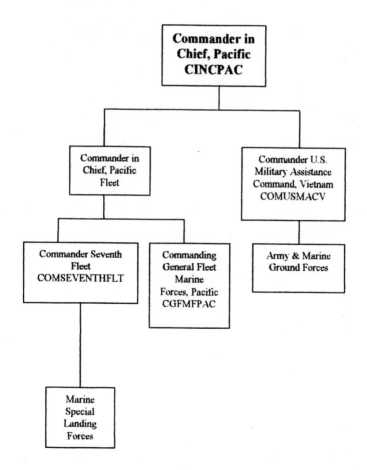

APPENDIX D

Operation Swift

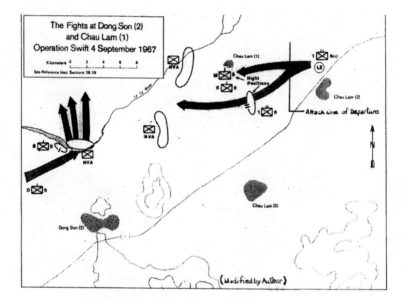

The Fights at Dong Son (2)
and Chau Lam (1)
Operation Swift 4 September 1967

Telfer et. al. for battle maps pp 66, 180, 300

INDEX OF NAMES

AUTHOR'S BIOGRAPHY

Peter L. Hilgartner

Colonel Peter L. Hilgartner, USMC, enlisted in the Marine Corps in 1945, graduated from the United States Naval Academy in1951, and served with distinction in the Marine Corps for 24 years. Four of those years were in combat zones in Korea and the Republic of Vietnam. As a Second Lieutenant in Korea, he fought against enemy forces in central and western Korea as an artillery forward observer. For his action against the enemy, he received the Bronze Star Medal with Combat V.

He served in Vietnam, and in 1966, while still a major, took command of the First Battalion, Fifth Marine Regiment, the most decorated regiment in the U.S. Marine Corps. He was promoted to lieutenant colonel, and continued to lead the First Battalion in its operations against the enemy in the Que Son Valley. He engaged Viet Cong forces in daily clear and sweep operations, and during 1967 fought in regiment size battles against the North Vietnamese Army in Operations Union I, Union II, and Swift. He commanded his front line Marine infantry battalion for ten and ½ months, one of the longest Marine command tours during the Vietnam War. For his combat service, he received the Silver Star, the Legion of Merit with Combat V, the Vietnamese Cross of Gallantry with Palm, and a second Vietnamese Cross of Gallantry with Gold Star.

Colonel Hilgartner holds an advanced degree in business management with emphasis in economics from the U.S. Naval Postgraduate School in Monterey, California.

BIOGRAPHY

For Samuel P. Ginder, Jr.

Sam Ginder began free-lance writing as a sideline to his thirty-five year career in the aerospace and defense industry. After retirement in 1993, he studied creative writing at Montgomery College and St. John's College, and became an author as a second career. His first novel, *McKinnon's Way*, was widely acclaimed as a well-researched story about submarine operations in World War II and Cold War intrigue with a thought-provoking underlying philosophical message. In addition to his writings on technical subjects ranging from shipboard and space-based systems to Very

High Speed Integrated Circuits (VHSIC), he has authored a number of magazine articles for wide distribution, and recently edited an important account of the fifty year record of achievements of the United States Naval Academy Class of 1951 in the last half of the twentieth century. In addition to his literary work, he has written scripts for special documentaries.

Prior to his aerospace and defense industry career, he served in the United States Navy aboard the battleship USS Wisconsin (BB-64), and saw action in the Korean War. He was selected for submarine service, qualified in submarines, and "rode the boats" for six years prior to leaving the Navy for civilian life.

He was graduated from the United States Naval Academy in Annapolis, Maryland and holds advanced degrees from the George Washington University, School of Engineering and Applied Science and the Georgetown University School of Liberal Studies. He taught computer systems graduate courses at the American University.

GI